The New
Where's That Poem?

An index of poems for children
Arranged by subject,
with a bibliography of
books of poetry

Helen Morris
Formerly Principal Lecturer in English
Homerton College, Cambridge

STANLEY
THORNES

Fourth edition © Helen Morris 1992
Previous editions 1967, 1974, 1985

Published in 1992 in Great Britain by
Simon and Schuster Education

Reprinted in 1994 by
Stanley Thornes (Publishers) Ltd
Ellenborough House
Wellington Street
CHELTENHAM GL50 1YD
England

A catalogue record for this book is available from the British Library.

ISBN 0 7487 1963 6

Photoset in North Wales by
Derek Doyle & Associates, Mold, Clwyd
Cover design by Miller, Craig & Cocking
Printed in Great Britain by
T. J. Press (Padstow) Ltd

Contents

Foreword

The first *Where's that Poem?* was produced because I was so often asked by my students, 'Do you remember that poem about . . . goats, or goblins, or Goliath, or gossiping? And where can I find it?' I began to list poems and keep references, and in 1967 the lists became a book which I believe has proved useful to teachers and students of poetry. New anthologies appear in increasing numbers, and the first edition had to be revised and enlarged in 1974, and again in 1984 as *The New Where's that Poem?* Now over half the anthologies in that edition are out of print, and there are many new books of poetry available. Many contain poetry by people of other lands, and by members of the ethnic minorities in Britain, so when it clarifies the meaning of the poem I have added the nationality, or sometimes the dates, of the writer.

I have not included any anthologies of poems written by children; to the reader wishing examples of fine work of this kind I strongly recommend Jill Pirrie's *On Common Ground* (Hodder & Stoughton, 1987).

The poems have been chosen with children of approximately five to fifteen in mind. Children of five and six are usually best suited by nursery rhymes and jingles, of which there are several admirable collections (particularly, for the teacher, *Ox Dic* and *Ox NR*, and for the children *Fab NV*, *Lob*, *Puf NR*, *Puf Y*, *Voa* and *Walk*, see page 195). But many of the poems listed can be read to, and with, even the youngest children in the infant school. The secondary teacher of upper forms will naturally use the widest selection of adult poetry to suit various groups. How arbitrary and how artificial these divisions are! Much really great poetry can be appreciated (admittedly at very different levels) both by small children and by adults: parts of *The Ancient Mariner*, some of Blake's songs, and the most often reprinted poem in this book, Robert Frost's *Stopping by Woods on a Snowy Evening*, illustrate this point.

To classify poems as suitable for a particular age-group is to make two mistakes: it is to expect a poem to speak exclusively to children at a certain stage of development, and to assume that children of a certain age are all at the same stage of poetic education and appreciation. The appreciation of poetry has to be learnt, as much as the appreciation of music and art. Though some poems, like some music and paintings, may at first hearing or sight be obvious enough to appeal to the uneducated, it is the teacher's business to foster real enjoyment and appreciation of more difficult poetry by a sensitive choice of poems for each class – and if possible, for each individual child. Once poems have been established as worth reading because they are interesting or even exciting, then pupils should browse in as many different books as possible, find a poem that says something particularly relevant, and copy it into a personal anthology, or read it aloud to the teacher or the class. For those who dismiss poetry as 'soppy', there are many really tough ballads, traditional and modern, and it is often useful to sing them with a guitar and impromptu percussion.

Since grouping by children's ages seems impracticable, the poems have been grouped under subject headings, with ample cross-reference. Carols, ballads and nursery rhymes are not listed as such, but many occur under relevant subject headings.

Some songs by Shakespeare are here, and children often enjoy snatches from the plays. Very few of the latter have been included, from lack of space, but every teacher must have favourite Shakespearean passages, a few lines to quote at an appropriate moment, which pupils may remember, and later grow to comprehend.

Reference is given to a wide variety of sources – pages 196-230 list 291 volumes. It is to be hoped that teachers will procure as many different poetry books as possible, to give children the opportunity to browse widely. In the list of books, each is identified by a symbol, a group of letters giving some indication of its title if it is an anthology, or of its author if it is by a single poet. These symbols are explained on page 195 and arranged alphabetically on pages 196-230 for convenient reference and identification. I hope the few words of comment on each book may assist the teacher who is building up a poetry library to decide whether any particular book is worth closer inspection. For more detailed and illuminating descriptions of available books of poems see *Poetry 0-16* by Morag Styles and Pat Triggs (Books for Keeps, 1988).

This index is by no means comprehensive, but highly selective and personal. No poem is included that I would not, in particular circumstances, be happy to offer to a class. No one person can choose poems for another to teach with any certainty of success, though many poems are widely popular with a majority of teachers and pupils. No teacher should ever give a class a poem unless she herself, or he himself, receives genuine pleasure from it. Enjoyment and boredom are both infectious.

In laying great emphasis upon the *enjoyment* of poetry I find myself in good company. Sir Philip Sidney wrote that the end of poesie is 'to teach and delight'; Dr Johnson declared that 'the end of poetry is to instruct by pleasing'; Robert Frost said that a poem 'begins in delight and ends in wisdom'. I hope that this book may help teachers to find poems which will both delight and enlighten their classes.

Helen Morris
Cambridge 1991

The Grouping of Poems

The poems are grouped according to their subjects, but certain *kinds* of poems will be found under the following headings: COUNTING RHYMES, COUNTING-OUT RHYMES, CUMULATIVE RHYMES, FABLES, LIMERICKS, NONSENSE, PAINTING:POEMS FOR PICTURE-MAKING, PARODY, QUESTION AND ANSWER, RIDDLES, TALES (CAUTIONARY) and TALES (TALL).

Sometimes a large group of poems on the same subject is divided into two sections, (L & D) for 'Lyric and Descriptive' and (N) for 'Narrative', so that the reader looking for a few vivid lines will not find a long story, and vice versa.

The poems are arranged alphabetically, by title, under each heading. The articles 'A', 'An' and 'The' have been ignored. When only part of a poem is given, this is preceded by either 'from' or 'part'.

Explanation of the letters and numbers following each poem will be found on page 195.

The Index

ABORIGINES

Bwalla the Hunter (Kath Walker)
In the hard famine time, in the long drought
Aus R 108

Last of his Tribe (Kath Walker)
Change is the law. The new must oust the old
Aus B 117

Spirit Belong Mother (Eva Johnson)
I not see you long time now
Aus R 126

Spiritual Song of the Aborigine (Hyllus Maris)
I am a child of the Dreamtime people
Aus B 15

ABRAHAM AND ISAAC

from the *Chester Miracle Play* (anon.)
Abraham, my servant, Abraham
Floc 78
O Isaac, Isaac, my darling dear
Sun 60

The Parable of the Old Man and the Young (Wilfred Owen)
So Abram rose, and clave the wood and went
Cam I 119; Floc 250; FWW 101; Sun 212; Voi III 127

ACCIDENTS: AT HOME

Advice to Children (Roy Fuller)
Caterpillars living on lettuce
Sort 9; Young 66

Dad and the Cat and the Tree (Kit Wright)
This morning a cat got
All 26; Once 84; Ox T 60; P Sev 54; Wri R 23

Daddy Fell into the Pond (Alfred Noyes)
Everyone grumbled. The sky was grey.
Like 20; Mad 58; Nine 87; Walk 156

Dahn the Plug'ole (anon.)
A muvver was barfing 'er biby one night
CBC 93; Mad 39; Rat 120; Voi II 164; Young 61

Dear Mum (Brian Patten)
While you were out
Pat T 123

The Gas Man Cometh (M. Flanders and D. Swann)
'Twas on a Monday morning
Face 62

I Used to Have a Little Red Alarm Clock (Michael Rosen)
I used to have a little red alarm clock
McRo 67

Micky Always (John Agard)
Bambalitty-Bambam
Five 113

Motor Accident (Vernon Scannell)
When he set off the sun was bright
Sca T 34

'Out, Out —' (Robert Frost)
The buzz saw snarled and rattled in the yard
Cam II 15; Rat 329; Voi II 10; Touch V 14; Wind 58

Richard's Brother Speaks (Desmond Strachan)
Richard . . ./ What's the matter?
Stuf 19

Sir Smasham Uppe (E. V. Rieu)
Good afternoon, Sir Smasham Uppe
CCV 32; King 240; P Sev 103; OWN 46; Puf Q 115; Walk 167

Wendy in Winter (Kaye Starbird)
No wonder Wendy's coat blew off
Mea 46

ACCIDENTS: MINES

The Avondale Mine Disaster (anon.)
Good Christians all, both great and small
Iron 75

Ballad of Springhill (Ewan MacColl and Peggy Seeger)
In the town of Springhill, Nova Scotia
KCP 126

The Brothers (Wilfrid Gibson)
All morning they had quarrelled as they worked
Nar 152

1

The Collier's Wife (D. H. Lawrence)
Somebody's knockin' at th' door
Speak 114; Wind 94

The Explosion (Philip Larkin)
On the day of the explosion
Ang II 46; Foc 156; Gold 28; Rat 144; Story 22

Flynn of Virginia (Bret Harte)
Didn't know Flynn –
KWP 85

The Gresford Disaster (trad.)
You've heard of the Gresford disaster
Ax 33; Nar 139; Voi III 142

ACCIDENTS: SCHOOL

An Accident (Wes Magee)
The playground noise stilled
Mea 48

ACCIDENTS: TRANSPORT

Auto Wreck (Karl Shapiro)
Its quick soft silver bell beating, beating
Floc 131; Rat 54

Drunk, or Stunned, or Dead? (James Aitchison)
Drunk, or stunned, or dead? I couldn't say
Scot 132

Casey Jones (anon.)
Come all you rounders I want you to hear
KWP 223

The Fallen Birdman (Roger McGough)
The old man in the cripplechair
Fire 43

A Farmer Went Trotting (anon.)
A farmer went trotting upon his grey mare
Cow 56

Fifteen (William Stafford)
South of the bridge on Seventeenth
Voi II 89

Interruption to a Journey (Norman MacCaig)
The hare we had run over
CCC 123; Rat 214

Meditation on the A30 (Sir John Betjeman)
A man on his own in a car
Ax 42; Rat 283

Mid-Term Break (Seamus Heaney)
I sat all morning in the college sick bay
Fire 133

Solitude (from Swedish, Robert Bly)
Right here I was nearly killed one night in February
Rat 397

Travelling through the Dark (William Stafford)
Travelling through the dark I found a deer
Ax 60; Floc 225; Foc 56; Open 95; Voi II 65

ACROBATS

Acrobats (Shel Silverstein)
I'll swing / By my ankles
PoWo I 48; Sil 10

The Man on the Flying Trapeze (anon.)
Oh the girl that I loved she was handsome
Story 24

The Man on the Flying Trapeze (Jack Prelutsky)
Sporting and capering high in the breeze
FF 64; ATP 112

ADAM AND EVE

from *Adam's Apple: Forbidden Fruit* (John Fuller)
Adam and Eve, Adam and Eve
Quin 93

Ancient History (Siegfried Sassoon)
Adam, a brown old vulture in the rain
Mes 219; Sun 51

Paradise Tint (Alexander Scott)
Said Adam til Eve
Scot 93

They Wondered Why the Fruit had been Forbidden (W. H. Auden)
They wondered why the fruit had been forbidden
Sun 49i

ADDERS

Charm for an Adder Bite (anon.)
Underneath this hazelen mot
Puf M 28

ADVERTISING

The Adman (A. S. J. Tessimond)
This trumpeter of nothingness, employed
Show III 14

Adman (Nigel Gray)
I'm the new man
Ang I 106

Defence of the Ad-Man (A. S. J. Tessimond)
He brings us aims and dreams and drugs; he tells
Show III 15

Mad Ad (Roger McGough)
A Madison Avenue whizzkid
Ang I 106; McG G 40

AEROPLANES

Sonic Boom (John Updike)
I'm sitting in the living room
Earth 29

AFRICA

Mango, Little Mango (anon.)
The mango stands for Africa
Pic 38, Wheel 27

AGINCOURT

Agincourt (Michael Drayton)
Fair stood the wind for France
Fab CV 237; Iron 70; NTP 172

from *Henry V*, before Agincourt (William Shakespeare)
Chorus: Now entertain conjecture of a time
Cam II 66
Westmoreland: O that we now had here
ND 162, PW 48

This day is called the feast of Crispian
Brave 129

AIR RAIDS

See Wars

ALCHEMISTS

The Alchemist (Gareth Owen)
There's a mysterious light
AFP 52

'ALIENS' FROM SPACE

Alien Humour (John Agard)
A visiting alien from out of space
Aga L 30

A Close Encounter (Adrian Rumble)
I was returning from a friend's one night
Shad 66; Spa 68; UD 36

Creature from Outer Space (Robert Heidbreder)
'I come from outer space . . .'
Hei 47

A Day on the Planet (Brian Morse)
We landed ten and a half hours local time
Mor 104

Four Children, One Being (Julie Holder)
The small ship
Spa 74

The Marrog (R. C. Scriven)
My desk's at the back of the class
AM 11; Like 85; MCF 60; Mons 8; Nine 158; Sk 60; Spa 77; Walk 125

Mars (anon.)
And then in my dream I slipped away
Shad 32

Never Since Eden (Raymond Wilson)
The Thing that came from Outer Space
Spa 78; Story 34

Out of a Cloud (Richard Edwards)
I have never seen one
Boo 85

3

Visitor (Adrian Henri)
Prepare to decelerate.
Hen 51

Zonky Zizzibug (Brian Patten)
I've just appeared in this classroom
SO 36

ALLIGATORS

Alligator (Grace Nichols)
If you want to see an alligator
Nic 4

THE ALPHABET

The Twenty-Sixers (Philip Gross)
We are the twenty-sixers
Gro 3

Twenty-Six Letters (James Rees)
Twenty-six cards in half a pack
Ree 3, Ree C 146

ALPHABET RHYMES

See *Ox Dic 47-52, Ox NR 105-9, Ree C 147-73*

Alphabestiary (Mark Burgess)
A was an ass that didn't eat grass
Bur F 8

An A-Z of the Items Found on the School Roof (Wes Magee)
Apple core (brown)
Mag W 30

The ABC (Spike Milligan)
'Twas midnight in the schoolroom
Bell 57; CBC 60; HH 58; Like 101; Sk 46

An Alphabet of Horrible Habits (Colin West)
A is for Albert who makes lots of noise
West 20

An Alphabet of Questions (Charles Edward Carryl)
Have Angleworms attractive homes?
CBC 22; OSF 20; PG 53

The Alphabet Speaks Up (David Horner)
A YOU / B QUIET
Rhy 126

An Animal Alphabet (Edward Lear)
The Absolutely Abstemious Ass
Chat 252; Rat 32; Show II 37; illustrated Lea B 103

Animal Alphabet (Zoe Goodall, aged 12)
Antelopes stare at you
HH 56

A Tumbled Down (Edward Lear)
And hurt his Arm
Lea C 270

A Was an Ant (Edward Lear)
Who seldom stood still
Lea C 131

A Was an Ape (Edward Lear)
Who stole some white tape
Lea C 145, RT 21

A Was an Apple-pie (anon.)
A was an apple-pie / B bit it
Lob 126; Ox Dic 47; Puf NR 12; Voa 4; Young 42

A Was an Archer (anon.)
A was an Archer who shot at a frog
B was a Butcher who kept a bull-dog
Fab NV 43; NV 24; Ox Dic 48; Ox NR 106

A Was an Archer (anon. c.1700)
A was an Archer and shot at a frog
B was a Blindman, and led by a dog
Ox CV 43; Ox Dic 49; Sk 48

A Was Once an Apple-Pie (Edward Lear)
A was once an apple-pie
Fab NV 186; Lea C 138; Ox CV 192; Ox NR 108

A Bestiary of the Garden (Phyllis Gotlieb)
On and between the blades of grass
Can 88

The New England Primer (anon. 1727 and 1768)
In Adam's fall / We sinned all
Ox A 7

Proverbial Alphabet (Michael Richards)
Acorns were good till bread was found
WP 22

Sally's Alphabet (Edwin Brock)
A is for alphabet
IC 45

AMERICANS, NATIVE

See Indians, American

ANGELS

The Barranong Angel Case (Les A. Murray)
You see that bench in front of Meagher's store?
Sun 86

The Fullness of Time (James Stephens)
On a rusty iron throne
Sun 82

Michael, Archangel (Alcuin, trans. Helen Waddell)
Michael, Archangel
Sun 85

The Seventh Angel (Zbigniew Herbert, trans. P. D. Scott)
The seventh angel / is completely different
Sun 83

ANGER

Anger Lay by Me all Night Long (Elizabeth Daryush)
Anger lay by me all night long
Rat 32; Show II 5

Anger's Freeing Power (Stevie Smith)
I had a dream three walls stood up wherein a raven bird
NTP 154

A Poison Tree (William Blake)
I was angry with my friend
Cam I 19; Choice 50; Fire 85; NTP 153; Rat 349; Story 1, Voi II 86; WS 57; YD 32

The Quarrel (Eleanor Farjeon)
I quarrelled with my brother
Nine 95

ANIMALS

See also Pets
See also Alligators, Antelopes, Apes and Monkeys, Baboons, Badgers, Bandicoots, Bats, Bears, Buffaloes, Bulls, Camels, Cats, Crocodiles, Deer, Dogs, Donkeys, Dormice, Dromedaries, Elephants, Fieldmice, Foxes, Frogs, Gerbils, Giraffes, Goats, Gorillas, Guinea-Pigs, Hamsters, Hares, Hedgehogs, Hippopotami, Horses, Hyenas, Jaguars, Kangaroos, Kittens, Lambs, Leopards, Mice, Moles, Monkeys *see* Apes, Mooses, Mountain Lions, Oxen, Pandas, Panthers, Pigs, Platypuses, Possums, Rabbits, Racehorses, Rams, Sheep, Skunks, Sloths, Squirrels, Stags, Tigers, Tortoises, Turtles, Weasels, Whales, Wolverines, Wombats, Yaks, Zebras

The Air was Filled with a Clamour (Ogden Nash)
The air was filled with a clamour appalling
Howl 54

Allie (Robert Graves)
Allie, call the birds in
Name 8; NTP 95; PoWo I 68; Spi 98; Tick 152

Animals' Houses (James Reeves)
Of animals' houses
Ox T 87; Puf Q 75; Ree C 19

At the Waterhole (Richard Edwards)
Hysterics at the waterhole
Edw M 36

from *The Bells of Heaven* (Ralph Hodgson)
'Twould ring the bells of heaven
Jung 101; Poem I 29; Ring 89

Better be Kind to Them Now (D. J. Enright)
A squirrel is digging up the bulbs
KWP 67; Pets 83; Sort 56; WZ 16

The Day the Animals Talked (Terry Jones)
I woke up one morning
Jon 66

Jump or Jiggle (Evelyn Beyer)
Frogs jump / Caterpillars hump
Day 31; Fab NV 74; Fun 11; Read 7; Tick 107; Tim 19

Over in the Meadow (anon.)
Over in the meadow in the sand in the sun
Fab NV 24; P Sev 30

The Vet (Guy Boas)
To be a successful and competent vet
Open 42

What in the World? (Eve Merriam)
What in the world
Pop 63; PoWo I 28

What They Said (German, trans. Rose Fyleman)
It's four o'clock
Fab NV 75; Pop 7

Poor Old Horse (anon.)
My clothing was once of the linset woolsey fine
Iron 21; Tick 136

Prayers (Leonard Clark)
Pray for the millions of battery hens
Cla C 21

The Righteous Mother (Eden Philpotts)
'Wretch!' cried the mother to her infant son
CCC 110, King 80

ANIMALS, CRUELTY TO

from *Auguries of Innocence* (William Blake)
To see a World in a grain of sand
Choice 48; Earth 38; Fab CV 63; ND 58; Puf V 60; Rat 47
(part) A dog starved at his master's gate
Sun 26

Family Holiday (Raymond Wilson)
Eight months ago, on Christmas Day
Ani 14; Foot 38; Pets 9

I Had a Little Pony (anon.)
I had a little pony
Ani 26; Ox Dic 143; Ox NR 99; NV 96; Ox PC 115; Puf NR 32; Puf V 41; Voa 45

Mole (Robert Sykes, aged 14)
Tapered black barrel with excavator paws
Rab 68

A Mouse Lived in a Laboratory (Kathryn Boydell, aged 15)
The scientists dyed a mouse bright blue
Rab 74

The Newcomer (Brian Patten)
There's something new in the river
Pat 14

The Old Nag's Song (Charles E. Carryl)
It's very confining this living in stables
CBC 50

The Owl's Trick (Brian Patten)
From its hollow and aged tree
Pat T 18

ANIMALS, FANTASTIC

See also Dragons, Monsters
See also Hug MW, McG M, throughout; *Ree C* 119-42

An Animal Alphabet (Edward Lear)
The Absolutely Abstemious Ass
Chat 252; Lea B 103; Rat 32; Show II 37

The Burrow Wolf (Ted Hughes)
A kind of wolf lives in the moon's holes
Hug MW 14

The Earth-Owl (Ted Hughes)
Far undergrounded
Hug MW 30

The Kwackagee (James Reeves)
Back in the bleak and blurry days
Fun 300

The Midnightmouse (Christian Morgenstern, trans. W. D. Snodgrass and Lore Segal)
It midnights, not a moon is out
Chat 347

Moon-Whales (Ted Hughes)
They plough through the moon stuff
Hug MW 10

Oliphaunt (J. R. R. Tolkien)
Grey as a mouuse
RT 144

A Perfect Pet (Barbara Giles)
Now you have a papagouli
UD 9

The Phoenix (Michael Rosen)
On the banks of the Nile
Ros W 63

6

'Quack!' said the Billy-Goat
(Charles Causley)
'Quack!' said the billy-goat
Ani 23; Cau F 20; Rog 15

The Roc (Edward Lowbury)
Scattered like flotsam on the
erupting sea
MCF 63

Silly Old Baboon (Spike Milligan)
There was a Baboon
Like 77

The Snitterjipe (James Reeves)
In mellow orchards, rich and ripe
Like 57, Ree C 137

Some Called him Rover (Michael
Rosen)
Some called him Rover
Ros M 43

The Wonderful Derby Ram (anon.)
As I was going to Derby
*Fab NV 70; Nine 162; Ox Dic 145; Ox
NR 205*

ANTELOPES

Kob Antelope (from Yoruba, Ulli
Beier)
A creature to pet and spoil
Rat 202

APES AND MONKEYS

Colobus Monkey (from Yoruba,
Ulli Beier)
We invite him to die
Rat 200

Red Monkey (from Yoruba, Ulli
Beier)
Child of maize!
Rat 203

The Ship of Rio (Walter de la
Mare)
There was a ship of Rio
de la M P 28; Fab NV 242; PG 75

APOLOGIES

Dear Sir (Stephen Dow, aged 11)
Dear Sir, I'm sorry about my
misbehaviour
WS 90

Laurie and Dorrie (Kit Wright)
The first thing that you'll notice if
Wri H 66

This is Just to Say (William Carlos
Williams)
I have eaten / the plums
*Cal 88; Floc 232; NTP 72; Tick 35;
Walk 146*

APPLES: COOKED

A – Apple Pie (Walter de la Mare)
Little Polly Pillikins
Pic 134

Apple-Pie (William King 1663-
1712)
Of all the delicates which Britons try
Pic 67

Mother Eve's Pudding (anon.)
If you want a good pudding to teach
you I'm willing
Pic 72

Sunday Special (Tom Durham)
'Come along, troops!'
Pic 116

APPLES: RAW

After Apple-Picking (Robert Frost)
My long two-pointed ladder's
sticking through a tree
*Choice 279; NTP 246; Touch V 48;
WP 110*

And God Said to the Little Boy
(George Barker)
And God said to the little boy
Pic 149

The Apple-Raid (Vernon
Scannell)
Darkness came early, though not yet
cold
*All 104; Poem I 86; Quin 182; Story
148*

Apple Song (Brian Jones)
I am an apple
Pic 27; WP 107

Apples (Laurie Lee)
Behold the apples' rounded worlds
Pic 29; WP 109

The Apple's Song (Edwin Morgan)
Tap me with your finger
*Nif 40; Pic 135; PoWo II 84; Strict 40;
WP 106*

I Bit an Apple (Vernon Scannell)
I bit an apple and the flesh was sweet
Sca 55

Moonlit Apples (John Drinkwater)
At the top of the house the apples
are laid in rows
Gold 44, Pic 30, WP 108

APRIL

All Fools' Day (John Agard)
First Voice: Look you bicycle wheel /
turning round
Aga 30; Cele 34

April (Ted Robinson)
So here we are in April, in showy,
blowy April
GTP 273, Occ 34

April Birthday (Ted Hughes)
When your birthday brings the
world under your window
Fifth 56

April Rise (Laurie Lee)
If ever I saw blessing in the air
Floc 13; ND 8; Out 33

A Day in Spring (Richard
Edwards)
I was lying in the bath
Edw M 74; Occ 35

School Dinner Menu for April 1
(Wes Magee)
Solid Soup / Grilled Carrots
Cele 35

ARITHMETIC

See also Maths, Numbers

Arithmetic (Carl Sandburg)
Arithmetic is where numbers fly
Bell 29; Floc 238; Pop 93; Walk 218

Stable's Tables (Roy Fuller)
There was a girl called Sheila Stables
Sort 92

THE ARK

See Noah

ARMADA

See also Drake

The Armada (Lord Macaulay)
Attend all ye who list to hear our
noble England's praise
Fab CV 243

The Armada, 1588 (John Wilson
1588-1677)
Our little fleet in July first
Ox CV 24

Some Years of Late (anon.)
Some years of late in eighty-eight
Fab CV 241

ARTHUR, KING

from *The Passing of Arthur* (Lord
Tennyson)
And answer made King Arthur,
breathing hard
ND 203

ASPARAGUS

Fields of Asparagus (Andrew
Young)
From their long narrow beds
Pic 19

ASPENS

Aspens (Edward Thomas)
All day and night, save winter, every
weather
Choice 176

ASTRONAUTS

If He Cried, He Cried in Private
(John Kitching)
If he cried, he cried in private
Spa 97

The Doomed Spaceman (Ted
Walker)
I remember one winter-night
meadow
Spa 100

Retired (Iain Crichton Smith)
He was tired after his voyages
Spa 106

AUGUST

August (Christina Rossetti)
And is this August weather? Nay,
not so
Occ 45

AUNTS

Anteater (Roger McGough)
Anteater, Anteater / Where have you been?
McG S 39

from *Aunts and Uncles* (Mervyn Peake)
When Aunty Jane
Nine 99

Big Aunt Flo' (Wes Magee)
Every Sunday afternoon
All 20; Mag M 20

Hearts and Flowers (Roger McGough)
Aunty Marge / Spinster of the parish
McG F 10

Hugger Mugger (Kit Wright)
I'd sooner be / Jumped and thumped
Gold 56; Speak 12

My Aunt (Ted Hughes)
You've heard how a green thumb
Hug F 37

My Aunt Flo (Ted Hughes)
Horrible! Horrible! Horrible is my old Aunt Flo
Hug F 41

AUSTRALIA (L and D)

See also Pat A throughout
See also Bushrangers, Corroboree

Australia! (Gavin Ewart)
Australian animals / haunt my dreams
Ewar 76

Australian Scenery (A. B. Paterson)
A land of sombre, silent hills, where mountain cattle go
Pat A 8

Australian Windmill Song (Max Fatchen)
By the clay-red creek on the dry summer day
Fat S 60; Pud 80

Buffalo Country (A. B. Paterson)
Out where the grey streams glide
Pat A 48; WZ 66

The Dead Swagman (Nancy Cato)
His rusted billy left beside the tree
O & A 125; Voi II 12

Down Under (Gavin Ewart)
Kookaburras and Currawongs
Ewar 50

In the Bush (Anne Le Roy)
In the bush / you might see
WZ 54

The Numbat (Michael Rosen)
The numbat / isn't a bat / OK?
Ark 62

From Old Australian Ways (A. B. Paterson)
The wind is in the barley grass
Pos 128

AUSTRALIA (N)

A Bushman's Song (A. B. Paterson)
I'm travelling down the Castlereagh, and I'm a station-hand
Iron 89

The Man from Snowy River (A. B. Paterson)
There was movement at the station, for the word had passed around
Nar 44

The Shearer's Wife (Louis Esson)
Before the glare o' dawn I rise
World 39

AUTUMN

Autumn (John Clare)
I love the fitful gust that shakes
Sing 18; WAS 139

From Autumn (Vernon Scannell)
It is the football season once more
Floc 264

Autumn Fires (Robert Louis Stevenson)
In the other gardens
Abi 24; NTP 114; Sing 17; Ste 102

The Computer's Ode to Autumn (Laurence Lerner)
Season of probabilities! Of seeds
Strict 100

A Day in Autumn (R. S. Thomas)
It will not always be like this
Choice 309

Gathering Leaves (Robert Frost)
Spades take up leaves
Earth 45

Late Autumn (Andrew Young)
The boy called to his team
Out 48

Leaves (Ted Hughes)
Who's killed the leaves?
Pro II 59

Ode to Autumn (John Keats)
Season of mists and mellow
fruitfulness
*Cam II 126; Choice 66; Fav 137; Fire
143; GTP 279; Like 174; Mes 97;
NTP 125; Rat 434; Show III 75*

Something Told the Wild Geese
(Rachel Field)
Something told the wild geese
*Cal 90; Once 51; Open 73; Out 60; Ox
A 240; Walk 85; WAS 109; YD 67*

Song (R. W. Dixon)
The feathers of the willow
Fab CV 55; Ox PC 134; This W 61

Summer is Gone (from the Irish,
Kuno Meyer)
My tidings for you: the stag bells
Fab CV 55

There Came a Day (Ted Hughes)
There came a day that caught the
summer
KCP 101; WS 96

Three Autumns in Regent's Park
(Gerda Mayer)
The footballers
Candy 10

When the Frost is on the Punkin
(J. W. Riley)
When the frost is on the punkin
Out 50

BABEL

The Tower of Babel (Nathaniel
Crouch)
After the dreadful Flood was past
Sun 58

BABIES

from *After the Christening* (Ogden
Nash)
Come along, everybody, see the
pretty baby
Face 19

Babies are Boring (Peter
Mortimer)
(Oh yes they are)
Gold 82

The First Tooth (Charles and
Mary Lamb)
Through the house what busy joy
NV 20; Ox CV 143; Walk 135; WS 89

Infant Joy (William Blake)
I have no name
GTP 10; Name 49; NTP 22; This W 52

The First Year No VIII (E. J.
Scovell)
The baby in his blue night-jacket
propped on hands
Moon 45

Little Flower (Cecil Rajendra
[Malaysia])
Your arrrival was unplanned
Stuf II 11

Looking Upwards (Richard
Edwards)
Those big pink faces
Edw M 21

Morning Song (Sylvia Plath)
Love set you going like a fat gold
watch
Foc 108; NTP 23; Touch V 135

New Baby (Valerie Bloom)
Mi baby sista come home las' week
ATP 18

The Rival Arrives (Brian Patten)
Tom, take the baby out the fridge
Pat T 91

Seven Activities for a Young Child
(Alan Brownjohn)
Turn on the tap for straight and
silver water
Rhy 28

When I Was Young (Allan
Ahlberg)
When I was young and had no sense
Ahl P 44

You're (Sylvia Plath)
Clownlike, happiest on your hands
Cam II 10

BADGERS

The Badger (John Clare)
The badger grunting on his
woodland track

Fav 119; Rat 57; Show I 31
(part) *Cla J 50*
When midnight comes a host of dogs
and men
Story 146

The Badgers (Eden Philpotts)
Brocks snuffle from their holt within
CCC 197

Badgers (Richard Edwards)
Badgers come creeping from dark
underground
Edw P 17

Bess my Badger (Ted Hughes)
Bess my badger grew up
Mes 110

The Combe (Edward Thomas)
The Combe was ever dark, ancient
and dark
Rab 78; Earth 61; Voi II 39

The Six Badgers (Robert Graves)
As I was a-hoeing, a-hoeing my lands
Fab NV 22

BAD TEMPER

To Beat Bad Temper (Cynthia
Mitchell)
An angry tiger in a cage
Gold 43

BAKERS

Our Village (John Yeoman and
Quentin Blake)
Down in the bakery
Vil 4

BAKING

Baking Day (Rosemary Joseph)
Thursday was baking day in our
house
Pic 61

The Friday Night Smell (Marc
Matthews [Caribbean])
I love the Friday night smell
ASP 54; Blac 24; Nif 51; Stuf 60

Wake Up, Sleepy Head (Gregory
Harrison)
Wake up, wake up, sleepy head
Tick 40

BALLOONS

Balloons (Sylvia Plath)
Since Christmas they have lived with
us
Touch IV 87

Hot Air Balloon (Philip Gross)
*Here Be Dragons . . . Old maps bred
them*
Gro 45

BALLS

My Ball (Eva May)
Why does my ball
Pos 100

BANANAS

See also Jamaica

Banana Man (Grace Nichols)
I'm a banana man
Five 14; Nic 21

Banana Talk (Brian Jones)
Bananas, said his mother, are curved
and yellow
AVF 56

BANDICOOTS

Benjamin Bandicoot (A. B.
Paterson)
If you walk in the bush at night
Pat A 29

BANDS

The Ceremonial Band (James
Reeves)
The old King of Dorchester
Nine 344; Noisy 2; Once 136; Ree C 68

Here Comes the Band (William
Cole)
The band comes booming down the
street
Pop 90

The Howling Pandemonium
(Eleanor Farjeon)
Crash and CLANG! *Bash* and BANG!
Howl 17

Old King Cole's Band (anon.)
Old King Cole was a merry old soul
Lob 161; Ox T 12; Puf NR 120; (part)
Voa 75

our school band (Wes Magee)
our school band
Mag W 6

BANJOS

The Song of the Banjo (Rudyard Kipling)
You couldn't pack a Broadwood half a mile
Fab CV 37

BARBERS

Alex at the Barber's (John Fuller)
He is having his hair cut. Towels are tucked
Quin 86

Haircut (Allan Ahlberg)
I hate having my hair cut
Ahl P 89; SS 22

I'll Get One Tomorrow (Ogden Nash)
Barber, barber, come and get me
Nas C 60

Solu the Barber (Russell Hoban)
I know a barber named Solu
Six 167

from *Suzanne at the Hairdresser's* (Ian Serraillier)
Robed in white on a lofty throne
Occ 138

BARLEY

The Golden Boy (Ted Hughes)
In March he was buried
Out 46; WAS 116; YD 85

John Barleycorn (anon.)
There was three kings into the east
Fab CV 197; ND 131; Rat 222
There came three men from out of the west
Iron 133

BASKETBALL

Foul Shot (Edwin A. Hoey)
With two 60s stuck on the scoreboard
Walk 220

BATHING: INDOORS

After a Bath (Aileen Fisher)
After my bath / I try, try, try
All 112; Day 39; Ox T 47; RT 62

Bathtime (Mark Burgess)
I love a bath
Bur 10

Bathtime (Michael Rosen)
Quite often / my mum used to say to me
Ros Q 47

Blur (Julie O'Callaghan)
A strange light
O'Ca 59

Come On In the Water's Lovely (Gareth Owen)
Come on in the water's lovely
King 26

Hello, I'm Home! (June Crebbin)
I'm not dirty –
Cre 78

Mum Takes a Bath (Mick Gowar)
On a normal, average day in our house
Gow T 32

The Tub (George S. Chappell)
My tub is an aquarium
Pos 84

Why is it? (Max Fatchen)
Why is it that / In our bathroom
Fat S 54; SS 24

BATHING: OUT OF DOORS

First Dip (John Walsh)
Wave after wavelet goes
DS 12

In Goes Robin (Eleanor Farjeon)
In goes Robin, bold as brass
Far R 84

Pater's Bathe (Edward Abbott Parry)
You can take a tub with a rub and a scrub
Ox CV 309; (part) Corn 68

BATS

Bat (D. H. Lawrence)
At evening, sitting on this terrace
Ten 54

The Bat (Gavin Ewart)
Consider the Bat.
Ewar 15

The Bat (Ogden Nash)
Myself, I rather like the bat
CCC 194; Nas C 123

The Bat (Ted Hughes)
The beggarly Bat, a cut out, scattily
CCC 193

The Bat (Theodore Roethke)
By day the bat is cousin to the mouse
CCC 195; Floc 209; GTP 56; Mons 74;
Ox A 257; Poem I 35; Pop 45; Pro I 18;
RMP 19; Shad 49; Ting 20; Walk 56;
Zoo 68

Bat Chant (Liz Lochhead)
I'm a bat / furry bat
King 225

Bats (Randall Jarrell)
A bat is born
CCC 195; Ox A 259; Rab 66

Ffangs the Vampire Bat (Ted
Hughes)
Ffangs the vampire landed in
London
Hug V 32

Man and Bat (D. H. Lawrence)
When I went into my room, at
mid-morning
Rat 262

Moon Bat (Sebastian Mays, aged
10)
Once I held a bat, its small helpless
Gold 67

BATTLES

See Fab CV 231-63
See also Sea Battles
See also Agincourt, Blenheim,
Otterbourne, Waterloo

BEACHCOMBING

Beachcomber (George Mackay
Brown)
Monday I found a boot
Cal 79; Gold 32; NTP 48; O & A 118;
Sea 63

BEACHES

The Beach (William Hart-Smith)
The beach is a quarter of golden
fruit
Show I 57

from *Dover Beach* (Matthew
Arnold)
The sea is calm tonight
Floc 53

BEARS

The Bear on the Delhi Road (Earle
Birney)
Unreal tall as a myth
Jung 102

A Big Bare Bear (Robert
Heidbreder)
A big bare bear bought a bear
balloon
Hei 5

Black Bear (Douglas Lepan)
Sweet-mouth, honey-paws, hairy
one!
Can 94

The Black Bear (Ted Hughes)
The Bear's black bulk / Is solid sulk
Hug U 18

Furry Bear (A. A. Milne)
If I were a bear
Mil NS 46; Pop 22; Stoc 22; Zoo 28

My Mother Saw a Dancing Bear
(Charles Causley)
My mother saw a dancing bear
Cal 58; Cau F 95; Foot 39; KWP 50;
PoWo II 60; Quin 48; Sort 65; WS 52

Nowhere Bear (John Mole)
I'm a nowhere bear, a threadbare
bear
Mol 50

Our Village (John Yeoman and
Quentin Blake)
The hurdy gurdy's playing
Vil 31

The Travelling Bear (Amy Lowell)
Grass-blades push up between the
cobblestones
Jung 104

BECKET

from *Murder in the Cathedral*
(T. S. Eliot)
Bar the door. Bar the door.
Sun 186

BEDS

from *The Bed Book* (Sylvia Plath)
Beds come in all sizes
P Sev 148
Most Beds are Beds / For sleeping or
resting
RMP 56

These are the Beds / for me and for
you!
Walk 217

The Great Bed of Ware (Mark
Burgess)
Oh, there's none to compare
Bur 50

BEDTIME

Bed! (Joni Akinrele)
When it is time to go to bed
Spi 33

Bed in Summer (Robert Louis
Stevenson)
In winter I get up at night
*Cal 71; NV 70; Ox CV 293; OX T 149;
Puf V 137; Sing 13; Ste 17*

Bed Time (Accabre Huntley)
Can I stay up five
Blac 40

Bedtime (Allan Ahlberg)
When I go upstairs to bed
AFP 56; Ahl P 93; Gold 76

Bedtime (Eleanor Farjeon)
Five minutes, five minutes more,
please!
*All 113; Day 36; Far R 25; Ox T 149;
Read 70*

Closing of the Door (Mick Gowar)
God keep us safe this night
Gow F 12

Escape at Bedtime (Robert Louis
Stevenson)
The lights from the parlour and
kitchen shone out
*GTP 13; KCP 193; KWP 200; Ox T
148; Shad 104; Ste 38; YD 129*

Going to Bed (Eleanor Farjeon)
Oh dear! need I brush my hair?
DS 60; Far M 40

Half Asleep (Gareth Owen)
Half asleep / And half awake
Ox T 156; YD 133

Hard Cheese (Justin St John)
The grown-ups are all safe
KWP 181

I Don't Want to Go to Bed (Mark
Burgess)
I don't want to go to bed
Bur 8

I Like to Stay Up (Grace Nichols)
I like to stay up
*ASP 59; Blac 100; Five 10; Nic 6; Stuf
72*

In the Dark (A. A. Milne)
I've had my supper
S Sun 85

In the Summer When I Go to Bed
(Thomas Hood)
In the summer when I go to bed
KCP 98

Not in Bed Yet! (Max Fatchen)
Getting Albert off to bed
Fat S 22

Now the Day is Over (Sabine
Baring Gould)
Now the day is over
Bed 46

Nurse's Song (William Blake)
When the voices of children are
heard on the green
GTP 11; O & A 73; This W 90

A Poem Just Like This (G. and A.
Mortimer Waterford)
Daddy came home and he read to
me
Nine 28

Sweet Dreams (Ogden Nash)
I wonder as into bed I creep
Nine 180; Once 120

BEES

See also Honey

The Bee (Isaac Watts)
How doth the little busy bee
GTP 69; Sk 32

Bee (George Barker)
I buzz, I buzz, I buzz
CCC 46

The Bees' Song (Walter de la
Mare)
Thousandz of thornz there be
de la M P 113

Buzz Along (Max Fatchen)
The flight of the bee
TG 32

City Bees (J. and G. Curry)
In a drab back yard
Down 46
from *The Georgics* (Virgil, trans.
C. Day Lewis)

14

Next I come to the manna, the
heavenly gift of honey
Floc 113

BEETLES

Forgiven (A. A. Milne)
I found a little beetle so that Beetle
was his name
CCC 180; Mil NS 48

I Knew a Black Beetle
(Christopher Morley)
I knew a black beetle who lived down
a drain
Young 19

Rendez-vous with a Beetle (E. V.
Rieu)
Meet me in Usk
Puf Q 114

BEING BLACK

See also Race Relations

Africa's Plea (Roland Tombekai
Demptster)
I am not you
Voi III 24

Always a Suspect (Oswald
Mbuyiseni Mtshali)
I get up in the morning
Wind 103

Black Bottom (Jackie Kay)
We're practising for the school show
Face 33

Blackness (Glyne Walrond, Carib-
bean)
Blackness is me
Stuf 10; Touch IV 94

Checking Out me History (John
Agard)
Dem tell me / Dem tell me
Ang II 80

Confession (James Berry)
I had a condition, she said
Bab 192

Dream Variation (Langston
Hughes)
To fling my arms wide
PG 50; Touch IV 23

Happy Birthday, Dilroy (John
Agard)
My name is Dilroy
Aga 3; Name 25

Historical Rights (Jawiattika
Blacksheep)
To my darling Mother and my dear
Daddy
Bab 95

I, Too (Langston Hughes)
I, too, sing America
Like 119; NTP 156

Incident (Countee Cullen)
Once riding in old Baltimore
Ox A 253

Killing Me for I (Jawiattika
Blacksheep)
Mansfield (Scotti) Rose
Bab 96

Ku Klux (Langston Hughes)
They took me out
Touch V 131

The Little Black Boy (William
Blake)
My mother bore me in the southron
wild
Iron 22; Ox CV 85; Show II 3

Me, Coloured (Peter Abrahams)
Aunt Liza / Yes? / What am I?
Afr II 46

Prayer of a Black Boy (Guy
Tirolien)
Lord I am so tired
Touch V 114

Sonny's Lettah (Linton Kwesi
Johnson)
Dear Mama / Good Day
Bab 62; FS 54

Stereotype (John Agard)
I'm a full-blooded
Touch IV 163

Strange Fruit (Lewis Allan)
Southern trees bear a strange fruit
Touch V 130

A Strange Meeting (W. H. Davies)
The moon is full and so am I
Ox PC 148

Telephone Conversation (Wole
Soyinka)
The price seemed reasonable,
location
*Face 134; Fire 34; Floc 134; Touch V
116; Voi III 26*

Trench Town shock (Valerie
Bloom)
Waia, Miss May, trouble dey yah
FS 54

BELFAST

Kill the Children (James Simmons)
On Hallowe'en in Ship Street
Ax 81

BELLS

The Bells (Edgar Allan Poe)
Hear the sledges with the bells
Ox A 71; (part) *O & A 70; Puf V 29*

The Bells of London or *Oranges and Lemons* (anon.)
Gay go up and gay go down
Chat 150; Ox Dic 337; Fab NV 116; OX NR 68; Puf V 178; Young 47
(part) Oranges and lemons
NV 47; Puf NR 40

Jingle Bells (James Pierpont)
Dashing through the snow
Chris 35; Stoc 52

BENBOW, ADMIRAL

The Death of Admiral Benbow (anon.)
Come all you sailors bold
Ox PC 44

BICYCLES

See also Motorbikes

Biker's Haikus (Vernon Scannell)
The keen cyclist comes
Sca T 26

Biking (Judith Nicholls)
Fingers grip / toes curl
Nic F 31

Cycling Down the Street to Meet my Friend John (Gareth Owen)
On my bike and down our street
Gold 38; Owe K 13; PG 57

The Cyclist (Louis MacNeice)
Freewheeling down the escarpment past the unpassing horse
Foc 73; Mot 117

Downhill (Sheila Simmons)
I'm rushing / I'm dashing
AFP 24

Esme on her Brother's Bicycle (Russell Hoban)
One foot on, one foot pushing
Cham 89

Going Down Hill on a Bicycle (Henry Charles Beeching)
With lifted feet, hands still
Occ 94

Mulga Bill's Bicycle (A. B. Paterson, Australia)
'Twas Mulga Bill, from Eaglehawk, that caught the cycling craze
Aus B 78

Riding on my Bike (Lois Lenski)
Riding on my bike
Pos 103

The Saga of the Doomed Cyclist (Brian Patten)
When Harry Harris knocked a witch
Pat 76

Tinkering (Diane Dawber)
I love beginning with / a clean sheet
Til 51

BIRCHES

Birches (Robert Frost)
When I see birches bend to left and right
Choice 281; Rat 78; Touch V 46

BIRDS

See also CCC throughout

See also Blackbirds, Bullfinches, Cockatoos, Cocks, Corbies *see* Crows, Cormorants, Crows, Cuckoos, Dotterels, Ducks, Eagles, Egrets, Geese, Hawks, Hens, Herons, Hoopoes, Humming-Birds, Jackdaws, Kestrels, Kingfishers, Lapwings, Larks *see* Skylarks, Linnets, Loons, Magpies, Moor-Hens, Nightingales, Owls, Parrots, Penguins, Pheasants, Pigeons, Ravens, Robins, Rooks, Sandpipers, Shags *see* Cormorants, Skylarks, Sparrows, Starlings, Storm Petrels, Swallows, Swans, Swifts, Thrushes, Turkeys, Vultures, Wagtails, Woodpeckers

See also Sea Birds

Answer to a Child's Question (Samuel Taylor Coleridge)
Do you ask what the birds say? The sparrow, the dove

NTP 94; Ox PC 68; Ox CV 111; Puf V
53; This W 42; WAS 69

A Bird Came Down the Walk
(Emily Dickinson)
A bird came down the walk
KCP 61; Mes 105; ND 72; Ox A 107;
Pop 122

Birds (Ray Fabrizio)
A bird flies and has wings
CCC 91

Birds of Paradise (Christina
Rossetti)
Golden-winged, silver-winged
Jung 46

The Bowerbird (Gavin Ewart)
The male Bowerbird builds
complicated bowers
Ewar 66

Field-Glasses (Andrew Young)
Though buds still speak in hints
Rat 152

The Flight of Birds (John Clare)
The crow goes flopping on from
wood to wood
Show II 56

A Footprint on the Air (Naomi
Lewis)
'Stay!' said the child. The bird said,
'No, . . .'
Foot 13

Magpies in Picardy (T. P.
Cameron Wilson)
The magpies in Picardy
FWW 64; PW 162; War 48

Michael's Song (Wilfrid Gibson)
Because I set no snare
NTP 99

Proud Songsters (Thomas Hardy)
The thrushes sing as the sun is going
Floc 90

Saint Francis and the Birds
(Seamus Heaney)
When Francis preached love to the
birds
Floc 89; NTP 69; Sun 182; WAS 124;
WS 47

To Paint the Portrait of a Bird
(Jacques Prevert, trans.
Lawrence Ferlinghetti)
First paint a cage
Chat 409; Floc 96

The Singing Garden (Irene
Rawnsley)
Mr Barley next door hates birds
Raw 28

A Way Out (Fleur Adcock)
The other option's to become a bird
Show III 30

What Bird So Sings (John Lyly)
What bird so sings, yet so doth wail?
Ox PC 67; This W 70

BIRDS, CAGED

The Birdcatcher's Boy (Thomas
Hardy)
'Father, I fear your trade . . .'
Nar 37

Caged Bird (Maya Angelou)
A free bird leaps
Jung 26

The Caged Bird in Springtime
(James Kirkup)
What can it be
CCC 158; Pets 66; Rab 76; WS 53; Zoo
72

One day at a Perranporth Pet-shop
(Charles Causley)
One day at a Perranporth pet-shop
Fun 26; Pets 70; Sort 44

BIRDS' NESTS

See Cla J 12, 32, 45

Birds' Nests (Edward Thomas)
The summer nests uncovered by
autumn wind
Gold 87

The Blackbird (John Walsh)
She builds her nest on a bare branch
Quin 226

A Cautionary Tale (Nigel Lewis)
Every addled egg
Ten 150

House Hunters (Eleanor Farjeon)
Birds will be house-hunting
Far R 99

The Nest (Jean Kenward)
Don't move / don't touch
Ani 36; Cal 40

The Pettichap's Nest (John Clare)
Well! in my many walks I've rarely
found
Iron 56

Rhyme (Christina Rossetti)
Hear what the mournful linnets say:
WAS 57

The Thrush's Nest (John Clare)
Within a thick and spreading
hawthorn bush
Ark 123; Floc 12; GTP 64; This W 117

BIRTHDAYS

See *Occ 68-80*

BLACKBERRIES

Blackberries (John Walsh)
Wind roaring loud
Cal 85; Pic 36

Blackberry (Harold Monro)
Hedge is like a breaking wave
Pic 37

Blackberrying (Leonard Clark)
'Time to go blackberrying' our
mother said
Cla C 25

Blackberry-Picking (Seamus
Heaney)
Late August, given heavy rain and
sun
Voi II 10

J is for Jam (Eleanor Farjeon)
Blackberries on the brambles
Sing 16

BLACKBIRDS

See also *CCC 102-3*

The Blackbird (Humbert Wolfe)
In the far corner, / close by the
swings
*Like 70; Name 12; Nine 139; Walk 83;
Zoo 64*

The Blackbird by Belfast Lough
(from Irish, AD 800, Frank
O'Connor)
What little throat
Irish 23; WS 46

A Blackbird Singing (R. S.
Thomas)
It seems wrong that out of this bird
Choice 310; Floc 90

The Blackbirds (Walter de la
Mare)
There was an old man, in reproof
CCC 102

I Watched a Blackbird (Thomas Hardy)

I watched a blackbird on a budding
sycamore
CCC 102; WAS 56

*Thirteen Ways of Looking at a
Blackbird* (Wallace Stevens)
Among twenty snowy mountains
Rat 421; Voi III 155

BLACKMAIL

Dane-geld (Rudyard Kipling)
It is always a temptation to an armed
and agile nation
Ten 151

BLACKSMITHS

The Blacksmiths (anon., Medieval
English)
Swart swarthy smiths besmattered
with smoke
Rat 82
Swarte-smeked smethes, smatered
with smoke
Earth 12
Swarthy smoke-blackened smiths,
smudged with soot
KWP 16

Brand the Blacksmith (James
Reeves)
Brand the blacksmith with his hard
hammer
Ree B; Ree C 148

Felix Randall (Gerard Manley
Hopkins)
Felix Randall, the farrier, O he is
dead then?
Choice 114; Fire 24; Voi III 171

Our Village (John Yeoman and
Quentin Blake)
When the darkness falls and the air
grows chill
Vil 36

The Village Blacksmith (Henry
Wadsworth Longfellow)
Under a spreading chestnut tree
Brave 25; Ox A 50

BLENHEIM

After Blenheim (Robert Southey)
It was a summer evening
Brave 32; GTP 146; PW 50

18

BLINDNESS

The Blind Men and the Elephant
(John Godfrey Saxe)
It was six men of Indostan
CBC 119; GTP 200; Once 22; Ox A 82; Ox T 116

Charles (Leonard Clark)
He was born blind with the snow on a winter's day
Six 116

BLUEBERRIES

from *Blueberries* (Robert Frost)
You ought to have seen what I saw on my way
Pic 35

BOATS

The Canoe Speaks (Robert Louis Stevenson)
On the great streams the ships may go
Mot 79

Eton Boating Song (William Cory Johnson)
Jolly boating weather
Cham 74

Paper Boats (Rabindranath Tagore)
Day by day I float my paper boats one by one
Blac 137; O & A 64

Sampan (anon.)
Waves lap lap / Fish fins clap clap
Noisy 9; RT 109; World 48

Where Go the Boats? (Robert Louis Stevenson)
Dark brown is the river
Fab CV 99; Like 49; Mes 41; NTP 30; Ox CV 294; RMP 7; Ste 30; WAS 71

BOOMERANGS

Boomerang (William Hart-Smith)
Behold wood into bird and bird to wood again
NTP 202

BOREDOM

Boredom (Eleanor Farjeon)
Oh dear! What shall I do?
Far M 69; Far R 22

Boredom (Gareth Owen)
Boredom / Is / Me
Owe K 37; Pro III 16; WP 58

Nothing to Do? (Shel Silverstein)
Nothing to do?
All 75; CBC 16

Round the Town (Charles Causley)
Round the town with Billy
WP 27

What Shall I Do? (Brian Lee)
The wind pulls the smoke from the chimney-pots
Sort 78

BOXING

See Cham 43-9

The Ballad of Billy Rose (Leslie Norris)
Outside Bristol Rovers Football Ground
Wind 52

Boxer Man in-a Skippin Workout (James Berry)
Skip on big man, steady steady.
Ber 62; Blac 86; Cham 43

Comeback (Vernon Scannell)
The wind is in a whipping mood tonight
Nar 175

Elegy for Lyn James (Leslie Norris)
I saw your manager fight. He was
Like 140

Epitaph (Rev Emmanuel Collins)
Skidmore, a bruiser of renown
Mot 9

from *First Fight* (Vernon Scannell)
Bite on gumshield
Quin 177
Tonight, then, is the night
Cham 46

The Greatest (Muhammad Ali)
This is a story about a man
Mot 171

Joe Frazier (Muhammad Ali)
I'm gonna come out smokin'
Mot 173

Last Fight (Vernon Scannell)
This is the one you know that you
can't win
Cham 47

Mastering the Craft (Vernon
Scannell)
To make the big time you must learn
Show II 63

Peerless Jim Driscoll (Vernon
Scannell)
I saw Jim Driscoll fight in nineteen
ten
Ax 4; Face 971

Who Killed Davey Moore? (Bob
Dylan)
Who killed Davey Moore
Cam I 122; KCP 66

BOYS

See Side throughout

A Boy's Song (James Hogg)
Where the pools are bright and deep
*All 60; Fav 17; Like 120; Nine 14; O &
A 24; Once 55; Ox PC 138; Ox T 43;
Puf V 134; Rab 45; Side 46(B)*

A Boy's Head (Miroslav Holub)
In it there is a space-ship
*Cam I 7; Chat 450; Floc 71; Like 156;
Open 34; Voi III 167; YD 13*

The Cowpat Throwing Contest
(Brian Moses)
Malc and me and Ian Grey, we
couldn't believe
Nif 29

Farm Child (R. S. Thomas)
Look at this village boy, his head is
stuffed
Choice 304; Floc 77; Poem I 79; WS 73

I Am (Chun Po Man, Hong Kong)
I am a human being, a boy
Stuf 9

Mart was my Best Friend (Michael
Rosen)
Mart was my best friend
McRo 27

Nooligan (Roger McGough)
I'm a nooligan
*Ax 76; Bell 72; McG G 11; McRo 25;
Sk 58; Speak 37*

Percival Mandeville, the Perfect Boy
(John Betjeman)
Percival Mandeville the perfect boy
Bell 61; ND 115

A Song about Myself (John Keats)
There was a naughty boy
*Chat 202; Fab CV 284; Fab NV 97;
Fav 29; KCP 108; Like 79; ND 97;
NTP 64; Once 107; Ox CV 148; P Sev
114; Puf V 122*

The Tunnel (Brian Lee)
This is the way that I have to go
Brave 53; Six 208

Wrestling (Kathleen Fraser)
I like wrestling with Herbie because
KWP 70

BREAKFAST

Breakfast (Adrian Rumble)
Sausages, sausages sizzling in the
pan
SS 35

Breakfast (Eleanor Farjeon)
Is it coffee for breakfast?
Pac 51

Breakfast Song in Time of Diet
(Stoddard King)
Take, O take the cream away
Pic 81

The King's Breakfast (A. A. Milne)
The King asked
*Fab NV 267; Mil VY 55; Nine 107; Ox
CV 341; Ox T 70; Pac 14*

The Meal (Karla Kuskin)
Timothy Tompkins had turnips and
tea
Pac 28; Read 68

BRIDESMAIDS

The Bridesmaid (Alfred Lord
Tennyson)
O bridesmaid, ere the happy knot
was tied
Love 111

Why am I Always the Bridesmaid?
(C. Collins and F. W.
Leigh)
Why am I dressed in these beautiful
clothes?
Love 110

20

BROADCASTING

Here is the News (Michael Rosen)
In Manchester today a man was seen
Pro I 70

BROKEN HOMES

The Child's Tale (Eric Millward)
My Dad was just no good, so
Mummy says
Face 29

Daddy (Mick Gowar)
Daddy lives in Tate Street now
Gow S 66; Mad 21

Divorce (Tove Ditlevsen,
Denmark)
He would / in the case of a divorce
Life 38

Fred (Nigel Gray)
I haven't got a dad. / But I'm not sad
IC 25

Looking for Dad (Brian Patten)
Whenever Mum and Dad
Pat 42

One Parent Family (John
Kitching)
I wish that I had more than just
Fifth 34

The Shoes (John Mole)
These are the shoes / Dad walked
about in
Rhy 119

Sunday Visiting (Barrie Wade)
On Sunday mornings I leave home
Wad 41

*There are Four Chairs Round the
Table* (Derek Stuart)
There are four chairs round the
table
Fifth 34

BROTHERS

Brother (Mary Ann Hoberman)
I had a little brother
PG 40; Pop 100

I Share my Bedroom with my Brother
(Michael Rosen)
I share my bedroom with my brother
Ros M 67

Me and my Bruv (Stephen
Mulrine)
Me and my bruv get along just great
IC 110

My Brother Bert (Ted Hughes)
Pets are the hobby of my brother
Bert
FF 10; Hug F 33

My Noisy Brother (Kashim
Chowdhury, aged 11)
My noisy brother's always noisy
World 36

My Obnoxious Brother Bobby (Colin
West)
Has a most revolting hobby
Pets 76; West 12

Tiny Tim (anon.)
I had a little brother
Tim 8

Tricks (Michael Rosen)
Nearly every morning
ASP 69; Ros Q 6

Willy's Stone (Vyanne Samuels)
Willy picked up a stone
Sam 16

Younger Brother (Trevor Millum)
He collects bottle tops
Mill 74

BUFFALOES

Buffalo (from Yoruba, Ulli
Beier)
The buffalo is the death
Rat 199

Buffalo Dusk (Carl Sandburg)
The buffaloes are gone.
*Jung 89; Ox A 216; Pop 81; Rab 82;
Rhy 79; Walk 58; WZ 120*

The Buffalo Skinners (anon.)
Come all you jolly cowboys and listen
to my song
Rat 88

The Flower-Fed Buffaloes (Vachell
Lindsay)
The flower-fed buffaloes of the
spring
*Earth 66; Jung 88; Ox A 218; Rat 158;
Ten 47; This W 123; World 50; WS 32;
YD 66*

I Rise, I Rise (Osage prayer
before buffalo hunt)

I, whose tread makes the earth to
rumble
TPS 29

BUGLES

from *The Princess* (Alfred Lord
Tennyson)
The splendour falls on castle walls
*Choice 83; Fab CV 36; MT 94; Ox PC
142; This W 86*

BULLDOZERS

*The Chant of the Awakening
Bulldozers* (Patricia Hubbell)
We are the bulldozers, bulldozers,
bulldozers
Open 119; Rab 53; S Sun 44

BULLFINCHES

The Bullfinch (Betty Hughes)
I saw upon a winter's day
WAS 148

BULLS

The Bull Moses (Ted Hughes)
A hoist up and I could lean over
Touch V 201

The Magnificent Bull (from the
Dinka, Africa)
My bull is white like the silver fish in
the river
*Ark 39; HH 108; Pets 28; Pro III 35;
Stuf 50; Talk 57*

Revelation (Liz Lochhead)
I remember once being shown the
black bull
Touch V 200

BULLYING

Back in the Playground Blues
(Adrian Mitchell)
Dreamed I was in a school
playground
KCP 142; Touch IV 149

Barry (Mick Gowar)
The teachers saw
Gow T 50

The Bully (Fay Maschler)
One of the girls at Audrey's school
Sk 117

from *A Bully and his Victim*
(Ambar Lone)
A bully, a person who picks on
others weaker
Stuf II 48

The Bully Asleep (John Walsh)
One afternoon when grassy
Bell 75; Pro I 69; Quin 199; Sk 56

Four O'Clock Friday (Derek
Stuart)
Four o'clock Friday. I'm home at last
Fifth 32

Going Home (Jean Kenward)
There were two ways of going home
SO 105

I've Got an Apple Ready (John
Walsh)
My hair's tightly plaited
*All 66; Bell 17; Brave 56; Open 33;
Quin 189; Sk 16*

King of the Toilets (Peter Dixon)
Maurice was King of the Toilets
Bell 74; SO 33

Lick-Me-If-You're-Bad (Vyanne
Samuels)
The worst girl our class ever had
Sam 39

My Enemy (Charles Causley)
My enemy was the pork butcher's
son
Strict 56

Pocket Money (Mick Gowar)
I can't explain what happens to my
cash
Fifth 33; Gow F 14

Stevie Scared (Richard Edwards)
Stevie scared, scared of the dark
Side 25(B)

BUREAUCRACY

Kipling Mishandled (U. A.
Fanthorpe)
Lo, we are the ones that uncover
Crys 37

This Letter's to Say (Raymond Wilson)
Dear Sir or Madam
Earth 47

BURGLARS

The Burglary (Tony Connor)
It's two o'clock now, somebody's pausing in the street
Cam I 25

BUSES

Walking Song (William E. Hickson)
We waited for an omnibus
Ox CV 230

BUSHRANGERS

The Death of Ben Hall (Will Ogilvie)
Ben Hall was out on Lachlan side
Nar 97

Rafferty Rides Again (Thomas V. Tierney)
There's a road outback that becomes a track
Story 136

The Wild Colonial Boy (trad.)
'Tis of a wild Colonial boy, Jack Doolan was his name
Nar 91; Story 82

BUSYNESS

Busy (A. A. Milne)
I think I am a Muffin Man. I haven't got a bell
Mil NS 7

Busy (Mbundu)
I've got some dust in my eye
Afr II 17

Busy Day (Michael Rosen)
Pop in / pop out
AVF 26; Corn 86; McRo 36; P Sev 113

Busy Week (Tony Bradman)
On Mondays / It's my Brownie night
Bra A 102

BUTCHERS

The Butcher's Cat (U. A. Fanthorpe)
The scuffled blood-stains on the sawdust floor
Crys 34

BUTTERFLIES

Blue-Butterfly Day (Robert Frost)
It is blue-butterfly day here in spring
Like 36

The Butterfly (Arun Kolatkur, India)
There is no story behind it
Blac 119; Stuf 37

Butterfly (D. H. Lawrence)
Butterfly, the wind blows sea-ward
Talk 65

The Butterfly (Stanley Cook)
The sun is on fire
AFP 93

The Butterfly in Church (William Cowper)
Butterfly, butterfly, why come you here?
CCC 38; Foot 61

The Cabbage White Butterfly (Elizabeth Jennings)
I look like a flower you could pick. My delicate wings
CCC 40

Flying Crooked (Robert Graves)
The butterfly, a cabbage white
Choice 256; Floc 208; Rat 160; WS 44; Young 24

The Saffron Butterfly (Teresa Hooley)
Out of its dark cocoon
CCC 38

This Loafer (Cecil Day Lewis)
In a sun-crazed orchard
CCC 41

To a Butterfly (William Wordsworth)
I've watched you now a full half-hour
GTP 74; Like 142; NTP 94; NV 92

Was Worm (May Swenson)
Was worm / swaddled in white
Pro I 68

CALVES

The Calf (Thomas Hardy)
You may have seen, in road or street
CCC 56

Happy Calf (Ted Hughes)
Mother is worried, her low, short
moos
CCC 55

A March Calf (Ted Hughes)
*Right from the start he is dressed in
his best*
WAS 32

A Newly-Born Calf (Oswald
Mtshali)
A newly-born calf
WZ 12

CAMELS

The Camel's Hump (Rudyard
Kipling)
The Camel's hump is an ugly lump
Fab NV 104; Ten 58; Young 70

The Plaint of the Camel (C. E.
Carryl)
Canary birds feed on sugar and seed
*CBC 147; Fab NV 80; Fun 16; GTP
37; Ox A 140; Ox CV 305; Ox T 118;
Walk 57*

CANADA

The Shooting of Dan McGrew
(Robert W. Service)
A bunch of the boys were whooping
it up
Can 22; Nar 100; Ten 106

CANDLEMAS (FEBRUARY 2)

At Candlemas (Charles Causley)
If Candlemas be fine and clear
Cau F 46; Ox CP 151; WAS 183

Candlemas Eve (Robert Herrick)
Down with the rosemary and bays
Sun 129; WAS 182

Ceremony upon Candlemas Eve
(Robert Herrick)
Down with the rosemary, and so
Ox CP 150

CARROLL, LEWIS

Lewis Carroll (Eleanor Farjeon)
You are wise, Mr Dodgson, the
young child said
Ox CV 331

CATERPILLARS

Caterpillar (Christina Rossetti)
Brown and furry
*Ani 33; Ark 41; CCC 36; GTP 72; Like
30; Ox CV 27; Pop 77; Pos 79; Pud 22;
Walk 76; WS 43*

The Tickle Rhyme (Ian Serraillier)
'Who's that tickling my back?' said
the wall
*Fab NV 57; King 227; Like 12; Once
124; OWN 68; Pos 80; P Sev 140; Puf
Q 174; RMP 47; Rog 12*

Was Worm (May Swenson)
Was worm/ swaddled in white
GTP 73; Pro I 68

CATS (L AND D)

See also **Death of Cats, Kittens**

A Cat (Edward Thomas)
She had a name among the children
ND 83; Iron 108; Ox PC 109

The Cat (Gareth Owen)
When the moon is leering yellow
Owe K 26

Cat (J. R. R. Tolkien)
The fat cat on the mat
Zoo 38

Cat (Mick Gowar)
He hasn't got a name
Gow S 11

Cat (Vernon Scannell)
My cat has got no name
Pets 18; Quin 169; WZ 22

The Cat (W. H. Davies)
Within that porch across the way
Ox PC 109; Shad 54; Tick 65

Cat (William Dunlop)
Cat, nine days old, knit out of soot
CCC 143

The Cat and the Moon (W. B.
Yeats)
The cat went here and there
*CCC 212; Fab CV 69; Floc 57; Irish
172; Iron 117; MT 104; Talk 63; YD
58*

Cat in the Dark (John Agard)
Look at that!
*Aga 36; Ani 15; DS 23; Five 117; Stuf
44*

Catalogue (Rosalie Moore)
Cats sleep fat and walk thin
GTP 50; Nine 142

Cats (Eleanor Farjeon)
Cats sleep / Anywhere
Ox T 95; Pos 49; Pro I 9; Walk 68; Zoo 30

Cats (Phoebe Hesketh)
Cats are contradictions: tooth and claw
Six 129

Cats no Less Liquid than their Shadows (A. S. J. Tessimond)
Cats no less liquid than their shadows
ND 81

Diamond Cut Diamond (Ewart Milne)
Two cats
CCC 142; Fab CV 76; Gold 66

Esther's Tomcat (Ted Hughes)
Daylong this tomcat lies stretched flat
Touch IV 189

Five Eyes (Walter de la Mare)
In Hans' old mill his three black cats
de la M P 84; Fab NV 28; Like 90; P Sev 18

Fourteen Ways of Touching the Peter (George Macbeth)
You can push / your thumb
Floc 59; Gold 26; Pro 28; YD 59

from *Jubilate Agno* (Christopher Smart)
For I will consider my Cat Jeoffrey
Fab CV 22; Foot 26; GTP 46; NTP 85; Ox PC 107; Pets 16; Rat 301; Talk 62

The Lover whose Mistress Feared a Mouse (George Turberville)
If I might alter kind
NTP 84

Mawgan Porth (Charles Causley)
Mawgan Porth / The Siamese cat
Cau J 37

The Meerkats of Africa (Gavin Ewart)
Meerkats go about in packs
Ewar 28

Milk for the Cat (Harold Monro)
When the tea is brought in at five o'clock
Gold 52; GTP 47; Ox PC 109; Pro I 75; This W 21

Montague Michael (anon.)
Montague Michael
Ox T 94

More About Tompkins (Roy Fuller)
One evening Tompkins' 'Mummy' calls
Trio 28

The Mysterious Cat (Vachell Lindsay)
I saw a proud, mysterious cat
Fab NV 174; Ox A 221; Pop 65

My Uncle Paul of Pimlico (Mervyn Peake)
My Uncle Paul of Pimlico
Nine 149; Ox T 94; PG 85; YD 35

Nodding (Stevie Smith)
Tizdal my beautiiful cat
CCC 182

On a Cat Ageing (Alexander Gray)
He blinks upon the hearth-rug
Pos 53

Our Cats (Wes Magee)
Our cats stay out all night . . . moonlighting
AVF 92; Mag W 38

Pangur Ban (from Gaelic, Robin Flower)
I and Pangur Ban, my cat
Fab CV 70; Irish 18; Rat 333

This and That (Gareth Owen)
Two cats together
Nine 144; Owe K 31; Ox T 92

Tibs (Daphne Lister)
Tibs is a cat
Pos 50

Two Songs of a Fool (W. B. Yeats)
A speckled cat and a tame hare
Foot 36

CATS (N)

An Alley Cat with One Life Left (Jack Prelutsky)
I'm an alley cat with one life left
Pre 82

Amber (Shirley Toulson)
I think that the tortoise-shell cat
Pets 22

Cat! (Eleanor Farjeon)
Cat! / Scat!
Ani 12; Far M 33; Once 45; Ox PC 104; Pos 51; Puf Q 38; Show 32; Tick 64

The Cat's Muse (Philip Gross)
I'm a tabby, flabby house cat, just a fusty ball of fur
Gro 22

The Cats of Kilkenny (anon.)
There were once two cats of Kilkenny
Walk 67

Explorer (Alan Brownjohn)
Two o'clock./ Let out of the back door
ATP 44

Hunting with Henry the Cat (Mick Gowar)
Small black-and-white cat
Gow T 34

from *Lady Feeding the Cats* (Douglas Stewart)
Shuffling along in her broken shoes from the slums
Floc 61

The Lost Cat (E. V. Rieu)
She took a last and simple meal
Puf Q 102

My Cat (Colin McNaughton)
My cat gives me serious cause for concern
McN 53

My Cat Plumduff (Charles Causley)
My cat Plumduff
Cau E 18

On a Night of Snow (Elizabeth Coatsworth)
Cat, if you go outside you must walk in the snow
GTP 48; Ox A 236; Stoc 25; Young 30

The Owl and the Pussycat (Edward Lear)
See Nonsense: (Edward Lear)

The Rescue (Hal Summers)
The boy climbed up into the tree
Poem I 88

That Cat (Ben King)
The cat that comes to my window sill
CCC 213

The Tom-Cat (Don Marquis)
At midnight in the alley
Open 82; Shad 55

Two Cats (Michael Rosen)
When we opened the door late
PoWo II 62

CATS: T. S. ELIOT

The Ad-Dressing of Cats (T. S. Eliot)
You've read of several kinds of Cat
GTP 54

Growltiger's Last Stand (T. S. Eliot)
Growltiger was a Bravo Cat, who lived upon a barge
Fab CV 182; Ox A 226; Pos 60

Gus: The Theatre Cat (T. S. Eliot)
Gus is the Cat at the Theatre Door
Ox A 229

Macavity: The Mystery Cat (T. S. Eliot)
Macavity's a Mystery Cat; he's called the Hidden Paw
CBC 64; Choice 225; Like 45; ND 82; Once 110; Ox A 225; Ox CV 346; Pos 56; Rat 255

Mr Mistoffelees (T. S. Eliot)
You ought to know Mr Mistoffelees
Chat 384; Pud 118

Of the Awefull Battle of the Pekes and the Pollicles (T. S. Eliot)
The Pekes and the Pollicles everyone knows
Brave 101

The Old Gumbie Cat (T. S. Eliot)
I have a Gumbie Cat in mind
Fab NV 168; Fun 19; GTP 44; P Sev 33

The Rum Tum Tugger (T. S. Eliot)
The Rum Tum Tugger is a Curious Cat
Nine 147; NTP 87; Pets 20

Skimbleshanks the Railway Cat (T. S. Eliot)
There's a whisper down the line at 11.39
Fab CV 285; KCP 74; Pos 58; Young 14

The Song of the Jellicles (T. S. Eliot)
Jellicle Cats come out tonight
Fab CV 75; Fab NV 175; Fav 98; Ox PC 105; Ox CV 347

CATTLE

See also Bulls, Calves

Bags of Meat (Thomas Hardy)
'Here's a fine bag of meat'
Rat 60; Touch V 179; Voi 62

Belinda and Jill (Diana Harland)
There once were two cows named
Belinda and Jill
Sort 58

Birth of Rainbow (Ted Hughes)
This morning blue vast clarity of
March sky
Hug MT 35; Sun 229

Cow in Meadow (Clive Sansom)
All day / In a leisurely, kindly sort of
way
CCC 86

Cows (James Reeves)
Half the time they munched the
grass
*NTP 110; Ox PC 118; P Sev 70; Puf Q
64; Ree C 79; Spi 64; Zoo 32*

Cow's Complaint (Grace Nichols)
Somebody calls somebody
Nic 30

Fetching Cows (Norman
MacCaig)
The black one, last as usual, swings
her head
Floc 227; Show I 63

The Gracious and the Gentle Thing
(R. P. Tristram Coffin)
The three young heifers were at
Summer supper
CCC 59

Highland Cattle (Gavin Ewart)
The pride of Scotland, see the
Highland Cattle
Ewar 45

Macartney's Cow (Michael Dugan)
Returning, tadpole laden, from the
creek
Aus R 7

Milking before Dawn (Ruth Dallas)
In the drifting rain the cows in the
yard are as black
NTP 109

Milking Song (Christina Rossetti)
Brownie, Brownie, let down your
milk
CCC 87

CHANGELINGS

The Changeling (Shirley Toulson)
Mary's mother is tall and fair
Puf M 94

Peak and Puke (Walter de la
Mare)
From his cradle in the glamourie
Mes 159

The Stolen Child (W. B. Yeats)
Where dips the rocky highland
PoWo II 34; Puf M 90

The Three Beggars (Walter de la
Mare)
'Twas autumn daybreak gold and
wild
Puf M 92

CHARLES I

As I was Going by Charing Cross
(anon.)
As I was going by Charing Cross
*Fab CV 139; Ox Dic 114; Ox NR 81;
Ox PC 146; Puf NR 53*

CHARLES II

On Charles II (John Wilmot, Earl
of Rochester, 1648-80)
Here lies a Great and Mighty King
Face 153; ND 151; NTP 56; WS 81

When the King enjoys his own again
(Martin Parker)
What Booker can prognosticate
Fab CV 140

CHARLIE, BONNIE PRINCE

Moy Castle (anon.)
There are seven men in Moy Castle
GTP 112

The Skye Boat Song (Robert Louis
Stevenson)
Sing me a song of a lad that is gone
NTP 43; Puf V 181; Ten 180

CHARMS AND SPELLS

See Ox NR 74-5, Puf M
throughout

Bye Now / Goodbye (James Berry)
Walk good / Walk well
IC 44

A Charm (Anglo-Saxon, trans.
Richard Hamer)
O wen, wen, O little wennikins
Rat 105

Charm (Maori, New Zealand)
Whispering ghosts of the west
HH 4

from *Comus* (John Milton)
Sabrina fair
Fab CV 217; Puf M 199

Good Wish (from Gaelic
Alexander Carmichael)
Power of raven be thine
Fab CV 229

Here's to Thee! (anon.)
Here's to thee, / Old apple-tree!
Ox PC 139; PPP 22; Puf NR 29

from *The Lord of the Rings* (J. R.
R. Tolkien)
Three rings for the Elven-Kings
under the sky
PG 35

from *Macbeth* (William
Shakespeare)
Round about the cauldron go
Open 109; Ting 29
Thrice the brinded cat hath mewed
Rat 429

Mary, Mary Magdalene (Charles
Causley)
Mary, Mary Magdalene
Cau F 87; Quin 37

The Night-piece, to Julia (Robert
Herrick)
Her eyes the glow-worm lend thee
Puf M 45

Rain Magic (Yoruba)
Gentle breeze is the father of rain
Afr I 40

Sabrina's Song (John Milton)
By the rushy-fringed bank
Fab CV 217; Puf M 199

Song for the Head (George Peele)
Gently dip, but not too deep
*Chat 77; Fab CV 227; Ox PC158; Puf
M 42; Rat 401; This W 66*

Song to . . . the Apple-Tree (trad.)
Here stands the good apple-tree
PoWo II 85

*Spell to Make your Teacher
Disappear* (S. J. Saunders)
From the blackboard gather chalk-
dust
Boo 63

Spells (James Reeves)
I dance and dance without any feet
*NTP 224; Puf M 51; Puf Q 66; Ree C
4; Ting 34*

Thief's Spell (Gazelle Peninsula,
New Britain)
Black concealment be about me!
HH 19

This is the Key of the Kingdom
(anon.)
This is the key of the kingdom
*Chat 232; Fab CV 227; Lob 62; Nine
31; NTP 158; Ox NR 125; Ox PC 158;
Ox T 13; PG 48; Star 52; This W 43;
WS 64*

Thrice Toss these Oaken Ashes
(Thomas Campion)
Thrice toss these oaken ashes in the
air
Fab CV 226

*A Very Old Spell . . . to Get Rid of
Warts* (anon. Middle English,
trans. Michael Rosen)
Wart, wart, wart-chicken
KWP 26

Witches' Charm (Ben Jonson)
The owl is abroad, the bat and the
toad
*Fab CV 224; Iron 48; KCP 106; Ox PC
88; Rat 469; This W 36; Ting 23*

CHAUCER

Sir Geoffrey Chaucer (Robert
Greene)
His stature was not very tall
Fab CV 116

CHEESE

Say Cheese (Kit Wright)
At Christmas the STILTON
Pac 25; Pic 122; Wri R 72

CHEMICAL WARFARE

Open Day at Porton (Adrian
Mitchell)
These bottles are being filled with
madness
Foc 150

28

CHERRIES

Bread and Cherries (Walter de la Mare)
'Cherries, ripe cherries!'
Pic 40

CHERRY TREES

Cherry Tree (Ivy Eastwick)
The Chaffinch flies fast
WAS 85

Loveliest of trees, the cherry now (A. E. Housman)
Loveliest of trees, the cherry now
Cal 45; Floc 13; ND 9; NTP 119; Out 29, Ox PC 136; Puf V 23; Rat 253; Ten 30; WAS 45

CHESTNUTS

Horse Chestnuts (John Cotton)
Autumn's special toys
Crys 12

Sweet Chestnuts (John Walsh)
How still the woods were! Not a redbreast whistled
Pic 24

Two Penn'orth of Chestnuts (Eleanor Farjeon)
Two penn'orth of chestnuts!
Pic 24

CHILDHOOD RECOLLECTED

A Child of our Time (Roger Woddis)
I remember, I remember
Fav 24

Childhood (John Clare)
O dear to us ever the scenes of our childhood
KWP 55

Helping Gran Remember (Hiawyn Oram)
When Gran feels sad and lonely
Ora 32

I Remember, I Remember (Philip Larkin)
Coming up England by a different line
NTP 38

I Remember, I Remember (Thomas Hood)
I remember, I remember
Fav 22; GTP 95; NTP 38; NV 60; (part) Abi 10

Nikki-Rosa (Nikki Giovanni)
childhood remembrances are always a drag
Show II 1

Rough (Stephen Spender)
My parents kept me from children who were rough
Brave 55; Floc 52; Foc 115; ND 119

Soap Suds (Louis MacNeice)
This brand of soap has the same smell as once in the big
NTP 42

The Place's Fault (Philip Hobsbaum)
Once, after a rotten day at school
Fire 124

CHILDREN

Bunches of Grapes (Walter de la Mare)
'Bunches of grapes,' says Timothy
Fab NV 123; Name 42; NTP 209; Ox CV 326

Children's Song (R. S. Thomas)
We live in our own world
Choice 305

The Place's Fault (Philip Hobsbaum)
Once, after a rotten day at school
Touch IV 142

CHILDREN, AWKWARD

The Car Trip (Michael Rosen)
Mum says: / 'Right, you two
PG 54

Colin (Allan Ahlberg)
When you frown at me like that, Colin
Name 21

David (Eleanor Farjeon)
Yes, David puts his toys away
Far R 74

The Experiment (Brian Patten)
I did an experiment to prove groan-ups
Pat T 24

I Say: What are you Doing? (Michael Rosen)
And our little boy Joe says, Mm?
Name 48; Ros Y 11

If You Don't Put Your Shoes On
(Michael Rosen)
If you don't put your shoes on
before I count fifteen
Ox T 46; Ros M 24; Ros Y 8

Just Fancy That (Max Fatchen)
'Just fancy that!' my parents say
Fat W 26

Late Home (Brian Lee)
I looked up – the sun had gone
down
Poem I 90, Six 199

The National Union of Children
(Roy Fuller)
NUC has just passed a weighty
resolution
Ax 74; Bell 148; Like 123

Not Now, Nigel (Allan Ahlberg)
Not now, Nigel
Ahl H 25

One of Those Days (June Crebbin)
Kevin's ripped his paper
Cre 28

Problem Child (J. E. Faulks)
How shall I deal with Roger, Mrs
Prodger?
Name 73

Snarl (Kit Wright)
When Dave Dirt left the dentist
Wri C 76

'We Won't Tell You Again!' (Max
Fatchen)
It makes me sullen and wilful and
wild
Fat W 25

What For! (Noel Petty)
One more word, said my dad
Rhy 99

When I'm Ready (Max Fatchen)
Doing things immediately
Aus B 18

CHILDREN, ILL-TREATED

Arithmetic (Gavin Ewart)
I'm 11. And I don't really know
Bell 80; Brave 139; Strict 19

Beatings (Roger McGough)
My father beats me up
Ang I 14

from *Child Labour* (Elizabeth
Barrett Browning)
'For oh,' say the children, 'we are
weary . . .'
KWP 45

Double Glazing (Brian Patten)
Jenny lives in a flat on the
nineteenth floor
Pat 101

Timothy Winters (Charles
Causley)
Timothy Winters comes to school
*Bell 60; Gang 38; Gold 80; ND 113;
Quin 9; Rat 432; Sk 111; Voi II 90*

The Unfairest Thing of All
(Hiawyn Oram)
But it's not fair / I yell
Ora 28

The Watercress Seller (Thomas
Miller 1807-74)
Now all aloud the wind and rain
Ox CV 21

CHILDREN, NAUGHTY

See also Tales, Cautionary

Abigail (Kaye Starbird)
Abigail knew when she was born
Face 43

The Class (Michael Rosen)
Quite often / you sit with your back
to the teacher
Speak 24

Crazy Frankie (Colin
McNaughton)
Crazy Frankie's round the twist
McN 20

Dave Dirt was on the 259 (Kit
Wright)
Dave Dirt was on the 259
KWP 218; Wri C 62

Don't Go Ova Dere (Valerie
Bloom)
Barry madda tell im
AFP 36; Stuf II 38

EE SHYNTA DUCKED (Barry
Heath)
Ken Dado / an / ah Lez
Pro III 59

Extremely Naughty Children
(Elizabeth Godley)
By far / The Naughtiest / Children
Like 83; Mad 43

Humphrey Hughes of Highbury (Colin West)
Goes to his local library
West 160

If Only (June Crebbin)
I'm waiting to see the headmaster
Cre 30

Inconsiderate Hannah (D. Streamer, 1899)
Naughty little Hannah said
Name 35

Knock-A-Door Run (Irene Rawnsley)
Come on, Lucy, / let's have fun
Raw 6

Lettuce Pray (Brian Patten)
I'm standing outside the headmaster's office
Pat T 106

The Miscreant (Jean Kenward)
Standing outside the door
SO 61

Monday's Child is Red and Spotty (Colin McNaughton)
Monday's child is red and spotty
McN 36

Think of Eight Numbers (Shelley Silverstein)
Think of eight numbers from one to nine
BBGG 30

Tom's Bomb (David Hornsby)
There was a boy whose name was Tom
Nine 49

The Trial of Derek Drew (Allan Ahlberg)
The charges: Derek Drew
Ahl H 47

Trouble? (Wes Magee)
Has someone told? And if so, who?
Mag M 44

A Visit to the Aquarium (Kit Wright)
Watching the Conger Eel
Wri R 63

Who Did It? (Irene Rawnsley)
Who put pudding
Raw 32

Who the Cap Fit, Let Dem Wear It (John Agard)
If it wasn't you / who tek de chalk
ASP 74; Gran 25

CHILDREN'S PARTIES

Betty at the Party (anon.)
When I was at the party
Occ 72

Birthday Party (Julie O'Callaghan)
Aiming clothespins at the mouths of jars
O'Ca 52

Joan Who Hates Parties (John Walsh)
Today's little Doreen's party-day
Name 47; Quin 219

Marty's Party (David McCord)
Marty's party? / Jamie came. He
Occ 76

My Party (Kit Wright)
My parents said I could have a party
Poem I 92; Wri R 12

A Party (Laura E. Richards)
On Willie's birthday, as you see
Nine 61

Waiting (James Reeves)
Waiting, waiting, waiting
Occ 77; Ox T 33; Poem I 100; Puf Q 67; Ree C 5; Tick 51

When the Tricky Man Comes (Brian Lee)
When the Tricky Man comes
SS 28

CHIMNEY SWEEPS

The Chimney Sweeper (William Blake)
A little black thing among the snow
Rat 108

The Chimney Sweeper (William Blake)
When my mother died I was very young
Ox CV 86; Puf V 211; This W 142

'Sooeep' (Walter de la Mare)
Black as a chimney is his face
Tick 165

CHOICE

The Choosing (Liz Lochhead)
We were first equal Mary and I

Bell 151; Moon 23; Speak 68; Strict 22; Wind 89

Iffy Butty (Vyanne Samuels)
Iffy Butty never knew
Sam 22

Mary and Sarah (Richard Edwards)
Mary likes smooth things
IC 115

Minnie (Eleanor Farjeon)
Minnie can't make her mind up
GTP 102; Pac 57

The Road Not Taken (Robert Frost)
Two roads diverged in a yellow wood
Fab CV 292; Foc 147; KCP 86; NTP 158; O & A 44; Open 62; Poem I 85; Show III 74

CHRIST

Ballad of the Bread Man (Charles Causley)
Mary stood in the kitchen
Brave 150; Gang 53; Rat 64; Sun 132; Voi III 63

The Birds (Hilaire Belloc)
When Jesus Christ was four years old
Chris 23; Sun 120

The Bitter Withy (anon.)
As it fell out on a Holy Day
Nar 8; Sun 121

Carol (John Short)
There was a Boy bedded in bracken
Fab CV 358

A Child my Choice (Robert Southwell)
Let folly praise that fancy love
Ring 67

Christ Harrows Hell (Langland, trans. R. Tamplin)
Hold still / Truth said: I hear some spirit
Sun 148

The Holy Well (anon.)
As it fell out one May morning
Fab CV 360; Sun 122

Joseph was an Old Man (anon.)
Joseph was an old man
Ox PC 20

Lord of the Dance (Sydney Carter)
I danced in the morning
Ten 169

On the Morning of Christ's Nativity (John Milton)
But peaceful was the night
Fab CV 355

Three Rusty Nails (Roger McGough)
Mother, there's a strange man
McG G 33

Yet if His Majesty (anon.)
Yet if His Majesty our sovereign Lord
Fab CV 364

CHRISTMAS CAROLS

The Animals' Carol (Charles Causley)
Christus natus est! the cock
Sun 102; Touch IV 204; WAS 164

Carolling Around the Estate (Wes Magee)
The six of us met at Alan's house
Cal 120; Mag M 58; Stoc 14

The Wicked Singers (Kit Wright)
And have you been out carol singing
Chris 76; SS 57; Stoc 18; Wri R 10

CHRISTMAS EVE

Christmas Eve at Sea (John Masefield)
A wind is rustling 'south and soft'
Sun 94

Just Before Christmas (Kit Wright)
Down the Holloway Road on the top of a bus
Wri C 72

The Oxen (Thomas Hardy)
Christmas Eve and twelve of the clock
Chris 92; NTP 111; Rat 331; WAS 159; Wind 10

Questions on Christmas Eve (Wes Magee)
But how can his reindeer fly without wings?
Cele 102; Stoc 73

Reindeer Report (U. A. Fanthorpe)
Chimneys: colder
Ox CP 106

A Visit from St Nicholas (Clement C. Moore)
'Twas the night before Christmas,
Chris 93; Gold 90; GTP 292; Ox A 15; Ox CP 93; Ox CV 154; Walk 50

CHRISTMAS: RELIGIOUS

See Ox CP, Star, Stoc throughout

Advent 1955 (John Betjeman)
The Advent wind begins to stir
Ox CP 17

The Burning Babe (Robert Southwell)
As I in hoary winter's night stood shivering in the snow
Chris 33; Fab CV 358; Floc 288; Ox CP 112; Rat 98; Sun 101

Carol (anon.)
As I sat on a sunny bank
Ox NR 204

Carol (Ronald Deadman)
The Palm Court Lounge is snug and warm
Poem I 76

Christmas (John Betjeman)
The bells of waiting Advent ring
Chris 79; Fav 104; Like 127; Ox CP 128

Christmas Bells (H. W. Longfellow)
I heard the bells on Christmas Day
Ox CP 110

from *A Christmas Childhood* (Patrick Kavanagh)
My father played the melodeon
Chris 111; Rat 303; Sun 110

Christmas Day (Andrew Young)
Last night in the open shippen
Ox CP 46

Christmas Day (Christopher Smart)
Nature's decorations glisten
Ox CP 111

Christmas is Really for the Children (Steve Turner)
Christmas is really
Chris 109; Ox CP 91

Eddi's Service (Rudyard Kipling)
Eddi, priest of Saint Wilfred
Ox CP 88; Ring 54; Star 27

Forty Days of Christmas (anon.)
Make we mirth / For Christ's birth
WAS 156

Kid Stuff (Frank Horne)
The wise guys / tell me
Blac 46

The Party's Over (Richard Edwards)
It's late and I'm tired but I don't want to sleep
Cele 104

Well, So That is That (W. H. Auden)
Well, so that is that. Now we must dismantle the tree
Ox CP 142

What the Donkey Saw (U. A. Fanthorpe)
No room in the inn, of course
WS 114

CHRISTMAS: SECULAR

See Ox CP; Star, Stoc throughout

Adrian Henri's Talking After-Christmas Blues (Adrian Henri)
Well I woke up this morning it was Christmas Day
Ax 94

The Boots of Father Christmas (Richard Edwards)
We're the boots of Father Christmas
Edw M 24

The Boy who Laughed at Santa Claus (Ogden Nash)
In Baltimore there lived a boy
BBGG 16; Nas C 50; Stoc 116

The Children's Carol (Eleanor Farjeon)
Here we come again, again
Far M 88; Star 11

Christmas at Sea (Robert Louis Stevenson)
The sheets were frozen hard and they cut the naked hand
Mes 72

Christmas Breeze (John Figueroa)
Auntie would say 'Ah! Christmas breeze'
Bab 171

Christmas in Martinique (Aimé Césaire)
Then time passed quickly, very quickly
FS 67

Christmas Day (Roy Fuller)
Small girls on trikes
Trio 27

Christmas Dinner (Michael Rosen)
We were all sitting round the table
Ox CP 116

The Computer's First Christmas Card (Edwin Morgan)
jollymerry / hollyberry / jollyberry
Chris 90; Corn 94; KCP 144; Poem I 77; Star 16; Stoc 81

December (John Clare)
Glad Christmas comes, and every hearth
Ox CP 101

Doctor Christmas (Edward Lowbury)
My first thought, 'Have they sterilized the beard?'
Fifth 50; Mea 83

Ghost Story (Dylan Thomas)
Bring out the tall tales
Ox CP 104

Goodwill to Men, Give us your Money (Pam Ayres)
It was Christmas Eve on a Friday
Ring 56

Keeping Christmas (Eleanor Farjeon)
How will you your Christmas keep?
Ox CP 98; Puf Q 48

A Mersey Christmas (Roger McGough)
De rain / De snows / De cold in
McG S 77

Santa Go Home (Ogden Nash)
My fellow parents
Chris 107

The Twelve Days of Christmas (anon.)
The first day of Christmas
Chris 51; Lob 104; Ox Dic 119; Ox NR 198; Puf NR 184
The king sent his lady on the first Yule day
NTP 212

CHRISTMAS PRESENTS

Afterthought (Elizabeth Jennings)
For weeks before it comes I feel excited, yet when it
Quin 117; Star 59

Christmas (Michael Rosen)
It was Christmas Eve
Ros H 66

Christmas Presents (Eric James)
Have you ever noticed how grown-ups give each other presents?
Stoc 84

Christmas Shopping (Louis MacNeice)
Spending beyond their income on gifts for Christmas
Ox CP 72

Christmas Stocking (Eleanor Farjeon)
What will go into the Christmas Stocking
Far R 148; Stoc 69

Christmas Stocking (Michael Rosen)
They say: Leave a stocking out for Santa
Ros Q 74

Christmas Thank You's (Mick Gowar)
Dear Auntie
Ang I 20; Chris 134; Gow S 73; King 133; Ox CP 134; Stoc 95

Dave Dirt's Christmas Presents (Kit Wright)
Dave Dirt wrapped his Christmas presents
Wri C 46

Horace's Christmas Disappointment (Anthony Thwaite)
Young Horace Giraffe on Christmas Eve
Sort 94

King John's Christmas (A. A. Milne)
King John was not a good man
Chris 100; Mil NS 2

Letters to Santa (Jacqueline Brown)
Dere Farther Crismus pleas cum soon
AFP 110

Now Thrice Welcome Christmas (anon.)
Now thrice welcome Christmas
Puf V 253

Presents (Michael Rosen)
I gave my mum and dad
Ros H 58

Thank-you Letter (Robin Klein)
Dear Aunty Grace Mum said I had to
KWP 117

CHRISTMAS TREES

The Christmas Tree (C. Day Lewis)
Put out the lights now!
Chris 64; Star 76; Stoc 68

The Christmas Tree (Eleanor Farjeon)
I set a little Christmas tree
Far R 150

The Christmas Tree (John Walsh)
They chopped her down in some far wood
Quin 233

Christmas Tree (Stanley Cook)
Stores and filling stations prefer a roof
Ox CP 97

little tree (e. e. cummings)
little tree
Chris 66; Floc 286; Ox CP 95; RT 181; Young 51

To a Young Wretch (Robert Frost)
As gay for you to take your father's axe
Sun 105

CHURCH GOING

A Boy in Church (Robert Graves)
Gabble-gabble . . . brethren . . . gabble-gabble
Ring 95

Church Going (Philip Larkin)
Once I am sure there's nothing going on
Fire 60; Touch V 99; Wind 12

Diary of a Church Mouse (John Betjeman)
Here among long-discarded cassocks
Cal 86; Fire 158; Ring 96

In a Country Church (R. S. Thomas)
To one kneeling down no word came
Foc 149

In Church (Thomas Hardy)
'And now to God the Father' he ends
Touch IV 147

In Church (William Barnes)
The Church do seem a touching sight
Sun 218

In Westminster Abbey (John Betjeman)
Let me take this other glove off
Fir 64; Touch IV 147

St Mark's, Cheetham Hill (Tony Connor)
Designed to dominate the district
Wind 14

CIRCUSES

See also Acrobats, Clowns

Be a Circus Clown (Robert Heidbreder)
Mom said to me, 'You like to clown around? . . .'
Hei 13

The Big Tent Under the Roof (Ogden Nash)
Noises new to sea and land
Nas C 109

The Big Top (John Mole)
Cacophony polyphonous / The circus comes to town
Mol 55

The Circus (C. J. Dennis)
Hey there! Hoop-la! The circus is in town!
Pos 13; Stoc 53

Circus (Eleanor Farjeon)
The brass band blares
Pos 14

Circus (Margaret Stanley-Wrench)
Saucer of sand, the circus ring
Open 90

A Circus Garland (Rachel Field)
This is the day the circus comes
Pos 13; Ox A 239

The Crunch (Gerda Mayer)
The lion and his tamer
Candy 20; WP 42

The Famous Human Cannon Ball (Jack Prelutsky)
The famous human cannon ball
RT 105

Hazardous Occupations (Carl Sandburg)
Jugglers keep six bottles in the air
Voi III 162

The Man on the Flying Trapeze (Jack Prelutsky)
Sporting and capering high in the breeze
RT 106

CITIES AND TOWNS

See also Belfast, Glasgow, Jerusalem, London

Birmingham (Laurence Smith)
The children play over brick walls
Trio 20; WP 121

City Song (Fran Landesman)
I'm not a nature poet. I sing a city song
Ang II 41

Municipal Gum (Kath Walker)
Gumtree in the city street
Foc 70

November Night, Edinburgh (Norman MacCaig)
the night tinkles like ice in glasses
Pro III 94

Out in the City (Gareth Owen)
When you're out in the city
WP 116

Preludes I–IV (T. S. Eliot)
The winter evening settles down
Choice 217; Fire 145; Show III 54 and 64
(part) *KCP 76*

Sing a Song of People (Lois Lenski)
Sing a song of people
PPP 20; Walk 95

CLERIHEWS

See Chat 358; HH 29-31; Pro II 8

CLOCKS

The Clockmaker's Shop (Colin West)
The clockmaker's shop is the strangest of places
West 122

CLOTHES

Agatha's Trousers (Helen Slavin)
When Angela arrives in her yellow trousers
Speak 76

Chaos on the Catwalk (Brian Patten)
The snakeskin hissed 'I hate this show!'
Pat T 49

Clothes (Elizabeth Jennings)
My mother keeps on telling me
Life 22

Fur Coats (J. K. Annand)
Said the whitrick to the stoat
Scot 27

The Revolt of the Clothes (Terry Jones)
My shirt was sitting next to me
Jon 9

CLOUDS

The Black Cloud (W. H. Davies)
Little flocks of peaceful clouds
Rat 81

Cloudburst (Richard Edwards)
There was a young cloud
Edw P 28; S Sun 78

The Cloud-Mobile (May Swenson)
Above my face is a map
O & A 87

The Moon and a Cloud (W. H. Davies)
Sometimes I watch the moon at night
Rat 291

White Sheep (W. H. Davies, *not* C. Rossetti)
White sheep, white sheep
Pop 17; Tick 128

CLOWNS

Bring on the Clowns (Jack Prelutsky)
Bring on the clowns!
Ox T 64; RT 104; Stoc 54

The Clown III (Elizabeth Jennings)
Others are noble and admired
Touch V 32

Clowns (Margaret Mahy)
Zing! goes the cymbal. Bang! goes
the drum
Like 172

Said the Clown (Charles Causley)
Said the clown in the seven-ring
circus
Cau E 27

COCKATOOS

The Red Cockatoo (Po Chu-i,
trans. Arthur Waley)
Sent as a present from Annam
*All 32; Iron 108; KCP 51; Voi III 149;
Zoo 70*

COCKS

Chanticleer and Pertelote
(Chaucer, trans. N. Coghill)
She had a yard that was enclosed
about
ND 74

Cock-Crow (Edward Thomas)
Out of the wood of thoughts that
grows by night
*CCC 16; Choice 174; ND 73; NTP
143; Rat 110; WAS 112*

Cock Crow Song (Chinese, trans.
Arthur Waley)
In the eastern quarter dawn breaks
Stuf 78

The Cockerel Proclaims (Elizabeth
Jennings)
I am proud of my pride
CCC 15

from *An Evening Walk* (William
Wordsworth)
Sweetly ferocious, round his native
walks
Zoo 74

from *Hamlet* (William
Shakespeare)
Some say that ever 'gainst that
season comes
Chris 30

I Sometimes Think (anon.)
I sometimes think I'd rather crow
CBC 39; Cow 90; GTP 228; Walk 194

COLLECTING

Dave Dirt's Jacket Pocket (Kit
Wright)
In Dave's jacket pocket
Wri C 30

Hector the Collector (Shel
Silverstein)
Hector the collector
Gang 32; Name 37

COLOURS

The Colourblind Birdwatcher
(U. A. Fanthorpe)
In sallow summer
WP 51

Colours (Frances Evans)
Red is death, for people who are
dying
YD 49

Crayoning (Stanley Cook)
The sheet of paper is white
DS 47

Grandpa Dropped his Glasses
(Leroy F. Jackson)
Grandpa dropped his glasses once
SS 15

Grey (James Reeves)
Grey is the sky and grey the
woodman's cot
Ree C 17; WP 51

I Asked the Little Boy (anon.)
I asked the little boy who cannot see
Once 26

King Rufus (Y. Y. Segal)
To a king who had
Can 9

The Paint Box (E. V. Rieu)
Cobalt and umber and ultramarine
Like 158; Puf Q 106; Walk 226

Pencil and Paint (Eleanor
Farjeon)
Winter has a pencil
Far R 131

Rhinos Purple, Hippos Green
(Michael P. Hearn)
My sister says / I shouldn't colour
Walk 129

Sam Said (Richard Edwards)
Sam said, 'Do you know what's pink?'
Edw M 16

Uncle Edward's Affliction (Vernon Scannell)
Uncle Edward was colour-blind
Quin 172; Strict 68

What is Black? (Mary O'Neil)
Black is the night
Tick 80

What is Blue? (Mary O'Neil)
Blue is a lake
Pos 107

What is Orange? (Mary O'Neil)
Orange is a tiger-lily
Walk 218

What is Pink? (Christina Rossetti)
What is pink? A rose is pink
Fav 101; Foot 50; NV 64; Once 59; Ox CV 280; Pop 114; Pos 107; Walk 218; WP 47

What is Red? (Mary O'Neil)
Red is a sunset
Pos 108; RT 18; Walk 219

What is White? (Mary O'Neil)
White is a dove
Tick 78

Yellow (Olive Dove)
Yellow for melons
SS 15

COLTS

The Runaway (Robert Frost)
Once when the snow of the year was beginning to fall
Zoo 36

COLUMBUS

The Discovery (J. C. Squire)
There was an Indian, who had known no change
Gold 94; KCP 192; ND 136; O & A 160; Sea 60

COMMUNICATION

Alpha – B375 – Earth Visitors' Guide (John Cunliffe)

Galactic Government Health Warning
Spa 114

I Speak, I Say, I Talk (Arnold L. Shapiro)
Cats purr / Lions roar
Tick 102

The Telephone (Robert Frost)
When I was just as far as I could walk
Voi III 95

COMPUTERS

Out of Line (Adrian Henri)
Our computer keeps going on the blink
Hen 50

What a Calamity! (Max Fatchen)
Little Harold, I'll be frank
ATP 84

CONCEIT

I'm the Single Most Wonderful Person I Know (Jack Prelutsky)
I'm the single most wonderful person I know
Pre 137

CONSERVATION

See Pollution
See Earth throughout

CORBIES

See Crows

CORMORANTS

The Common Cormorant (anon.)
The common cormorant or shag
CBC 143; Cow 82; Fab CV 88; Fab NV 82; Fun 20; GTP 223; Ox PC 66; P Sev 22; RMP 46; Walk 171

The Cormorant (John Heath-Stubbs)
A lone black crag stands offshore
Sea 46

Cormorants (John Blight)
The sea has it this way: if you see
Floc 94

CORNWALL

Delectable Duchy (Sir John Betjeman)
Where yonder villa hogs the sea
Sea 80

CORROBOREE

Corroboree (Kath Walker)
Hot day dies, cook time comes
Cele 14

Corroboree (Max Fatchen)
The clap, clap, clap of the clapsticks beat
Cele 16

COUNTING-OUT RHYMES

See Fab NV 19; PG 58-9

Counting-out Rhyme (Edna St Vincent Millay)
Silver bark of beech, and sallow
WS 1

Salt, Mustard, Vinegar, Pepper (trad.)
Salt, Mustard, Vinegar, Pepper
Pac 63

COUNTING RHYMES

See Ox NR 110-12

COUNTING RHYMES (DOWN)

Five Little Monkeys (anon.)
Five little monkeys walked along the shore
Tim 17

Ten to One (Ivy O. Eastwick)
Ten tired tortoises lying in the sun
Read 37

Twelve Huntsmen with Horns and Hounds (anon.)
Twelve huntsmen with horns and hounds
Fab NV 141; Iron 141

COUNTING RHYMES (UP)

Counting's Easy (Robert Heidbreder)
Counting's easy – 1 2 3
Hei 17

The Gaping, Wide-mouthed Waddling Frog (anon.)
A gaping, wide-mouthed, waddling frog
Corn 36; Ox Dic 181

A New Dial (anon.)
In these twelve days let us be glad
Sun 79

Count Me Out (John Rice)
One football player scored his second goal
SS 56

One Old Oxford Ox (anon.)
One old Oxford ox opening oysters
Chat 235; Rhy 127

Over in the Meadow (anon.)
Over in the meadow in the sand in the sun
Fab NV 24; P Sev 30

Ten Little Indian Boys (anon.)
One little Indian boy making a canoe
Fab NV 110

This Old Man (anon.)
This old man, he played one
Fab NV 125

COURAGE

The Dare (Judith Nicholls)
Go on. I dare you / come on down
Nic F 26; YD 24

If – (Rudyard Kipling)
If you can keep your head when all about you
Fav 32; GTP 314; Like 165; ND 230 (part) *Brave 25*

Life Doesn't Frighten Me (Maya Angelou)
Shadows on the wall
Life 88

Mississippi Water IV (Alice Walker)
My father and mother both
Moon 75

Mother to Son (Langston Hughes)
Well, son, I'll tell you
Brave 13

The Door (Miroslav Holub, trans.
Ian Milner)
Go and open the door
PoWo II 30

from *The Women of Mumbles Head*
(Clement Scott)
Up at a lighthouse window two
women beheld the storm
Brave 46

COURTSHIP (L AND D)

Billy and Betty (anon.)
When shall we be married
Ox NR 194

Blackberry Sweet (Dudley Randall)
Black girl black girl
Love 44

Johnnie Groat Says (Charles
Causley)
Johnnie Groat says my eyes are blue
Cau F 30

The Key of my Heart (anon.)
Madam I will give you a new lace cap
Puf NR 82

The Little Man and the Little Maid
(anon.)
There was a little man
NV 121; Ox Dic 290; Ox NR 176

Love Letter (Louise Bennett)
Me darlin' love, me little dove
Afr II 43

The Milkmaid (anon.)
Where are you going to, my pretty
maid?
Nine 33; Puf NR 156

A Subaltern's Love-Song (John
Betjeman)
Miss J. Hunter-Dunn, Miss J.
Hunter-Dunn
Wind 98

Taking the Plunge (John Mole)
Flipping eck, cor blimey, strewth
Love 16; Pro I 73

To his Coy Mistress (Andrew
Marvell)
Had we but world enough and time
*Cam II 53; Fire 155; Love 44; Touch V
72*

COURTSHIP (N)

Flowers in the Valley (anon.)
O there was a woman and she was a
widow
Ox PC 40

Green Broom (anon.)
There was an old man lived out in
the wood
Ox PC 38

The Laird o' Cockpen (Lady
Nairne)
The Laird o' Cockpen he's proud an'
he's great
Kist 61

My Young Man's a Cornishman
(Charles Causley)
My young man's a Cornishman
NTP 27

The One Answer (anon.)
On yonder hill there stands a
creature
GTP 169

The Saucy Sailor Boy (anon.)
Come, my only one, come, my fond
one
Sea 184

*Soldier, Soldier, Won't you Marry
me?* (anon.)
Soldier, soldier, won't you marry
me?
Ox PC 35; Puf NR 176

COWBOYS

Cowboy Song (Charles Causley)
I come from Salem County
Like 92; Strict 152; Voi II 132

Cowboys (Jon Stallworthy)
Panther-footed saunter in the street
ND 139; Voi II 120

A Night-Herding Song (Harry
Stephens)
Oh, slow up, dogies, quit your roving
round
NTP 241

The Streets of Laredo (anon.)
As I walked out in the streets of
Laredo
Rat 409; Story 16; WP 79

CRABS

The Dead Crab (Andrew Young)
A rosy shield upon its back
Rat 122

Crabwise (George Barker)
Sea-crabs live in / And near the sea
Six 51

CRAYONING

See Painting

CREATION

from *Adam's Apple* (John Fuller)
God leaned out of himself one day
Quin 91

The Creation (James Weldon Johnson)
And God stepped out on space
Open 2; Sun 46

Creation [of Phoots] (Richard Edwards)
On the first day
Edw Ph 15

Gin I was God (Charles Murray)
Gin I was God, sittin' up there abeen
Scot 1

In the beginning (Baluba)
In the beginning
Afr I 66

CRICKET

See Cham 29-39; also Mot

At Lord's (Francis Thompson)
It is little I repair to the matches of the southern folk
Mot 93

Cricket at Worcester, 1938 (John Arlott)
Dozing in deck-chair's gentle curve
Mot 121

Cricketer (R. C. Scriven)
Light / as the flight
Cham 29; Sk 125

The Extra Inch (Siegfried Sassoon)
O Batsman, rise to go and stop the rot
Mot 110

Incident at 'The Oval' (Wes Magee)
Here, sunk in memories of summer afternoons
Strict 155

Missed! (P. G. Wodehouse)
The sun in the heavens was beaming
Cham 36; Mot 99

Night Cricket (Max Fatchen)
Cricket at nights
Aus B 54

Quick Ball Man (James Berry)
Bowlerman, bowlerman
Cham 34

A Sporting Knock (Richard Heller)
'Leg stump, please.' The wicket feels hard
Cham 30

Street Cricket (Gareth Owen)
On August evenings by the lamppost
Owe C 26

from *Vitai Lampada* (Sir Henry Newbolt)
There's a breathlesss hush in the Close tonight
Cham 39; Like 38; Mot 94; Sk 126

Viv (for cricketer Vivian Richards) (Faustin Charles)
Like the sun rising and setting
Ang I 60; Bab 77

CRIME

There Was an Old Woman (Charles Causley)
There was an old woman of Chester-le-Street
Cau E 11

CROCODILES

Beware! (June Crebbin)
The crocodile is coming!
Cre 40

A Crocodile (Thomas Lovell Beddoes)
Hard by the lilied Nile I saw
Ark 120; Jung 37; Rat 114

Crocodile Tears (Irene Rawnsley)
I used to spend
Raw 22

The Dentist and the Crocodile (Roald Dahl)
The crocodile, with cunning smile, sat in the dentist's chair
Dah S 43

If You Should Meet a Crocodile
(anon.)
If you should meet a crocodile
*Aus B 74; Cow 84; Fab NV 76; Once
101; OSF 31; P Sev 60*

How Doth the Little Crocodile
(Lewis Carroll)
How doth the little crocodile
*Chat 283; Cow 87; GTP 70; Rat 194;
Talk 68; Ten 52; Walk 80*

The Purist (Ogden Nash)
I give you now Professor Twist
Nas C 116; Ox A 250; WS 80

CROWS

As He Lay Dying (Randolph Stow)
As he lay dying, two fat crows
Floc 257

The Carrion Crow (anon.)
A carrion crow sat on an oak
Ox Dic 111; Ox NR 186; Ox PC 21

Crow (Roger McGough)
A crow is a crow is a crow
McG S 36

The Crow (Russell Hoban)
Flying loose and easy, where does he
go?
Ark 40

Crows (David McCord)
I like to walk
AFP 94; CCC 93

Horrible Song (Ted Hughes)
The Crow is a wicked creature
Poem I 70

I Sometimes Think (anon.)
I sometimes think I'd rather crow
CBC 39; Cow 90; GTP 228; Walk 194

The Frog and the Crow (anon.)
There was a jolly frog in the river
did swim, O!
Puf NR 138

The Twa Corbies (anon.)
As I was walking all a-lane
*Fab CV 266; Floc 256; Puf V 98; Rat
440; Scot 49*

Why the Jackass Laughs (A. B.
Paterson)
The Boastful Crow and the
Laughing Jack
Pat A 33

THE CRUCIFIXION

Friday Morning (Sidney Carter)
It was on a Friday morning that they
took me from the cell
Story 90

The Song of the Hours (from
German, James Kirkup)
In the first hour of the day
Sun 136

Stations of the Cross (George
Mackay Brown)
Pilate: Our winter jar of grain and
malt
Sun 139

The Wood Fire (Thomas Hardy)
'This is a brightsome blaze you've lit
Sun 141; WAS 53

CUCKOOS

The Cuckoo (John Heath-Stubbs)
The cuckoo and the warty toad
CCC 94

The Cuckoo (anon.)
Cuckoo, cuckoo / What do you do?
Ani 34; Cal 57; Puf V 16; Tick 92

The Cuckoo (anon.)
O the cuckoo she's a pretty bird
Iron 118; Rat 119

Cuckoo Song (Rudyard Kipling)
Tell it to the locked-up trees
NTP 114; Puf M 169

The Gowk (William Soutar)
Half doun the hill, whaur fa's the
linn
Kist 127

Repeat that, Repeat (Gerard
Manley Hopkins)
Repeat that, repeat
Floc 11; KWP 92; NTP 97; Talk 81

The Woods and Banks (W. H.
Davies)
The woods and banks of England
now
WAS 43

CUDDLES

Who Likes Cuddles? (Michael
Rosen)
Who likes cuddles? / Me
Ros D 18

CUMULATIVE RHYMES

A Farmyard Song (anon.)
I had a cat and the cat pleased me
Ox NR 182

Frying Pan in the Moving Van
(Eve Merriam)
A new family's coming to live next
door to me
KCP 134

History (Mick Gowar)
When I was a lad so young
Gow S 39

The House that Jack Built (anon.)
This is the house that Jack built
*Lob 44; Ox Dic 229; Ox NR 47; Voa
110*

I Had a Cat (anon.)
I had a cat and the cat pleased me
Cow 70

John Ball (anon.)
John Ball shot them all
Corn 64; DS 30; Fab NV 189

The Mouse and the Fire Engines
(Wilma Horsbrugh)
Here is a house, a neat little place
RT 31

The Old Woman who Bought a Pig
(anon.)
An old woman went to market and
bought a pig
Ox NR 207

There Was an Old Woman (anon.)
There was an old woman who
swallowed a fly
*CBC 144; GTP 231; Ox A 156; Nine
59; Spi 30; Walk 164*

This is the House that Jack Built
(anon.)
This is the House that Jack built
*Chat 156; Ox Dic 229; Ox NR 49; Puf
NR 23*

The Train to Glasgow (Wilma
Horsbrugh)
Here is the train to Glasgow
*CBC 40; Fab NV 251; Nine 69; Once
11; Young 90*

CURRY

Nice Little Fish (from the
Subhasitaratnakosa, trans. John
Brough)

I rolled them in turmeric, cummin
and spice
Pic 70

CURSES

See Puf M 57-67

A Glass of Beer (James Stephens)
The lanky hank of a she in the inn
over there
Fire 167; Rat 179

Revenge (Robin Klein)
I hate you, I hate you, I hate you,
Anne Scully
Occ 79

To Curse Her (Keith Douglas)
You're handsome and false, and I
could cover
Show II 14

Traveller's Curse after Misdirection
(from Welsh, Robert Graves)
May they stumble, stage by stage
Poem I 59; Voi II 87

*The Wicked Who Would Do Me
Harm* (from Gaelic, A.
Carmichael)
The wicked who would do me harm
Rat 462

DAFFODILS

The Daffodils (William
Wordsworth)
I wandered lonely as a cloud
NTP 120

The Lent Lily (A. E. Housman)
'Tis spring; come out and ramble
WAS 51

To Daffodils (Robert Herrick)
Fair daffodils we weep to see
Fab CV 51; NTP 120

DANCING (L and D)

The Baby's Dance (Ann Taylor)
Dance, little baby, dance up high
Ox CV 120; Ox Dic 60

Break Dance (Grace Nichols)
I'm going to break dance
Life 76

The Dance (Thomas Campion ?)
Robin is a lovely lad
Fab CV 42

The Dancing Cabman (J. B. Morton)
Alone on the lawn
Fab NV 213

Disco Nite (Wes Magee)
In the girls' cloaks
Side 42G

Fancy's Knell (A. E. Housman)
When lads were home from labour
Fab CV 43

The Fiddler of Dooney (W. B. Yeats)
When I play on my fiddle in Dooney
Fab CV 41; Face 136; Irish 171

Limbo Dancer's Sound Poem (John Agard)
Go–down–low–low–low
Touch IV 40

Quickstep (Kit Wright)
Way down Geneva, / All along Vine
KCP 214

Rumba (José Tallet)
Zumba, mama, la rumba y tambo
Afr II 12

Russian Dance (Ogden Nash)
The Russian moujik is made for music
Nas C 107

Tarantella (Hilaire Belloc)
Do you remember an Inn, Miranda?
Fab CV 45; KCP 33; Like 111; Rat 416
(part) *Name 62*

When I Dance (James Berry)
When I dance it isn't merely
Ber 60

Yaa, the Adowa dancer (L. M. Asiedu)
The tune of Adowa
Afr I 39

DANCING (N)

Bad Dancer Mustn't Blame the Floor (John Agard)
You don't have to go to school
Gran 31

George Mackenzie (Richard Edwards)
Old George Mackenzie used to dance
Edw P 52

Lily (Richard Edwards)
Lily's always dancing
Edw W 44

The Lost Shoe (Walter de la Mare)
Poor litle Lucy
de la M P 46; Fab NV 95; Fun 99; Name 56

Off the Ground (Walter de la Mare)
Three jolly farmers
de la M P 52; Fab NV 60

A Piper (Seamus O'Sullivan)
A piper in the streets today
Like 115

DANGER

Good Taste (Christopher Logue)
Travelling, a man met a tiger, so
O & A 137; Ox SP 109

DANIEL

Daniel (Vachel Lindsay)
Darius the Mede was a king and a wonder
Brave 79; ND 126; Pud 88

The Plotting Princes Approach the King (W. H. Auden)
The plotting princes approach the king
Sun 73

DARKNESS

After Dark (Sheila Simmons)
What is it like / After dark
ASP 58

The Dark (Adrian Henri)
I don't like the dark coming down on my head
TG 14

The Dark (Roy Fuller)
I feared the darkness as a boy
Poem I 30

Darkness (Wes Magee)
Children, we burrowed beneath blankets
ATP 63

Fear of the Dark (Vernon Scannell)
Along the unlit lane on a night
YD 126

In the daytime (Michael Rosen)
In the daytime I am Rob Roy and a tiger
Poem I 30; Ros M 65

Leave the Stairs Light On (Brian Morse)
'Leave the stairs light on, please!'
Mor 98

The Longest Journey in the World (Michael Rosen)
Last one into bed
Pro II 58; Ros Y 12; RT 80

Out in the Dark (Edward Thomas)
Out in the dark over the snow
Foot 24

A Short Cut . . . After Dark (Wes Magee)
It's late / The night is icy
ATP 76

The Silent Spinney (Seamus Redmond)
What's that rustling behind me?
All 105; Gho 31

Walking in Autumn (Frances Horovitz)
We have overshot the wood
Wind 124

DARTS

Dart Board Dave (Danny Pollock)
I know / it's been said before
Mot 182

The Dartist (F. Scott Monument)
He watches Eric Bristow on the box
Mot 193

DAVID AND GOLIATH

David and Goliath (Judith Nicholls)
David was a shepherd boy
Nic F 33

David and Goliath (Nathaniel Crouch)
When Israel against Philistia
Ox CV 41

Goliath and David (Robert Graves)
Yet once an earlier David took
FWW 86

Goliath and the Pebble (Michael Baldwin)
David looking on Goliath saw
Sun 70

DAWN

The Black Turkey-Gobbler (Mescalero Apache)
The black turkey-gobbler, under the East
TPS 22

from *Fox-Trot: Aubade* (John Fuller)
As the earth's turning darkness ends
Quin 69

Hark! Hark! the Lark (William Shakespeare)
Hark! Hark! the lark at heaven's gate sings
Fab CV 47; Ox PC 94

DAYDREAMS

Hundreds and Thousands (Kit Wright)
Under the hair-drier
Ang I 10

DEATH

And Death Shall Have No Dominion (Dylan Thomas)
And death shall have no dominion
ND 243

Because I Could not Stop for Death (Emily Dickinson)
Because I could not stop for Death
Mes 142; Touch V 18

Calcas Speaks Over the Body of Ajax (James Shirley)
The glories of our blood and state
ND 241

The Dead Crab (Andrew Young)
A rosy shield upon its back
Rat 122

Death (from the Welsh, A. T. Davies)
One night as I lay on my bed
Rat 122; Story 155

Death Be Not Proud (John Donne)
Death be not proud, though some have called thee
Touch V 19

Death in Leamington (John Betjeman)
She died in the upstairs bedroom
Rat 123; Touch IV 90

Devonshire Street, W1 (John Betjeman)
The heavy mahogany door with its wrought iron screen
Foc 97

Do Not Go Gentle Into That Good Night (Dylan Thomas)
Do Not Go Gentle Into That Good Night
Cam II 158; Rat 131; Touch V 17; Wind 62

Grandad (Kit Wright)
Grandad's dead
Mad 54; Occ 146; Wri R 28

Harrybo (Michael Rosen)
Once my friend Harrybo
Five 99; Ros H 122

Janet Waking (John Crowe Ransom)
Beautifully Janet slept
This W 27

Lights Out (Edward Thomas)
I have come to the borders of sleep
Floc 177

Mid-Term Break (Seamus Heaney)
I sat all morning in the college sick-bay
Bell 88; Touch V 15

My Busconductor (Roger McGough)
My busconductor tells me
Brave 114; Voi III 50

On a Portrait of a Deaf Man (John Betjeman)
The kind old face, the egg-shaped head
KCP 35; Like 159

The Passing of Alfred (U. A. Fanthorpe)
Our fathers were good at dying
Fan 48

Piazza Piece (John Crowe Ransom)
I am a gentleman in a dustcoat trying
Show II 33

The Twin of Sleep (Robert Graves)
Death is the twin of sleep, they say
Voi III 138

Until Gran Died (Wes Magee)
The minnows I caught
Wes M 18

Up-hill (Christina Rossetti)
Does the road wind up-hill all the way?
O & A 173

DEATH OF CATS

A Case of Murder (Vernon Scannell)
They should not have left him there alone
Ax 62; KCP 173; Pro II 78; Ten 84; Wind 74

Cat's Funeral (E. V. Rieu)
Bury her deep, down deep
PoWo II 63; Puf Q 147

Dead Cat (Basil Payne)
Three boys / swinging / a dead cat
Irish 138

Death of a Cat (Anthony Thompson)
I rose early / On the fourth day
Ax 61; CCC 169

The Death of a Cat (George Barker)
No, it was nothing much. Just the ginger
Six 30

The Early Purges (Seamus Heaney)
I was six when I first saw kittens drown
Fire 31

The Golden Cat (Eleanor Farjeon)
My golden cat has dappled sides
CCC 187

My Old Cat (Hal Summers)
My old cat is dead
CCC 185

To a Siamese Cat (Michael Joseph)
I shall walk in the sun alone
CCC 184

DECEMBER

December (John Clare)
While snows the window-panes bedim
Ox CP 15

DEER

Deer (Clive Sansom)
Such gentle things they are
CCC 121

The Deers' Request (Elizabeth Jennings)
We are the disappearers
Ark 43; Rab 25

Earthy Anecdote (Wallace Stevens)
Every time the bucks went clattering
Zoo 58

The Fallow Deer at the Lonely House (Thomas Hardy)
One without looks in tonight
Gold 103; Ox PC 124; Rat 151; Stoc 26; Talk 61

The Fawn in the Snow (William Rose Benet)
The brown-dappled fawn
CCC 118

In Midwinter a Wood was (Peter Levi)
In midwinter a wood was
CCC 120; Sun 81; WAS 167

Roe-deer (Ted Hughes)
In the dawn-dirty light, in the biggest snow of the year
Hug MT 19

DEMOLITION

Different Views (Hiawyn Oram)
They're pulling down the clock tower
Ora 38

House Coming Down (Eleanor Farjeon)
They're pulling down the house
Pos 45

DENTISTS

See also Teeth, Toothache

After the Dentist (May Swenson)
My left upper / lip and half
Occ 139

In and Out of the Dentist's Chair (Hiawyn Oram)
I am at the dentist
Ora 47

The Dentist (Judith Nicholls)
I love to visit my dentist
AFP 47

The Dentist and the Crocodile (Roald Dahl)
The crocodile, with cunning smile, sat in the dentist's chair
Dah S 43

Dentist's Lament (Mick Gowar)
I give them 'Natural Nashers' badges
Gow T 60

Going to the Dentist (Gareth Owen)
After tea / Trev and me
Owe K 9

An Urgent Call (John Cunliffe)
Dentist! Dentist!
Straw 28

Visit to the Dentist (J. and G. Curry)
When Ulie woke up
Down 74

DEPRESSION

Blackest of Blues (Roger McGough)
I was born in Dread County
McG S 90

DESERT ISLANDS

The Castaways or Vote for Caliban (Adrian Mitchell)
The Pacific Ocean
Gang 86

Emperors of the Island (Dannie Abse)
There is the story of a deserted island
Gho 46; Poem I 64

DIGGING

Digging (Edward Thomas)
Today I think
Choice 174; Iron 53; Nif 36; Pic 10; WAS 138; WS 99

Digging (Seamus Heaney)
Between my finger and my thumb
Fire 183

The Digging Song (Wes Magee)
In your hands you hold the spade
AVF 24

DINOSAURS

See Mag M 52-4; Mons 63-9

Brontosaurus (Gail Kredenser)
The giant brontosaurus
Walk 79

Deinosaurs (Arthur J. Bull)
I love the Deinosaurs, their padded
bulk
Ark 96

Dinosaurs (Grace Nichols)
Diplodocus
Nic 29

Diplodocus (Bert L. Taylor)
Behold the mighty dinosaur
Mons 67

How the Dinosaur got Here (Spike
Milligan)
'Daddy, what's a dinosaur?'
Mons 64

Rhamphorhynchus (Wes Magee)
Look, as he swoops from the cliff's
rugged face
Mag M 52; Mons 69

So Big! (Max Fatchen)
The dinosaur, an ancient beast
AM 64; AVF 78; King 207

The Song of Tyrannosaurus Rex
(William Scammell)
I'm a rock, I'm a mountain, I'm a
hammer and a nail
Ten 71

Steam Shovel (Charles Malam)
The dinosaurs are not all dead
*Poem I 36; P Sev 150; RMP 25; Walk
216*

The Steam Shovel (Rowena
Bennett)
The steam digger
Pop 80

You'd Better Beware (Colin
McNaughton)
You'd better beware if you come
round here
McN 58

DIRGES AND LAMENTS

See Fab CV 264-75

Adieu, Farewell Earth's Bliss
(Thomas Nashe)
Adieu, farewell earth's bliss
Mes 124; Rat 21

The Bonnie Earl of Moray (anon.)
Ye Highlands and ye Lawlands
*Fab CV 270; Ox PC 152; Puf V 97;
Kist 36*

Bonnie George Campbell (anon.)
Hie upon Highlands
Kist 5

Call for the Robin Redbreast (John
Webster)
Call for the robin redbreast and the
wren
Fab CV 265; Ox PC 153; This W 30

Death of Cock Robin (anon.)
Who killed Cock Robin?
*Chat 146; Fab NV 113; GTP 62; Lob
138; Ox Dic 130; Ox NR 166; Puf NR
76; Puf V 38; RMP 44; Voa 102*

Elegy for Himself (Chidiock
Tichborne)
My prime of youth is but a frost of
cares
Rat 140; Voi II 149

Fear No More the Heat o' the Sun
(William Shakespeare)
Fear no more the heat o' the sun
*Fab CV 265; Like 154; Mes 126; ND
242; Puf V 244; Rat 151; WAS 180*

The Flowers of the Forest (Jean
Elliot)
I've heard them lilting at
the yowe-milking
Brave 135; Fab CV 269; Kist 109

Full Fathom Five (William
Shakespeare)
Full fathom five thy father lies
*Cam I 78; Fab CV 268; Floc 42; MT
85; NTP 217; Ox PC 52; P Sev 79;
This W 83; WS 23*

The Lament of the Border Widow
(anon.)
My love he built me a bonny bower
Mes 59

Li Fu-Jen (Wu-ti 157-87 BC,
trans. Arthur Waley)
The sound of her silk skirt has
stopped
WS 105

Lost in France: Jo's Requiem
(Ernest Rhys)
He had the plowman's strength
PW 115

A Lyke-Wake Dirge (anon.)
This ae nighte. this ae nighte
*Fab CV 264; Fire 65; Floc 258; Iron
137; NTP 228; Puf V 204; Voi II 156*

My Dearest Dust (Lady Catherine Dyer 1641)
My dearest dust, could not thy hasty day
Puf V 163

A Nocturnall upon St Lucies Day (John Donne)
'Tis the yeares midnight and it is the dayes
Fire 55

from *On the Death of Doctor Swift* (Jonathan Swift)
The time is not remote when I
Mes 133

Requiem (Robert Louis Stevenson)
Under the wide and starry sky
NTP 238

A Slumber Did my Spirit Seal (William Wordsworth)
A slumber did my spirit seal
Fab CV 273

Stop All the Clocks (W. H. Auden)
Stop all the clocks, cut off the telephone
Fab NV 170; Gold 61; Love 152; Rat 406

DIVING

The Diver (Ian Serraillier)
I put on my aqua-lung and plunge
KCP 178

DOGS (L AND D)

See Greyhounds, Puppies, Sheepdogs

Bad Dog (Brian Lee)
All day long Bones hasn't been seen
All 30; Pets 6

Binkie (Rudyard Kipling)
Pussy can sit by the fire and sing
NV 95

The Bloodhound (Edward Anthony)
I am the dog world's best detective
GTP 43; Nif 13

Boarding Kennels (U. A. Fanthorpe)
Here we lodge love when it grows inconvenient
Crys 35

The Country Dog (Max Fatchen)
The country dog with his eager grin
Fat S 8

Dead 'Wessex' the Dog to the Household (Thomas Hardy)
Do you think of me at all
CCC 189

A Dog's Life (Brian Patten)
Sigh, sob / gulp, bark, gush
Pat 115

A Dog's Tombstone (Greek, trans. Lord Hailsham)
This tombstone, stranger passing near
TC 37

Greedy Dog (James Hurley)
This dog will eat anything
WZ 14

Happy Dogday (Peter Dixon)
Today is our dog's birthday
TG 16

Heads or Tails? (Kit Wright)
Dave Dirt's dog is a horrible hound
Ox T 88; Wri H 16

I Have this Crazy Problem (Mohammed Khan)
When I was young
SS 19; WZ 18

An Introduction to Dogs (Ogden Nash)
The dog is man's best friend
GTP 38; Pud 13; Young 9

Lone Dog (Irene McLeod)
I'm a lean dog, a keen dog, a wild dog and lone
Ax 67; Like 35; Puf V 42; Walk 65; YD 65

Man and Dog (Siegfried Sassoon)
Who's this – alone with stone and sky?
CCC 179

Mick (James Reeves)
Mick my mongrel-O
Day 26

My Dog (Vernon Scannell)
My dog belongs to no known breed
ASP 100

Night Walk (Max Fatchen)
What are you doing away up there
ATP 75; CCC 201; Fat S 12; Ox T 151; Shad 51; Tick 173; YD 130

A Popular Personage at Home (Thomas Hardy)
'I live here: 'Wessex' is my name . . .'
CCC 188

Roger the Dog (Ted Hughes)
Asleep he wheezes at his ease
Pets 5; PoWo I 55; YD 64

Sunning (James S. Tippett)
Old Dog lay in the summer sun
Cal 66; Pos 64; Walk 66; WAS 86

To My Dog (Adrian Mitchell)
This gentle beast
Mit N 70

Who Rolled in the Mud (Mike Rosen)
Who rolled in the mud
Ani 10; Ros M 62; Ros Y 4

DOGS (N)

The Barkday Party (James Berry)
For my dog's birthday party
Occ 78

Beth Gelert (William R. Spencer)
The spearmen heard the bugle sound
GTP 138

Daley's Dorg Wattle (N. T. Goodge)
'You can talk about yer sheep dorgs' said the man from Allan's Creek
KWP 77

Dog in the Playground (Allan Ahlberg)
Dog in the playground
Ahl P 50; Ani 44; Bell 100; SS 52

The Dog Lovers (Spike Milligan)
So they bought you
Speak 16

Down Behind the Dustbin (Michael Rosen)
Down behind the dustbin
PoWo I 56; Pro I 21; WP 68
(part) *Tim 15*

Nemo Canem Impune Lacessit (Robert Garioch)
I kicked an Edinbro dug-lover's dug
Scot 41

Old Mother Hubbard (anon.)
Old Mother Hubbard
Chat 186; Fab NV 171; Lob 154 ; Ox CV 125; Ox Dic 317; Ox NR 28; Puf NR 146; Voa 62

P. C. Plod Versus the Dale St Dogstrangler (Roger McGough)
For several months
McRo 14; Ox SP 72; WP 118

A Playground Visitor (Brian Morse)
The queue for the toilet starts to thin
Mor 61

The Rescue (Ian Serraillier)
The wind is loud
Brave 98; Spi 11; Tick 58

Today Was Not (Michael Rosen)
Today was not / very warm
RMP 40

Where's Schell? (Frank McMahon)
He certainly detested George Schell's dog
Aus R 112

DONKEYS

The Donkey (G. K. Chesterton)
When fishes flew and forests walked
Fav 132; HH 50; KCP 50; Like 137; ND 76; NV 89; Rat 133; Show II 8; Sun 132; WAS 52

Francis Jammes: a Prayer to go to Paradise with the Donkeys (Richard Wilbur)
When I must come to you, O my God I pray
Rat 166

Nicholas Nye (Walter de la Mare)
Thistle and darnel and dock grew there
CCC 73; de la M P 81; Ox PC 120

Time Out (John Montague)
The donkey sat down on the roadside
Irish 117

What the Donkey Saw (U. A. Fanthorpe)
No room in the inn, of course
WS 114

DORMICE

The Christening (A. A. Milne)
What shall I call
Like 98; Young 28

DOTTEREL

Dotterel (Judith Wright)
Wild and impermanent
Aus B 33

DOVES

See Pigeons

DOWSERS

The Diviner (Seamus Heaney)
Cut from the green hedge a forked
hazel stick
Irish 61

DRAGONFLIES

A Dragonfly (Eleanor Farjeon)
When the heat of the summer
*Cal 66; CCC 49; Far M 15; Open 78;
Pos 132; Tick 131*

Second Birth (Lord Tennyson)
Today I saw the Dragon Fly
Ark 42; CCC 49; Zoo 21

DRAGONS

Beowulf's Fight with the Dragon
(Anglo-Saxon)
The treasure-guardian heard the
talk
HH 63

*Custard the Dragon and the Wicked
Knight* (Ogden Nash)
Guess what happened in the little
white house
*Nas C 96; Ox A 250; Ox T 120; RMP
22*

The Dragon (Edward Lowbury)
On the island of Komodo
Mons 43

The Dragon of Wantley (English
Folk Song)
Old stories tell how Hercules
Voi II 29
(part) This dragon had two furious
wings
Mons 42

The Dragon's Lament (Trevor
Harvey)
It isn't much fun to find out you're a
dragon
Cele 42

Fafnir (Stevie Smith)
In the quiet waters
Mes 156; MT 72; ND 189; Rab 89

The Gold-Tinted Dragon (Karla
Kuskin)
What's the good of a wagon
Read 34

Jocelyn, my Dragon (Colin West)
My dragon's name is Jocelyn
Pets 78; West 171

The Lonely Dragon (Theresa
Heine)
A dragon is sad
AFP 59

A Modern Dragon (Rowena
Bennett)
A train is a dragon that roars
through the dark
Read 35

Sir Eglamour (Samuel Rowlands)
Sir Eglamour that worthy knight
Fab CV 170; MT 130; Ox PC 25

A Small Dragon (Brian Patten)
I've found a small dragon in the
woodshed
*AM 20; Foot 35; Gang 112; Gold 36;
MCF 14; MT 71; ND 190; Puf M 174;
Tick 56; Ting 44*

St George and the Dragon (anon.)
Open your doors and let me in
Chris 126

Storytime (Judith Nicholls)
Once upon a time, children,
AFP 24; Nic F 39; Ox SP 23; Story 4

The Tale of Custard the Dragon
(Ogden Nash)
Belinda lived in a little white house
*Fab NV 170; GTP 166; Name 14; Nas
C 42; Once 130*

DRAKE, SIR FRANCIS

Drake's Drum (Sir Henry
Newbolt)
Drake he's in his hammock an' a
thousand miles away
*Brave 121; Fab CV 246; Sea 139; YD
44*

Of the Great . . . Sir Francis Drake
(Robert Hayman)
The Dragon that our Seas did raise
his Crest
Fab CV 145

Upon Sir Francis Drake's Return
(anon.)
Sir Francis, Sir Francis, Sir Francis is
come
Fab CV 144

DREAMS

See also Nightmares

A Child's Dream (Frances Cornford)
I had a little dog, and my dog was very small
CCC 155

Corners of the Night (Brian Morse)
In the box room Darren dreams of Samantha
Mor 59

Dog's Dinner (Irene Rawnsley)
On Thursday night / my mother said
Raw 2

Dream of a Bird (Bach Nga Thi Tran)
You ask me, what did I dream?
Aus R 122

The Dream of a Boy who Lived at Nine Elms (W. B. Rands)
Nine grenadiers with bayonets in their guns
Fab NV 138; Ox CV 235

The Dream of a Girl who Lived at Sevenoaks (W. B. Rands)
Seven sweet singing birds up in a tree
Fab NV 138; Ox CV 235

Waking Up (Eleanor Farjeon)
Oh! I have just had such a lovely dream
Far M 78

What Did I Dream? (Robert Graves)
What did I dream? I do not know
Shad 46; Tick 179; YD 138

wonder boy (Jeff Cloves)
and so / among the traded playground fagcards
Mot 159

DROMEDARIES

The Dromedary (A. Y. Campbell)
In dreams I see the dromedary still
Jung 59

DROVERS

A Drover (Padraic Colum)
To Meath of the pastures
Rat 135

King Ezra (Charles Causley)
King Ezra was a drover
IC 14

DROWNING

The Banished Duke of Grafton (anon.)
Three youths went a-fishing
Sea 55

The Sands of Dee (Charles Kingsley)
O Mary, go and call the cattle home
Fav 58; KCP 110; Ox PC 153; Story 154; Ten 175; YD 100

DRUGS

Hero (Mick Gowar)
Of course I took the drugs. Look, son
Ang I 58

DRUMS

Beat Drummers (Benjamin Zephaniah)
Come Zipporah come rock with I
Blac 91

The Bongo Man (Hugh Hailson Boatswain)
He drummed his fingers lightly
Bab 134

The Drum (John Scott of Amwell)
I hate that drum's discordant sound
Cam II 77; PW 85; Voi II 73

Percussionist (John Mole)
When the Gladiators enter hear him hurrying the beat
Mol 64

DRUNKENNESS

Melting into the Foreground (Roger McGough)
Head down and it's into the hangover.
McG F 22

DUCKS

Dilly, Dilly (anon.)
Oh, what have you got for dinner,
Mrs Bond?
Ox Dic 91; Ox NR 171

The Duck (Ogden Nash)
Behold the duck
*CBC 133; CCC 75; Nas C 74; Pud 24;
Rat 137; Zoo 76*

Ducks (Frederick William
Harvey)
From troubles of the world
CCC 78; Once 40

Ducks (Phoebe Hesketh)
A small procession waddles single
file
Six 128

Ducks' Ditty (Kenneth Grahame)
All along the backwater
*Fab NV 78; Like 114; Ox CV 328; Ox
T 101; P Sev 21; RMP 48; Walk 83;
Young 29*

Flo the White Duck (Gwen Dunn)
All white and smooth is Flo
Ani 24; P Sev 15; Show II 31

Four Ducks on a Pond (William
Allingham)
Four ducks on a pond
*Irish 27; Ox PC 66; Rab 43; This W
16; WAS 128*

Mallard (Rex Warner)
Squawking they rise from reeds into
the sun
Rhy 69

Mrs McPhee (Charles Causley)
Mrs McPhee / Who lived in South
Zeal
Cau E 10; PG 71

Quack! (Walter de la Mare)
The duck is whiter than whey is
CCC 76; RT 156

from *A Winchester Mosaic*
(Jeremy Hooker)
A smell of cut grass and growing
nettles
Face 120

Winter Ducks (Russell Hoban)
Small in the shrink of winter,
CCC 17; Out 84

DUMB INSOLENCE

Dumb Insolence (Adrian Mitchell)
I'm big for ten years old
*Ax 72; Bell 83; KCP 140; Mit N 66;
Speak 28; Strict 26*

Mart's Advice (Michael Rosen)
If someone's acting big with you
McRo 31

DUNCES

Arithmetic (Gavin Ewart)
I'm 11. And I don't really know
Bell 80; Brave 139; Strict 19

The Dunce (Jacques Prevert,
trans. John Dixon Hunt)
He says no with his head
Floc 72

In One Ear and Out the Other
(Colin West)
When Miss Tibbs talks
Bell 69; West 13

Progress (Barrie Wade)
We're in the progress group, which
means we get on slower
Wad 18

Slow Reader (Vicki Feaver)
He can make sculptures
Strict 51

Streemin (Roger McGough)
Im in the botom streme
*Ax 5; Bell 73; King 17; McG G 9;
McRo 26; Sk 55*

Truant (Phoebe Hesketh)
They call him dunce and yet he can
discern
Six 141

DUSTBIN MEN

The Dustbin Men (Gregory
Harrison)
The older ones have gone to school
RT 52

DWARVES

Two Songs of the Dwarves (J. R. R.
Tolkien)
Far over the misty mountains cold
Like 135; MT 128
Under the mountain dark and tall
MT 129

EAGLES

from *Child and Boatman* (Jean Inglelow)
Bless the child!
Jung 84

The Eagle (Alfred Lord Tennyson)
He clasps the crag with crooked hands
CCC 96; Fab CV 89; Gold 98; GTP 58; Iron 12; KCP 197; ND 64; NTP 98; Open 69; Ox PC 66; Pos 79; Rab 78; S Sun 19; Ten 44; This W 120; Walk 87; Zoo 66

The Eagle (Andrew Young)
He hangs between his wings outspread
Ark 44; CCC 95

EARTH

The Bonnie Broukit Bairn (Hugh Macdiarmid)
Mars is braw in crammasy
Scot 5

Gin I Was God (Charles Murray)
Gin I was God, sittin' up there abeen
Scot 1

EARTH: DESTROYED

See also Hiroshima, Nuclear Power

ALPHA – B375 – EARTH VISITORS GUIDE (John Cunliffe)
Galactic Government Health Warning
Spa 114

The Destroyers (Albert Rowe)
Through the spacescope's limitless eyes
Spa 116

Do You Think We'll Ever Get to See Earth, Sir? (Sheenagh Pugh)
I hear they're hoping to run trips
Spa 119; Wind 38

EARTHWORMS

The Earthworm (from Swedish, Robert Bly)
Who really respects the earthworm
Rat 139

The Earthworm's Monologue (Elizabeth Jennings)
Birds prey on me, fish are fond of my flesh
Quin 124

Guess Me (Richard Edwards)
Dear Reader, Guess me, I'm a riddle
Edw W 35

Nobody Loves Me, Everybody Hates Me (anon.)
I'm going in the garden to eat worms
HH 9

Worms and the Wind (Carl Sandburg)
Worms would rather be worms
WZ 39; Zoo 85

EASTER

Easter (Gerard Manley Hopkins)
Break the box and shed the nard
Sun 152

Easter Eggs (Russian, anon.)
Easter eggs! Easter eggs! Give to him that begs
Sun 154

Easter Morning – The African Intellectual (Abioseh Nicol)
Ding dong bell / Pussy's in the well
Fire 62

Easter Song (George Herbert)
I got me flowers to straw thy way
Sun 152

Easter Wings (George Herbert)
Lord, who createst man in wealth and store
Show II 16

ECHOES

Echo (Leonard Clark)
Walking for the first time
Six 119; Mes 236

Echo (Sara Asheron)
Hello! / Hello!
Gh P 9

The Lion and the Echo (Brian Patten)
The King of Beasts, deep in the wood
ASP 113; Ox SP 129; Pat 27

The Voice in the Tunnel (Robert Fisher)
The end of the tunnel was dark
DS 46

EELS

A Visit to the Aquarium (Kit Wright)
Watching the conger eel
Wri R 63; WZ 99

EGGS

Egg Thoughts (Russell Hoban)
Soft-Boiled: I do not like the way you slide
Day 12

Eggs (Jack Prelutsky)
Eggs! / You're excellent, exquisite
Pre 104

EGRETS

Egrets (Judith Wright)
Once as I travelled through a quiet evening
Aus R 100; Stuf II 61

ELDORADO

Eldorado (Edgar Allen Poe)
Gaily bedight / A gallant knight
Fab CV 187; Stuf 80

ELEPHANTS

The Blind Men and the Elephant (John Godfrey Saxe)
It was six men of Indostan
CBC 119; GTP 200; Once 22; Ox A 82; Ox T 116

The Circus Elephants (John Foster)
What are they thinking
AFP 71

Elephant (from Yoruba, trans. Ulli Beier)
Elephant, a spirit in the bush
Rat 201
Elephant, death-bringer!
Afr I 23; Stuf II 70; Talk 69

Elephant (Alan Brownjohn)
It is quite unfair to be
Once 33

Elephant (Barbara Juster Esbensen)
The word is too heavy / to lift
Esb 1

Ellie the Elephant (Robert Heidbreder)
I'm Ellie the elephant, elephant, elephant
Hei 21

Hunting Song (Gabon)
On the weeeping forest, under the wing of the evening
Afr II 23

Jumbo (Vernon Scannell)
He makes a useful vehicle
Sca T 14

Oliphaunt (J. R. R. Tolkien)
Gray as a mouse
AM 14; PoWo I 44; Walk 59

Two Performing Elephants (D. H. Lawrence)
He stands with his forefeet on the drum
Rat 442

ELEVATORS

See Lifts

ELIZABETH I

A Ditty (Edmund Spenser)
See where she sits upon the grassy green
Fab CV 137

The Looking-Glass (Rudyard Kipling)
The Queen was in her chamber, and she was middling old
Face 90; NTP 54

EMBARRASSMENT

Hot and Cold (Brian Lee)
Everybody all excited and hot
Six 214

New Shoes (Brian Lee)
I keep close to walls
Six 212

EMUS

The Emu (Leon Gellert)
The Emu makes, though prone to
fret
CBC 43

ENDANGERED SPECIES

Extinction of the 21st Century Dodo
(John Walsh)
The Dodo said / to the kangaroo
Rab 62

ENGINE DRIVERS

Casey Jones (anon.)
Come all you rounders if you want to
hear
Ox PC 76

The Fireman's Not for Me (Ewan
McColl)
Come all you young maidens, take
warning from me
Cam I 21

ENGLAND

Gaunt's Dying Speech (William
Shakespeare)
Methinks I am a prophet new-
inspir'd
ND 6
(part) This royal throne of kings this
sceptred isle
Fav 13

ENGLAND: HISTORY

Puck's Song (Rudyard Kipling)
See you the ferny ride that steals
Fab CV 129; Ox CV 320

ENGLISH LANGUAGE, THE

Blue Umbrellas (D. J. Enright)
The thing that makes a blue
umbrella with its tail
Voi III 156

*The Cheetah, My Dearest, is Known
not to Cheat* (George
Barker)

The cheetah, my dearest, is
known not to cheat
Six 31

Foolish Questions (American,
adapted William Cole)
Where can a man buy a cap for his
knee?
OSF 40; Pro II 52

Have You Ever Seen? (anon.)
Have you ever seen a sheet on a
river-bed?
Walk 195

Have You Ever Thought?
(Jacqueline Brown)
A comb has teeth but can't bite
ASP 122

*Hints on Pronunciation for
Foreigners* (T. S. W.)
I take it you already know
Floc 237; KCP 23; WS 85

J: Jargon (James Reeves)
Jerusalem, Joppa, Jericho
Ree C 156

A New Song of New Similes (John
Gay 1685-1732)
My passion is as mustard strong
Chat 136

'Ough!' A Phonetic Fansy (W. T.
Goodge)
The baker-man was kneading dough
Aus B 73

The Song of the Dumb-Waiter
(James Reeves)
Who went to sleep in the flower-bed?
Fab NV 118; Ree C 8

Why English is So Hard (anon.)
We'll begin with a box and the plural
is boxes
Bell 36; Fav 25

ENGLISHMEN

Mad Dogs and Englishmen (Noel
Coward)
In tropical climes there are certain
times of day
Wind 22

ENVIRONMENT, THE

See also Pollution

Bad Luck, Dead Duck (Nicholas
Davey)
Lying there amongst the muck
Aus B 121

Can You? (Nicholas Guillen)
Can you sell me the air as it slips
through your fingers
FS 65

Caul Kail (Ken Morrice)
Rigs stan erect, great iron teats
Scot107

Extinction Day (Terry Jones)
The Dodo and the Barbary Lion
Jon 78

5 Ways to Kill a Man (Edwin
Brock)
There are many cumbersome ways
to kill a man
Earth 30; Fire 111

Going, Going (Philip Larkin)
I thought it would last my time
Ang II 52

Moss-Gathering (Theodore
Roethke)
To loosen with all ten fingers held
wide and limber
Earth 19

The Rabbit (Alan Brownjohn)
We are going to see the rabbit.
*Earth 55; Gold 58; KCP 42; ND 85;
Open 76; Rab 70; Six 76; Ten 56; WAS
98*

EPIPHANY

The Adoration of the Magi
(Christopher Pilling)
It was the arrival of the kings
Ox CP 55

Camels of the Kings (Leslie Norris)
The Camels, the Kings' Camels,
Haie-aie!
Ox CP 52

Carol of the Brown King (Langston
Hughes)
Of the three Wise Men
RT 178

Journey of the Magi (T. S. Eliot)
'A cold coming we had of it . . .'
*Choice 219; Fab CV 359; ND 225; Ox
CP 53; Star 86; Wind 8*

The Journey of the Magi (W. R.
Rodgers)
It was a dark January night, cold and
snowing
Irish 144

Three Kings Came Riding (Henry
Wadsworth Longfellow)
Three kings came riding from far
away
Ring 25

EPITAPHS

See also WS 80-3

An Epitaph (Walter de la Mare)
Here lies a most beautiful lady
Rat 142

Epitaph on a New Army (Michael
Thwaites)
No drums they wished, whose
thoughts were tied
PW 89

Epitaph on an Army of Mercenaries
(A. E. Housman)
These, in the day when heaven was
falling
ND 183; PW 88; Rat 142

*Another Epitaph on an Army of
Mercenaries* (Hugh Macdiarmid
in reply to A. E. Housman)
It is a God-damned lie to say that
these
PW 88

Epitaph on a Tyrant (W. H.
Auden)
Perfection, of a kind, was what he
was after
*Choice 239; Foc 26; PW 59; Rat 142;
Voi III 58*

Epitaph on Salathiel Pavy (Ben
Jonson)
Weep with me, all you that read
Face 150

Here Dead Lie We (A. E. Housman)
Here dead lie we because we did not
choose
FWW 83

The Unknown Citizen (W. H.
Auden)
He was found by the Bureau of
Statistics to be
Choice 244

ESKIMOS

Eskimo Chant (trans. Knud
Rasmussen)
There is joy in
Can 64; Open 61

Eskimo Lullaby (anon.,
Greenland)
It's my fat baby
Spi 12

Hunger (anon., Canada)
Fear hung over me
Wheel 46

The Mother's Song (Eskimo, trans.
Peter Freuchen)
It is so still in the house
Rhy 121; Voi III 12

The Song of Kuk-Ook, the Bad Boy
(Eskimo, N. America)
I am going to run away from home,
hayah
Talk 24

When I'm Out of the House
(Eskimo, trans. William
Thelbitzer)
When I'm out of the house in the
open, I feel joy
PPP 14

EVENING

Twilight Time (Samuel Palmer)
And now the trembling light
NTP 232

EXAMS

Dear Mr Examiner (Gareth Owen)
Thank you so much for your
questions
SO 94

Exam (Trevor Millum)
Heads down in rows
Mill 34

Exams (David Harmer)
Exams aren't fun
SO 93

Revised Version (Barrie Wade)
Come ye blank-faced singers, come
Wad 22

EXCUSES

Blame (Allan Ahlberg)
Graham, look at Maureen's leg
Ahl P 22; Bell 116; Name 49; SO 26

Excuses (Allan Ahlberg)
I've writ on the wrong page, Miss
Ahl P 61

Excuses (Pamela Gillilan)
I only took it off
AFP 108

Explanation, on Coming Home Late
(Richard Hughes, aged 7)
We went down to the river's brink
This W 13

It's Not My Fault (John Kitching)
It's not my fault
SO 27

Jeremy (Paul Sayers)
Didn't do it, wasn't me
Name 46

Kidnapped! (Shel Silverstein)
This morning I got kidnapped
KCP 187

Mr Nobody (anon.)
I know a funny little man
Fav 88; Gho 27; Puf V 150; Voa 52

Where's Your Homework? (David
Jackson)
As soon as I got home last night, Sir
SO 79

EXPLORERS

See Columbus, Drake

The Ballad of Kon-Tiki: the Raft
(Ian Serraillier)
All day the plane had searched for
them
Puf Q 177

The Ever-touring Englishmen
(Gond)
The ever-touring Englishmen have
built their bungalows
Rhy 150

FABLES

The Ant and the Cricket (from
Aesop)
A silly young cricket accustomed to
sing
GTP 78

*The Country Mouse and the City
Mouse* (R. S. Sharpe)
In a snug little cot lived a fat little
mouse
NV 98; Ox CV 139

Fable (Ralph Waldo Emerson)
The mounain and the squirrel
GTP 57; Ox A 39

58

Tortoise and Hare Poem (Judith
Nicholls)
Slowly the tortoise raised her head
Nic F 10

The Tortoise and the Hare (Roald
Dahl)
The Tortoise long ago had learned
Dah S 19

FAIRIES (L AND D)

See also Dwarves, Goblins

I'd Love to be a Fairy's Child
(Robert Graves)
Children born of fairy stock
Fab NV 93

from *The Satyr* (Ben Jonson)
This is Mab, the mistress-fairy
Puf M 211

FAIRIES (N)

Bonny Kilmeny (James Hogg)
Bonny Kilmeny gaed up the glen
Kist 95

The Fairies (William Allingham)
Up the airy mountain
*Fab CV 209; Fav 115; Irish 26; Mes
162; MT 57; Ox CV 215; Ox PC 92;
Ox T 126; Puf V 190; Walk 207
(part) Pud 36*

The Fairies' Farewell (Bishop
Richard Corbet)
Farewell rewards and fairies
Fab CV 205

Fairy Story (Stevie Smith)
I went into the wood one day
Gold 37; Puf M 210

from *Romeo and Juliet* (William
Shakespeare)
O, then I see Queen Mab hath been
with you
Floc 186; GTP 108

Thomas Rymer (anon.)
True Thomas lay on Huntlie bank
*Fab CV 213; Floc 181; GTP 124; Kist
41; Puf V 94; Rat 425*

FAIRIES' SONGS

Ariel's Song (William
Shakespeare)
Come unto these yellow sands

*Fab CV 216; Like 50; Ox PC 90; Puf M
213; Talk 14; This W 74*

Ariel's Song (William
Shakespeare)
Where the bee sucks, there suck I
*ND 8; Ox PC 91; P Sev 90; Talk 66;
Ten 178; This W 76*

The Fairy Queen (anon.)
Come, follow, follow me
Puf M 215

Fairy's Song (John Keats)
Shed no tear – O shed no tear
Puf M 212

FAIRS

See also Roller-Coasters,
Roundabouts

The Fair (Vernon Scannell)
Music and yellow steam, the fizz
Cam II 19

Fairground (Marian Lines)
Organ-shout music, kaleidoscope
streamers
Pos 21; Tick 44

The Fun Fair (Isabel Best)
Round about / And round about
O & A 51

Good Friday Fair (Michael Rosen)
Good Friday fair / comes once a year
Ros W 93

Hamnavoe Market (George
Mackay Brown)
No school today! We drove in our
gig to the town
Occ 89

Home from the Carnival (Russell
Hoban)
Gone all the lights and all the noise
RT 167

FAIRY AND FOLK TALES

After Ever Happily (Ian
Serraillier)
And they both lived happily ever
after
Floc 145; Ox SP 30; Poem I 65

Ali Baba and the Forty Thieves
(Roald Dahl)
A very decent Arab sport
Dah S 47

Aladdin and the Magic Lamp
(Roald Dahl)
A very wicked old Chinese
Dah S 67

Any Prince to any Princess (Adrian Henri)
August is coming
Gang 145; Hen 67

The Apple-Tree Man (Charles Causley)
The farmer sleeps under a printed stone
Ox SP 95

Beauty and the Beast (L. J. Anderson)
A merchant, returning, remembered the gift for his *daughter*
Crys 24

The Babes in the Wood (anon.)
My dear do you know
Tick 166

Cinderella (Roald Dahl)
I guess you think you know this story
Dah R

Cinderella at the Ball (L. J. Anderson)
Though my sisters were there, I half believed
Crys 28

Count Carrots (Gerda Mayer)
He's the giant of the mountains
Candy 12

Dick Whittington and his Cat (Roald Dahl)
Dick Whittington had oft been told
Dah S 7

The Emperor's New Clothes (Roald Dahl)
The Royal Tailor, Mr Ho
Dah S 33

Fairy Story (Stevie Smith)
I went into the wood one day
Gold 37; Puf M 210

The Frog Prince (Stevie Smith)
I am a frog
Mes 160; NTP 57

The Gingerbread Lady (John Mole)
The gingerbread lady's
All 108; PG 88

Goldilocks and the Three Bears (Roald Dahl)
This famous wicked little tale
Dah R

Hansel and Gretel (Roald Dahl)
Mum said to Dad, 'These kids of ours! . . .'
Dah S 57

Interview [Cinderella] (Sara Henderson Hay)
Yes, this is where she lived before she won
Ox A 255

Jack and the Beanstalk (Roald Dahl)
Jack's mother said, 'We're stony broke!'
Dah R; SS 48

Legend (Kay Hargreaves)
Down-dripping water led her
Foot 70

Little Red Riding Hood and the Wolf (Roald Dahl)
As soon as Wolf began to feel
Dah R; Open 96

from *The Sleeping Beauty* (Edith Sitwell)
The fairies all received an invitation
Floc 189

Snow-White and the Seven Dwarfs (Roald Dahl)
When little Snow-White's mother died
Dah R

So They Went Deeper into the Forest (Roy Daniels)
'So they went deeper into the forest,' said Jacob Grimm
Can 16; Mes 49

Song of the Frog Prince (Judith Nicholls)
It's the royal bed I miss
Nic F 32

The Three Little Pigs (Roald Dahl)
The animal I really dig
Dah R; Open 98

The Twelve Princesses (L. J. Anderson)
The night is what we live for
Crys 22

Waiting for the Prince (Roy Fuller)
When the Bad Fairy cast her spell
Trio 24

FAMILIES

FANTASY

One Step from an Old Dance
(David Helwig)
Will the weasel lie down with the
snowshoe hare?
Can 95

Romance (Walter James Turner)
When I was but thirteen or so
*Bell 89; Like 130; MT 121; NTP 207;
Puf V 209; This W 135*

Sky in the Pie (Roger McGough)
Waiter, there's a sky in my pie
McG P 11

Snail of the Moon (Ted Hughes)
Saddest of all things on the moon is
the snail without a shell
ND 192

The Song of the Mad Prince
(Walter de la Mare)
Who said 'Peacock Pie'?
*Fab CV 282; NTP 217; Ox CV 327;
Puf V 203*

Tartary (Walter de la Mare)
If I were Lord of Tartary
*de la M V 9; GTP 105; Like 73; ND
111; Ox CV 325*

Topsy-Turvey World (W. B.
Rands)
If the butterfly courted the bee
Ox CV 232

Warning to Children (Robert
Graves)
Children, if you dare to think
*Chat 390; Choice 257; Fab CV 98; Fav
30; Floc 195; NTP 142; Ox PC 32; YD
132*

*What We Said Sitting Making
Fantasies* (James Berry)
I want a talking dog wearing a cap
Ber 47

You'd Better Believe Him (Brian
Patten)
He discovered an old rocking-horse
in Woolworth's
Gang 12; King 72; Story 70

FARMERS

The Hill Farmer Speaks (R. S.
Thomas)
I am the farmer, stripped of love
Choice 309

FARMING

See also Barley, Hay, Mowing,
Ploughing

Burning the Stubble (Jon
Stallworthy)
Another harvest gathered in
ND 25

The Pasture (Robert Frost)
I'm going out to clear the pasture
spring
*Choice 277; Nine 13; Open 60; Rog 39;
Talk 82*

The Rest of the Day's Your Own
(anon.)
One day when I was out of work a
job I went to seek
KWP 23

Rural Idyll (Margaret Toms)
A mild man, God-fearing
PW 19

Soil (R. S. Thomas)
A field with tall hedges and a young
Choice 305

FARM WORKERS

See also Tractors

The Herdboy (Lu Yu, China, 12th
cent., trans. Arthur Waley)
In the southern village the boy who
minds the ox
Floc 76

FATHERS AND
DAUGHTERS

Beattie is Three (Adrian Mitchell)
At the top of the stairs
Five 37

Girls Can We Educate We Dads?
(James Berry)
Listn the male chauvinist in mi dad
Ber 37

Growing Pains (Mick Gowar)
The twelfth of August
Gow F 31

Make Believe (Gerda Mayer)
Say I were not sixty
Moon 69

Poem for Jane (Vernon Scannell)
So many catalogues have been
Sca L 35

Tickle (Michael Rosen)
When I tickle Laura on the back of her neck
Ros H 12

You Being Born (Brian Jones)
I saw you born
Face 15

FATHERS AND SONS

Blaming Sons (T'ao Ch'ien, trans. Arthur Waley)
White hairs cover my temples
Bell 146

Dad (E. A. Markham)
You're a fat old man
Life 21

Dockery and Son (Philip Larkin)
Dockery was junior to you
Fire 113

Father (Tadeusz Rozewicz)
My old father walks through
Life 20

Follower (Seamus Heaney)
My father worked with a horse-plough
Fire 107; Touch IV 85; Voi III 14

For My Son (Alan Brownjohn)
Not ever to talk when merely requested
Touch V 143

Guess What Dad Does (Brian Patten)
When I went to junior school
Pat 63

The Identification (Roger McGough)
So you think it's Stephen?
Ax 80; KCP 130; Story 124; Strict 58

My Dad, Your Dad (Kit Wright)
My dad's fatter than your dad
King 141; Nine 88; Poem I 47; Wri R 31

My Father (Ted Hughes)
Some fathers work at the office
Hug F 57; Poem I 48; Ten 114

My Papa's Waltz (Theodore Roethke)
The whiskey on your breath
Floc 64; NTP 244; Show II 40; Stuf II 19; WS 14

Our Father (Ray Mathew)
She said my father had whiskers and looked like God
Floc 63; Voi II 92

Tavistock Goose Fair (Charles Causley)
The day my father took me to the Fair
Cau J 60

FATNESS

Fat Boy (Mick Gowar)
I know it
Gow S 18

FEAR

The Cave (Gregory Harrison)
I told the boatman to go deep
Fifth 10

Cold Feet (Brian Lee)
They have all gone across
Poem I 67; Six 206; Sort 82

Cornered (Barbara Giles)
In the corner by my bed
Trio 12

The Dare (Judith Nicholls)
Go on, I dare you / come on down
Nic F 26; YD 24

Don't Panic (Eric Finney)
That beating at my bedroom pane
ASP 66

Fear at the Crossroads (Yoruba)
I look to the right
Afr II 10

Gunpowder Plot (Vernon Scannell)
For days these curious cardboard buds have lain
Floc 267; Voi II 17

The Lion and the Echo (Brian Patten)
The King of Beasts, deep in the wood
ASP 113; Ox SP 129; Pat 27

O What is That Sound (W. H. Auden)
O what is that sound which so thrills the ear

Choice 237; Floc 254; KCP 27; Story 94
(part) *Howl 29; Wind 30*

Posting Letters (Gregory Harrison)
There are no lamps in our village
Shad 15

The Queer Moment (Brian Lee)
It was a queer moment when all on my own
Ting 18

The Tunnel (Brian Lee)
This is the way that I have to go
Brave 53; Six 208

When I Realised I Wasn't so Brave (Alex Chaplin)
Everyone had jumped the ditch on the building site
Speak 29

Who's There? (Ray Mather)
Who's there? / Just an eddy of air
Boo 7

Who's That? (James Kirkup)
Who's that / stopping at
MT 13; Open 108; Ox T 130; PG 98

FEBRUARY

At Middle-Field Gate in February (Thomas Hardy)
The bars are thick with drops that show
Choice 140

FERRYMEN

Ferry Me Across the Water (Christina Rossetti)
Ferry me across the water
NTP 221; Ox CV 277

FESTIVALS

See also Christmas, Easter, Hallowe'en, Seder

The Doll Festival (James Kirkup)
Lighted lanterns
Cele 30

Idh al-Fitr (Philip Gross)

In the ninth month of Ramadan, one moon to another
Cele 49

Once Upon a Great Holiday (Anne Wilkinson)
I remember or remember hearing
Can 82

Prince Rama Comes to Longsight (John Cunliffe)
A hundred points of flame
Cele 84

FIDDLERS

The Fiddler of Dooney (W. B. Yeats)
When I play on my fiddle in Dooney
Fab CV 41; Face 136; Irish 171; O & A 52; World 38

FIELDMICE

Anne and the Fieldmouse (Ian Serraillier)
We found a mouse in the chalk quarry today
Foot 19

The Fieldmouse (Cecil Frances Alexander)
Where the acorn tumbles down
CCC 145; Ox CV 204

The Meadow Mouse (Theodore Roethke)
In a shoe box stuffed in an old nylon stocking
Rat 282

FIGHTING

The Combat (Edwin Muir)
It was not meant for human eyes
Mes 193

FIREFLIES

Fireflies in the Garden (Robert Frost)
Here come real stars to fill the upper skies
Walk 76; Zoo 18

The Firefly (Edward Lowbury)
This beast is real but fabulous
Pud 33

FIRES

A Fire in London 1715 (John Gay)
But hark! distress with screaming
voice draws nigh'r
Iron 67

London Mourning in Ashes (anon.
1666)
Of Fire, Fire, Fire I sing
Nar 135

There's a Fire in the Forest (W. W.
E. Ross)
There's a fire in the forest
Can 57

FIREWORKS

See Mag M 52-7

Fireworks (James Reeves)
They rise like sudden fiery flowers
*Cal 104; Gold 33; Once 17; Poem I 75;
Puf Q 59; Ree C 95; WAS 134*

Let's Send a Rocket (Kit
Patrickson)
Ten, nine eight . . .
Tick 29

FISHERFOLK

Fisherman (George Mackay
Brown)
The west flushed, drove down its
shutter
Sea 97

Herring is King (Alfred P.
Graves)
Let all the fish that swim the sea
Irish 56

I Sit Up Here at Midnight (Robert
Louis Stevenson)
I sit up here at midnight
Sea 101

from *The Men of the Rocks*
(Joseph Macleod)
Our pastures are bitten and bare
Scot 22

from *The Nightfishing* (W. S.
Graham)
We are at the hauling then hoping
for it
Scot 70

Three Fishers went Sailing (Charles
Kingsley)
Three fishers went sailing out into
the west
Ten 126

Uncle Roderick (Norman
MacCaig)
His drifter swung in the night
Face 106, Sea 97

FISHES AND SEA CREATURES

See also Crabs, Eels, Goldfish,
Pike, Sardines, Seals, Sea
Monsters, Sea-Trout, Sharks,
Shrimps, Trout, Turtles, Whales

Alas, Alack! (Walter de la Mare)
Ann, Ann!
Fab NV 64; Ox CV 327; PoWo I 46

Animals' Houses (James Reeves)
Of animals' houses
Ox T 87; Puf Q 75; Ree C 19

The Coelacanth (Gavin Ewart)
The Coelacanth has a hollow spine
Ewar 30

Fish (Ivor Cutler)
Fish / are not / very bright
Pro II 68

Fish (Mary Ann Hoberman)
Look at them flit
S Sun 42

Fishes' Evening Song (Dahlov
Ipcar)
Flip flop, / Flip flap
Noisy 11

Flying Fish (John Agard)
Flying fish / flying fish
Five 116

from *Miss Thompson Goes
Shopping* (Martin Armstrong)
A little further down the way
Pic 52

FISHING

See Cham 65-71

The Angler (F. Scott Monument)
Now here's a nutter who looks
dressed to thrill
Mot 194

The Angler's Lament (anon.)
Sometimes over early
WS 37

Beginner's Luck (Stanley Cook)
Well, he had his fibreglass rod
Ang I 38

Boy Fishing (E. J. Scovell)
I am cold and alone
O & A 60; Pos 84; This W 14; WAS 93

The Fish (Elizabeth Bishop)
I caught a tremendous fish
Cham 68; Gang 126; GTP 128; NTP 91; Rat 153; Voi II 45; Wind 72

Fishermen (anon.)
Hiyamac / Lobuddy / Binearlong?
Pro III 60; Speak 43; WP 33

Fishing Song (Judith Nicholls)
Ragworm, lugworm, mackerel, maggot
Nic M 10; O & A 61

In the Deep Channel (William Stafford)
Setting a trotline after sundown
Rat 210

Live Baiting (Philip Oakes)
It isn't nice, the way I fish
Ang I 39; Earth 76

One Evening in the Bay of Lipari (Michael Rosen)
One evening in the bay of Lipari
Ros W 40

The Names of the Sea-trout (Tom Rawling)
He who would seek her in the clear stream
WS 36

The Salmon Fisher to the Salmon (Seamus Heaney)
The ridged lip set upstream, you flail
Ang I 40

FISHMONGERS

The Fishmonger (A. S. J. Tessimond)
Sleek through his fingers
Rhy 137

FLIES

The Fly (Walter de la Mare)
How large unto the tiny fly
Ox T 105

The Fly (William Blake)
Little fly
GTP 81; Ox PC 130; Puf V 47

THE FLIGHT INTO EGYPT

Joseph and Jesus (Robert Graves)
Said Joseph unto Mary
Sun 115

The Miraculous Harvest (anon.)
Rise up, rise up you merrymen all
Sun 113

FLOODS

The Flood (John Clare)
On Lolham Brigs in wild and lonely mood
Rat 156
The floods come o'er the meadow leas
Cla J 46

from *High Tide on the Coast of Lincolnshire, 1571* (Jean Ingelow)
The old mayor climb'd the belfry tower
Mes 60

FLOWERS

See Daffodils, Gentians

from *Children Gathering Flowers* (William Wordsworth)
Pull the primrose, sister Anne!
Abi 3

from *Midsummer Night's Dream* (William Shakespeare)
I know a bank whereon the wild thyme blows
Abi 13

FLYING

Hang-gliders in January (U. A. Fanthorpe)
Like all miracles it has a rational
Fan 70
I, Icarus (Alden Nowlan)

There was a time when I could fly. I
swear it
Ox T 43

Mama Dot Learns to Fly
(Frederick D'Aguiar)
Mama Dot watched reels of film
Bab 29

Night Flight (Vernon Scannell)
For ages I have kept my secret. I
Sca T 36

FLYING-FISH

The Flattered Flying-Fish (E. V.
Rieu)
Said the Shark to the Flying-Fish
over the phone
P Sev 68

FOALS

Birth of the Foal (Ferenc Juhasz,
trans. D. Wevill)
As May was opening the rosebuds
CCC 21; Rat 79; Stuf 47

*Yesterday he was Nowhere to be
Found* (Ted Hughes)
Yesterday he was nowhere to be
found
NTP 106

FOG

Fog (Carl Sandburg)
The fog comes
Floc 266; Out 68; Ox A 216; Open 16;
Pos 141; P Sev 124; RMP 18; Talk 94;
Walk 96

The Fog (W. H. Davies)
I saw the fog grow thick
Out 70

At Middle-Field Gate in February
(Thomas Hardy)
The bars are thick with drops that
show
Out 23

FOOD

See also Breakfast, Cheese, Fruit,
Greed, Over-fed and Under-
fed, Spaghetti, Vegetables

Chicken Dinner (Valerie Bloom)
Mama, don' do it please
ASP 78

Christmas Dinner (Michael Rosen)
We were all sitting round the table
Ros Q 110

The Clean Platter (Ogden Nash)
Some singers sing of women's eyes
Nas C 65

The Contrary Waiter (Edgar
Parker)
A tarsier worked as a waiter
OWN 26

Delicious (Leonard Clark)
O, the smell of fish and chips on a
winter's night
Cla C 19

Dinner Party Blues (Mick Gowar)
I eat / Children's food
Gow S 58

Dumplin (Martin Glyn)
It might be fried or boil
Stuf II 35

*E322 or Is My Mother Trying to
Kill Me?* (Trevor Millum)
I don't have school dinners
Mill 38

Eat Up Your Insects (Gavin Ewart)
Do you fancy a nice caterpillar stew?
Ewar 9

Figgie Hobbin (Charles Causley)
Nightingales' tongues, your majesty?
Cau F 26; NTP 218

Fish and Chips (A. Elliott-
Cannon)
Fish and chips today for tea
Pic 55

The Friendly Cinnamon Bun
(Russell Hoban)
Shining in his stickiness and
glistening with honey
King 94; Nine 113; Ox T 32; Pic 44;
RT 171; Sort 101

Hot Cake (Shu Hsi, trans. Arthur
Waley)
Winter has come; fierce is the cold
Floc 280

If We Didn't Have to Eat (Nixon
Waterman)
Life would be an easy matter
Pic 128

Jelly-lover (Vernon Scannell)
Jill likes stuff that wobbles, quivers
Sca 20

Lotus Flower Takeaway (J. and G. Curry)
Number One/ Egg Foo Yung
Down 57

Midnight Feast (Mark Burgess)
I'm often hungry in the night
Bur 35

Mincemeat (Elizabeth Gould)
Sing a song of mincemeat
Chris 57

Miss T (Walter de la Mare)
It's a very odd thing
FF 59; Iron 19; Once 90; Pud 87

Modern Cookery (Okot p'Bitek)
My husband says / He rejects me
Afr II 68

My Brother is Making a Protest about Bread (Michael Rosen)
My brother is making a protest about bread
Like 153; Ros M 76

The Olympic Eating Game (Vernon Scannell)
My dear old school friend, Pendleby Reid
Sca 44

The Pancake (Christina Rossetti)
Mix a pancake
Cal 24; Day 15; Read 50; WAS 27

The Pancake Collector (Jack Prelutsky)
Come visit my pancake collection
Ox A 286

Porridge (Clive Riche)
I didn't like my porridge
Pic 86

Rice Pudding (A. A. Milne)
What is the matter with Mary Jane?
KWP 142

Rubbery Chicken (Roger McGough)
Aye, Waiter – over 'ere!
McG S 78

Sky in the Pie (Roger McGough)
Waiter, there's a sky in my pie
McG P 11

Snow-Cone (John Agard)
Snow-cone nice
Aga 12; SS 41

Sources of Sauce (Vernon Scannell)
All those sauces
Sca 46

US Flies in Hamburgers (Roger McGough)
If you go down the High Street today
KWP 139; McG S 80

Wha Fe Call I' (Valerie Bloom)
Miss Ivy, tell mi supmn
Bab 104

Yellow Butter (Mary Ann Hoberman)
Yellow butter purple jelly red jam black bread
Corn 90; KCP 95; OSF 56; Pac 84; Read 67; Stuf 23; WS 28

FOOTBALL

Big Day (Robert Sparrow)
Playing for the School today
Mea 64

The Commentator (Gareth Owen)
Good afternoon and welcome
All 79; Owe C 21; Pro I 29

The Footballer (Tony Bradman)
I take the pass / in the crowded / playground
Bra A 67

Footy Poem (Roger McGough)
I'm an ordinary feller 6 days of the week
McG G 25; McRo 57

Kevin Scores! (Leslie Norris)
Kevin flicks the ball sideways, leaning
Occ 96

The Rovers (Kit Wright)
My Dad, he wears a Rovers' scarf
Cham 7; Wri H 48

Rhythm (Iain Crichton Smith)
They dunno how it is. I smack a ball
Cham 11

Sittn guzzlin (Tom Leonard)
sittn guzz-/ lin a can
Speak 39

Sonnet: A Footballer (Edward Cracroft Leroy)
If I could paint you, friend, as you stand there
Face 87

Sports Report (Gareth Owen)
Five o'clock of a Saturday night
Owe K 14

Stanley Matthews (Alan Ross)
Not often con brio, but andante,
andante
Mot 130

FORESTS

For Forest (Grace Nichols)
Forest could keep secrets
Five 17

FORGETFULNESS

Old Mrs Thing-um-e-bob (Charles
Causley)
Old Mrs Thing-um-e-bob
Cau F 35; FF 70; Nine 54; Ox T 67

The Reverend Sabine Baring-Gould
(Charles Causley)
The Reverend Sabine Baring-Gould
Cau F 28; CBC 145; Nine 89; Ring 87

FOXES

See also Hunting

The Fox (Adrian Mitchell)
A fox among the shadows of the
town
Mit N 23

Fox (Ted Hughes)
Who / Wears the smartest evening
dress in England ?
CCC 206

A Fox Came into my Garden
(Charles Causley)
A fox came into my garden
Cau F 17; Ox T 86; Pac 96

A Fox Jumped Up (anon.)
A fox jumped up one winter's night
*Cow 34; Ox Dic 173; Ox NR 190; Ox
PC 114; P Sev 107; Puf V 50*
A fox went out one chilly night
GTP 32

The Fox Rhyme (Ian Serraillier)
Aunt was on the garden seat
P Sev 32; Puf Q 168

from *Fox-Trot* (John Fuller)
The hounds are breathing at my tail
Quin 74

Foxy Comes to Town (Maureen
Duffy)
Have you seen the fox in our street
IC 11

John Clark (Charles Causley)
John Clark sat in the park
Cau E 7

Modereen Rue (Katharine Tynan-
Hickson)
Och Modereen Rue, you little red
rover
Brave 108

from *Reynard the Fox* (John
Masefield)
The fox was strong, he was full of
running
Ten 50
And here, as he ran to the hunts-
man's yelling
Brave 110

Stop, Thief! (anon., rewritten G.
Summerfield)
The false fox came to our house one
night
PoWo I 38

The Thought-Fox (Ted Hughes)
I imagine this midnight moment's
forest
*Cam II 32; NTP 105; Touch IV 57;
WZ 78*

The Three Foxes (A. A. Milne)
Once upon a time there were three
little foxes
Fab NV 90; Ox CV 341

The Tod (anon.)
'Eh' quo' the tod, it's a braw licht
nicht
Kist 14

Visitor (Wes Magee)
Sliding in slippers along the house-
side
Fifth 91; Mag M 59; Show I 81

The Vixen (John Clare)
Among the taller wood with ivy
hung
Ark 79; Cla J 64; P Sev 20; Rat 451

The Vixen (John Walsh)
On these dark nights
Quin 227

FREEDOM

We Will Keep On (Oku Onuora)
we have been struggling
FS 11

FRIENDS: ACTUAL

Best Friends (Adrian Henri)
It's Susan I talk to not Tracey
Hen 37; Pro I 37

Friends (Elizabeth Jennings)
I fear it's very wrong of me
Ax 11; Day 30; Quin 114

Friends (Gareth Owen)
When first I went to school
Bell 66

Friends (Nigel Gray)
I used to feel lonely every night
IC 26

Friends and Enemies (Theresa Heine)
I'll read with you and play with you
AFP 26

Friendship (Elizabeth Jennings)
Such love I cannot analyse
Moon 46

I Had No Friends (John Kitching)
I had no friends at all
AVF 18

It Is a Puzzle (Allan Ahlberg)
My friend / Is not my friend any more
Ahl P 48

My Best Pal (Colin McNaughton)
There's a boy in our class
McN 74

My Friend Thelma (Russell Hoban)
Such a friend as my friend Thelma everyone has not
Six 179

Since Hanna Moved Away (Judith Viorst)
The tyres on my bike are flat
AFP 35

Small Quarrel (Allan Ahlberg)
She didn't call for me as she usually does
Ahl P 26

Write a Poem about a Friend (Brian Morse)
Hayley is a nice person
Mor 13

FRIENDS: IMAGINARY

Billy Dreamer's Fantastic Friends (Brian Patten)

The Incredible Hulk came to tea
Pat 24

Binker (A. A. Milne)
Binker – what I call him – is a secret of my own
Mil NS 15

A Boy's Friend (Roy Fuller)
I have a secret friend
Gho 21; Puf M 105

Friendship Degree (Vyanne Samuels)
I'm looking for a friend
Sam 30

Friendship Poems (Roger McGough)
There's good mates and bad mates
McG P 51; Pro II 69

Nobody (Shel Silverstein)
Nobody loves me
Ox T 50

The Secret Brother (Elizabeth Jennings)
Jack lived in the greenhouse
Gho 18; Puf M 106; Quin 112

Skilly Oogan (Russell Hoban)
Skilly Oogan's no one you can see
Gho 23; PoWo II 20; RT 103; Six 162

The Unseen Playmate (Robert Louis Stevenson)
When children are playing alone on the green
Ste 73

Us Two (A. A. Milne)
Wherever I am there's always Pooh
Mil NS 33; Ox CV 345

FROGS

See also Tadpoles

Black Dot (Libby Houston)
a black dot / a jelly tot
CCC 134; Pro I 68; Tick 140

Bullfrog (Ted Hughes)
With their lithe long strong legs
Ark 47

Death of a Naturalist (Seamus Heaney)
All year the flax-dam festered in the heart
Cam II 17; Fire 77; Touch V 182

The Frog (Hilaire Belloc)
Be kind and tender to the Frog
Bel CV 108; Cow 85; Like 288; Walk 81

The Frog and the Crow (anon.)
There was a jolly frog in the river
did swim, O!
Puf NR 138

Frog and Toad (Christina
Rossetti)
Hopping frog, hop here and be seen
CCC 137

Frog Fable (Ian Seraillier)
Two frogs fell, splash
ATP 99

A Frog he Would a-Wooing Go
(anon.)
A frog he would a-wooing go
*Fab NV 114; Ox Dic 177; Ox NR 172;
RMP 50*
*Mr Froggie went a-courtin' and he did
ride*
GTP 19

The Frog Prince (Stevie Smith)
I am a frog
Mes160; NTP 57

The Frog on the Log (Ilo Orleans)
There once / was a green
S Sun 23

Frogs (Norman MacCaig)
Frogs sit more solid
CCC 139; Touch IV 193; Voi III 11

Frogs in Chorus (A. B. Paterson)
The chorus frogs in the big lagoon
Pat A 15

Frogspawn, I Love It (Berlie
Doherty)
Frogspawn, I love it
ATP 97

The Puddock (J. M. Caie)
A Puddock sat by the lochan's brim
Kist 22; Like 95

The Tin Frog (Russell Hoban)
I have hopped, when properly
wound up
Six 166; Walk 217; Zoo 43

FROST AND ICE

Cobweb Morning (June Crebbin)
On a Monday morning
Cre 14; Occ 127

Frozen-out Gardeners (anon., 19th
cent.)
We're broken-hearted gardeners,
scarce got a bit of shoe
Spi 68

Hard Frost (Andrew Young)
Frost called to water 'Halt!'
Like 129; Out 88

Ice (Jim Wong-Chu)
was the first time
KWP 216
Ice (Walter de la Mare)
The North Wind sighed
de la M V 18; Ox T 147

FRUIT

See Apples, Bananas,
Blackberries, Blueberries,
Cherries, Chestnuts,
Gooseberries, Lychees,
Mangoes, Quinces, Strawberries

A Bowl of Fruit (Roger McGough)
In the wooden bowl
McG P 59; Pic 136

Fiesta Melons (Sylvia Plath)
In Benidorm there are melons
World 57

Fruit in a Bowl (A. J. Seymour)
Full golden apples with veined skins
so fine
Blac 26

How to Eat a Strawberry (Judith
Nicholls)
First, sniff
Occ 131

To a Poor Old Woman (William
Carlos Williams)
munching a plum on
Talk 81

GALOSHES

Galoshes (Rhoda Bacmeister)
Susie's galoshes
Pop 18

GAMES

See also Cham throughout, *Far R
54-68*

See also Balls, Basketball, Cricket,
Darts, Football, Golf, Hide and
Seek, Marbles, Monopoly,
Rugby Football, Snooker

Confessions of a Born Spectator
(Ogden Nash)
One infant grows up and becomes a
jockey
Cham 114

Dart Board Dance (Danny
Pollock)
I know / it's been said before
Cham 108

The Game of Life (Roy Fuller)
Have you ever been in sight of
heaven
Poem I 84

The Hockey Field (Betty Parvin)
When Autumn swings a mace that
cleaves
Mot 123

Hug o' War (Shel Silverstein)
I will not play at tug o' war
Sil 19

The Jigsaw Puzzle (Russell
Hoban)
My beautiful picture of pirates and
treasure
ASP 85

Kicking a Ball (Allan Ahlberg)
What I like best / Yes, most of all
Ahl H 73

GARDENING

See Digging, Sowing

Garden Lore (Juliana Horatia
Ewing)
Every child who has gardening tools
Ox CV 260

Gathering Leaves (Robert Frost)
Spades take up leaves
Rat 176

GARDENS

The Garden (Andrew Marvell)
How vainly men themselves amaze
Fire 192
(part) *Abi 17*

My Garden (Rodney Bennett)
I've a garden of my own
Pic 11

GEESE

Complaint of the Wild Goose
(Western Mongolian lullaby)
We were nine to leave the lake in the
north
WZ 121

Goose (Ted Hughes)
The White Bear, with smoking
mouth, embraces All the North
Hug U 41

Something Told the Wild Geese
(Rachel Field)
Something told the wild geese
*Cal 90; Once 51; Open 71; Out 60; Ox
A 240; Walk 85; WAS 109; YD 67*

GENERALS

See Hannibal, Napoleon

GENTIANS

Bavarian Gentians (D. H.
Lawrence)
Not every man has gentians in his
house
*Cam II 160; Choice 198; Fab CV 54;
Talk 91*

GERBILS

The Gerbil (Stanley Cook)
The gerbil stands up
Ani 38

My Gerbil (John Kitching)
Once I had a gerbil
Pets 44

Verbal Gerbil (Philip Gross)
See him go / little scrabble rat
Pets 48

GHOSTS (L AND D)

See also Gho throughout, *Puf M
99-128*

Duppy Dan (John Agard)
Duppy Dan / aint no livin man
Blac 98

The Garden Seat (Thomas Hardy)
Its former green is blue and dim
Mes 88; Rat 175

Ghostly Lessons (Judith Nicholls)
Ma, I want some chocolate
Boo 62

The Ghosts' High Noon (W. S. Gilbert)
When the night wind howls in the chimney cowls
Gho 58; MT 37; Puf M 127

Ghosts in Our Suburban Homes (Jan Dean)
The creaking of a wicker chair
Pro II 57

hist whist (e. e. cummings)
hist whist
Fab NV 204; HH 3; MT 139; Nine 38; Ting 32; Walk 201; Wit 30

House Ghosts (Irene Rawnsley)
Airing cupboard ghosts
Raw 40

The Wandering Spectre (anon.)
Wae's me, wae's me
Fab CV 228; Ox PC 156; Puf V 186; Rat 455

GHOSTS (N)

Children Lost (Max Fatchen)
On a lonely beach the old wreck lies
Aus R 36

Colonel Fazackerley (Charles Causley)
Colonel Fazackerley Butterworth-Toast
Brave 39; Cau F 50; Gho 76; King 194; Like 116; MT 38; Once 118; OSF 24; Ox T 68; Pos 2; Puf M 103; Sort 22; Ten 90; Walk 204

Corporal Stare (Robert Graves)
Back from the line one night in June
War 28

Dicky (Robert Graves)
Oh, what a heavy sigh!
MT 41; Puf M 107

Emperors of the Island (Dannie Abse)
There is the story of a deserted island
Gho 46; MT 35; Poem I 64

Ghost (anon.)
In the dark, dark wood there was a dark, dark house
Tim 21

The Ghost-Cage (Leo Aylen)
The ghost / Made no attempt to struggle
Boo 87

Ghost Story (Dylan Thomas)
Bring out the tall tales now that we told
Ox CP 104; Star 70

The Ghost Teacher (Allan Ahlberg)
The school is closed, the children gone
Ahl H 16

Ghosts (Kit Wright)
That's right. Sit down and talk to me
Stoc 122; WP 40; Wri R 54

The Glimpse (Thomas Hardy)
She sped through the door
Gho 42; Puf M 118

The Late Express (Barbara Giles)
There's a train that runs through Hawthorn
Gold 23; Ox T 136; Trio 16

Locking Up (Ian Serraillier)
A frail old woman lived by herself
Boo 16

The Man Who Wasn't There (Brian Lee)
Yesterday upon the stair
Gho 12; Poem I 33; Pro II 33; Six 221

Miller's End (Charles Causley)
When we moved to Miller's End
Cau F 81; Story 152

Moon-Shadow Beggars (Ted Hughes)
Crossing the frontier from dark to light
Hug MW 28

The Old Wife and the Ghost (James Reeves)
There was an old wife and she lived all alone
Gho 56; Gh P 19; MT 39; Ox T 132; Pop 40; Pos 3; PoWo I 108; Puf Q 76; Ree C 63; Ten 88

The Phantom Lollipop Lady (Adrian Henri)
The phantom lollipop lady
Hen 95

Sweet William's Ghost (anon.)
There came a ghost to Margret's door
Gho 50; Puf M 123

Trespassers Will . . . (Philip Gross)
The sign says PRIVATE
Gro 1

The Two Old Women of Mumbling Hill (James Reeves)
The two old trees on Mumbling Hill
Poem I 26; Ree C 47

Two's Company (Raymond Wilson)
They said the house was haunted, but
Boo 88; Gho 78

The Visitor (Ian Serraillier)
A crumbling churchyard, the sea and the moon
KCP 179

The Visitors (Barrie Wade)
'Twenty-seven lamps is what it takes,' he said
Wad 52

Who's That? (James Kirkup)
Who's that / stopping at
MT 13; Open 108; Ox T 130; PG 98

Whose Boo is Whose? (X. J. Kennedy)
Two ghosts I know once traded heads
Gh P 24

The Wife of Usher's Well (anon.)
There lived a wife at Usher's Well
Kist 94; Rat 464; Story 43

GIANTS

Giant Thunder (James Reeves)
Giant Thunder, striding home
Mons 81; Pac 105; Ree C 105

Grim (Walter de la Mare)
Beside the blaze of forty fires
de la M P 87; PoWo II 13

Gulliver in Lilliput (Alexander Pope)
From his nose / Clouds he blows
FF 53

In the Orchard (James Stephens)
There was a giant by the orchard wall
Mons 79; Nine 18; Ting 42

Me and My Giant (Shel Silverstein)
I have a friend who is a giant
Sil 38
More about Blunderbore (Roy Fuller)
It seems the giant Blunderbore
Mons 84

My Brother Dreams of Giants (Bernard Logan)
My brother dreams the world is the size of a football
Gang 129

The Sleepy Giant (Charles E. Carryl)
My age is three hundred and seventy two
CBC 30; Mons 80; PG 78

GIPSIES

Gipsies (John Clare)
The gipsies seek wide sheltering woods again
O & A 110
The snow falls deep; the forest lies alone
ND 136

The Gipsy Laddie (anon.)
It was late in the night when the Squire came home
Fab CV 173; GTP 96; Ox PC 70

Gypsy Dance (Linda Davies, aged 11)
I saw the gypsy queen
O & A 111

The Idlers (Edmund Blunden)
The gipsies lit their fires by the chalk-pit gate anew
ND 137

Meg Merrilies (John Keats)
Old Meg she was a gipsy
Fab CV 117; Like 162; O & A 112; Ox CV 147; Ox PC 149; Puf V 235; Ten 32; This W 137

The Wraggle Taggle Gypsies (anon.)
Three gypsies stood at the Castle gate
Ten 167

GIRAFFES

Giraffe (Barbara Juster Esbensen)
Quietly nibbling
Esb 19

Giraffe (Carson McCullers)
At the zoo I saw: a long-necked, velvety Giraffe
Nif 47; Zoo 59

The Giraffe (Geoffrey Dearmer)
Hide of a leopard and hide of a deer
Jung 30

GIRLS

See *Side* throughout

Adventures of Isabel (Ogden Nash)
Isabel met an enormous bear
*Brave 44; Fab NV 105; MT 127; Nas
C 88; Once 143; Ox A 248; Pop 58;
Walk 179; Young 72*

Eat-it-All Elaine (Kaye Starbird)
I went away last August
Walk 108

Eugenie and the Ice (Richard
Edwards)
It grew cold. Puddles froze
Edw M 72; IC 115

Girls (Robert Sparrow)
The girls are huddled together
Side 16B

Good Girls (Irene Rawsley)
Good girls
Side 21G

The Good Little Girl (A. A. Milne)
It's funny how often they say to me
'Jane? . . .'
BBGG 37; Mil NS 66; Spi 58

Modern Girl (Okot p'Bitek)
Ocol is no longer in love with the old
type
Afr II 33

Who is de Girl? (John Agard)
who is de girl dat kick de ball
IC 16; Side 34G

GLASGOW

Glasgow Sonnet (Edwin Morgan)
A mean wind wanders through the
backcourt trash
Show III 2; Scot 89; Touch IV 48

The Hert o the City (Duncan Glen)
I'm juist passin through
Scot 126

GLIDERS

Gliders and Gulls (James Reeves)
What are they, these gliders in the
blue cold air
Open 115

GOATS

The Goat (anon.)
There was a man, now please take
note
Ani 55; Once 139

The Goat Paths (James Stephens)
The crooked paths go every way
Foot 20; Irish 156; ND 227

Old Hogan's Goat (anon.)
Old Hogan's goat was feeling fine
Pets 23; Pud 120

GOBLINS

Evening by Evening (Christina
Rossetti)
Evening by evening
Puf M 217

Little Orphant Annie (James
Whitcombe Riley)
Little Orphant Annie's come to our
house to stay
*BBGG 113; MT 143; Ox A 147; Ox CV
300*

Overheard on a Saltmarsh (Harold
Monro)
Nymph, nymph, what are your
beads?
*Gold 102; HH 71; KCP 143; Like 104;
Mes 158; MT 64; Puf M 207; This W
33*

GODIVA

Godiva (L. J. Anderson)
The worst was the beginning
Crys 30

GOLDFISH

My Pet Goldfish (Edward
Williams, aged 9)
I have a small aquarium
Pets 52

GOLF

Seaside Golf (John Betjeman)
How straight it flew, how long it flew
Cham 57; Mot 116

GOOSEBERRIES

The Gooseberry Tree (Herbert Palmer)
Some pilgrim-folk sing of the oak for bedsteads
Pic 34

GORILLAS

Au Jardin des Plantes (John Wain)
The gorilla lay on his back
Cam II 109; Floc 220; Jung 56

Gorilla (Class 4 S)
Hairy arms, egg-shaped head
WZ 73

Gorilla (Martin Honeysett)
A giant Gorilla came to tea
AFP 31

The Gorilla (Patricia Beer)
If the expression on a face
ND 84

GRACES

Grace before Beer (F. R. Higgins)
For what this house affords us
Irish 65

A Grace for Children (Robert Herrick)
What God gives, and what we take
Ox CV 31

Another Grace (Robert Herrick)
Here a little child I stand
NTP 22; Ox CV 31; PPP 6; P Sev 59; Sk 80; This W 98

GRANDFATHERS

Bucket (Roger McGough)
every evening after tea
CCV 15; McRo 54

The Folk Song (Ronald McCuaig)
'I'll sing a song I sung'
Aus B 61

Grampa (Dennis Scott)
Look him. As quiet as a July river
NTP 244

Grandad (Kit Wright)
Grandad's dead
Mad 54; Occ 146; Wri R 28

Grandad (Michael Rosen)
When we go over
P Sev 101

Grandpa Dropped his Glasses (Leroy F. Jackson)
Grandpa dropped his glasses once
OSF 13

Grandpa is Very Old (Gregory Harrison)
Grandpa is very old you know
AFP 20

Harrybo (Michael Rosen)
Once my friend Harrybo
Five 99; Ros H 122

My Grandpa (Ted Hughes)
The truth of the matter, the truth of the matter
Hug F 21

Newcomers (Michael Rosen)
My father came to England
Ros Q 71

No Sight of his Grave (Ernest Mbewe)
When my grandfather died
Afr II 79

Shed in Space (Gareth Owen)
My Grandad Lewis
Spa 16

GRANDMOTHERS

Grandma (Ted Hughes)
My grandmother's a peaceful person, and she loves to sit
Hug F 25; King 149

Grandma Gurney (A. E. Dudley)
Grandma Gurney / Gives to me
Tim 27

Granny Granny Please Comb my Hair (Grace Nichols)
Granny Granny / please comb my hair
AFP 18; Five 12; KCP 149; Mad 15; Nic 12; Stuf 16

Grans United (John Cunliffe)
Have you heard / Of Grans United?
Straw 37

In Praise of Grans (John Cunliffe)
I like grans
Straw 36

My Grandmother (Elizabeth Jennings)
She kept an antique shop – or it kept her
Touch V 146

My Grannies (June Crebbin)
I hate it, in the holiday
Cre 63

My Other Granny (Ted Hughes)
My Granny is an Octopus
Hug F 29

My Sparrow Gran (Berlie Doherty)
My Sparrow Gran
AFP 19

The Older the Violin the Sweeter the Tune (John Agard)
Me Granny old
Gran 3; Mad 47

Orders of the Day (John Cunliffe)
Get up! Get washed!
Straw 42

Sunday Visits (Jenny Craig)
I was a child straight-faced and plain and solemn
Nif 22

GREED

The Glutton (John Oakman)
The voice of the glutton I heard with disdain
Ox CV 83

The Glutton (Spike Milligan)
Oh Molly, Molly, Molly
Pac 67

Greedyguts (Kit Wright)
I sat in the cafe and sipped at a Coke
King 103; Ox T 76; SS 40; Wri H 32

Greedy Richard (Jane Taylor)
'I think I want some pies this morning'
Fab NV 100; Ox CV121; Puf V 136

Griselda (Eleanor Farjeon)
Griselda is greedy, I'm sorry to say
Far M 62; Far R 79; GTP 100; Young 53

Hungry Mungry (Shel Silverstein)
Hungry Mungry sat at supper
KCP 185; Pac 78; Sil 160

Ice-cream Poem (Gerda Mayer)
The chiefest of young Ethel's vices
Poem I 19

I'm Hungry (Jack Prelutsky)
Im hungry, so I think I'll take
Walk 145

Jimmy Jupp who Died of Over-Eating (H. A. C. Evans)
Oh, shed no tears for Jimmy Jupp
OSF 37

Little Thomas (F. Gwynne Evans)
Thomas was a little glutton
BBGG 45

The Mouse and the Cake (Eliza Cook)
A mouse found a beautiful piece of plum cake
NV 82; Ox CV 209

Mr Grin and Mr Groan (Derwent May)
When Mr Grin and Mr Groan
TC 41

The Other Day when I Met Dick (John Ciardi)
The other day when I met Dick
Pac 54

Robin the Bobbin (anon.)
Robin the Bobbin, the big fat Ben
Fab NV 59; Ox NR 84; Pac 88
Robin and Bobbin, two big-bellied men
Puf NR 133

Sneaky Billl (William Cole)
I'm Sneaky Bill, I'm terribly mean
Fun 47; OTR 36

GREMLINS

Song of the Gremlins (anon.)
When you're seven miles up in the heavens
Mons 46; Puf M 224

GREYHOUNDS

The Properties of a Good Greyhound (Dame Juliana Berners)
A greyhound should be headed like a Snake
Rat 352
To a Black Greyhound (Julian Grenfell)
Shining black in the shining light
CCC 178

GRIEF

Break, Break, Break (Lord Tennyson)
Break, break, break
Show II 10

The Woodspurge (Dante Gabriel Rossetti)
The wind flapped loose, the wind was still
Foot 57

GROWING UP

Adolescence (Alastair Mackie)
Gin they wad leave me alane
Scot 110

A Ball (Michael Rosen)
Laura laughs
Ros H 50

The End (A. A. Milne)
When I was One
Like 82; Mil NS 102

Good Questions. Bad Answers (Wes Magee)
Where's the rattle / I shook
IC 52; Mag M 14

Growing (Max Fatchen)
When I grow up I'll be so kind
Fat S 18; Pud 44

Growing Pains (Brian Patten)
Growing / bored
Pat T 51

Growing Up (U. A. Fanthorpe)
I wasn't good
Fan 98

Growing Up? (Wes Magee)
It must be / a month or more
Ang I 6; Mag M 23

Grown Up? (John Cunliffe)
When I'm grown up?
Fifth 30; Straw 30

Grown Up (Julie O'Callaghan)
Bored by the day
O'Ca 22

High Heels (John Agard)
I wonder / how it feels
Aga 13

Junior School Sports (Mick Gowar)
Sports Day's over
Gow T 46

My First Cup of Coffee (Carole Satyamurti)
I'm sophisticated in my Cuban heels
Face 46

Nursery Rhyme of Innocence and Experience (Charles Causley)
I had a silver penny
Fire 48; NTP 37; Sea 251; Ten 23

Poem for my Sister (Liz Lockhead)
My little sister likes to try my shoes
Speak 64

The Seven Ages of Man (William Shakespeare)
All the world's a stage
Cam II 6; GTP 85; ND 221

A Song in the Front Yard (Gwendolyn Brooks)
I've stayed in the front yard all my life
Foc 125

Sonnet: In Time of Revolt (Rupert Brooke)
The Thing must End. I am no boy. I AM
Face 47

A Toast for Everybody Who is Growin (James Berry)
Somebody who is growin
Ber 35

When You're No Longer a Child (Mark Ludwig)
You know you're not a child any more
Stuf II 24

GUINEA-PIGS

Gentle Rodent (Jake, aged 8)
Gentle rodent in its cage
Pets 40

Guinea-pig Silence (Nick, aged 10)
My best moment is when I come home
Five 119

A Guinea-pig Song (anon.)
There was a little guinea-pig
Cow 30; GTP 229; Ox CV 80; Ox Dic 195; Ox NR 138; Pets 41; Puf NR 65

GUITARS

Guitarist (Mick Gowar)
It looks so easy on the telly
Gow F 40

Guitarman (Gordon Phillips)
I play my Guild guitar like a sub-machine gun
Ang I 24

GUY FAWKES NIGHT

See also Fireworks

Gunpowder Plot (Vernon Scannell)
For days these curious cardboard buds have lain
Floc 267; Voi II 17

Gunpowder Plot Day (anon.)
Please to remember
Ox NR 129

Guy Fawkes (Barry Heath)
we wantud best Guy Fawkes
Speak 93

The Man Outside (Richard Edwards)
There's a man in the street
Edw W 13

November Story (Vernon Scannell)
The evening had caught cold
Poem I 74; Pro II 71; Quin 173

November the Fifth (Leonard Clark)
And you, big rocket
Once 14

November 3rd (Mick Gowar)
A rocket with its stick
Cal 102; Gow S 64; Occ 56

Please to Remember (Walter de la Mare)
Here am I / A poor old Guy
NTP 133; RT 86

Remember, Remember (anon.)
Please to remember
Cal 104

A Scarecrow Remembers (Colin West)
Head of straw and heart of wood
West 131

Why? (Charles Causley)
Why do you turn your head, Susanna?
Cau J 43

HAIKU

See HH 26-8, Pro II 12-15, Sca T 25-9, Show I 14-15, 22

Haiku (Eric Finney)
Poem in three lines
Rhy 18

HAIR

Hair (Max Fatchen)
I despair / About hair
Fat S 19; Tick 99

Hairstyle (John Agard)
What about my hairstyle?
Ang I 8

HALLOWE'EN

The Game at the Hallowe'en Party (Wes Magee)
Around the trees ran witches
O & A 71

Hallowe'en (A. Ruddich)
This is the night / When witches fly
Pos 6

Hallowe'en (Leonard Clark)
This is the night when witches fly
Puf M 72; Ting 36

Halloween (Marie Lawson)
Granny, I saw a witch go by
Shad 63

A Hallowe'en Pumpkin (Dorothy Aldis)
They chose me from my brother: 'That's the . . .'
Cal 99

Halloween Witches (Felice Holman)
Magical Prognosticator
Wit 26

October Nights (Harriet Cooper)
October means it's Hallowe'en
Til 41

HAMLET

Dear Sir (Brian Morse)
Dear Sir / This may sound like an excuse
Mor 82

HAMSTERS

Our Hamster's Life (Kit Wright)
Our hamster's life
Ani 7; CCC 160; Ox T 90; Pets 46; Wri R 80; WZ 20

HANG-GLIDING

See Flying

HANGING

The Death of Parker (anon.)
Ye gods above protect the widows
and with pity look down
on me
Sea 151

The Faking Boy (anon.)
The faking boy to the trap has gone
Rat 150

The Hangman's Tree (anon.)
Hangman, hangman, hold your
hand
WS 4

Let Him Dangle (Elvis Costello)
Bentley said to Craig, 'Let him have
it, Chris'
Pro III 8

HANNIBAL

Hannibal (Eleanor Farjeon)
Hannibal crossed the Alps
Fav 81; RT 112

HAPPINESS

The Enchanted Shirt (John Hay)
The king was sick. His cheek was red
WP 76

HARDY, THOMAS

Afterwards (Thomas Hardy)
When the Present has latched its
postern
*Choice 144; Fire 29; ND 237; Rat 23;
Touch V 207*

HARES

Epitaph on a Hare (William
Cowper)
Here lies, whom hound did ne'er
pursue
Ox PC 121; Pets 38; Puf V 55

Hare (Molly Holden)
He lives on edge throughout his days
CCC 126

The Hare (Walter de la Mare)
In the black furrow of a field
PoWo I 34

Hares at Play (John Clare)
The birds are gone to bed the cows
are still
CCC 200; Cla J 9; NTP 90; Rat 184

Have Hare (Ted Hughes)
There's something eerie aboout a
hare . . .
CCC 125

The Names of the Hare (from
Middle English, Seamus
Heaney)
The man the hare has met
Rat 305

The Snow-Shoe Hare (Ted
Hughes)
The Snow-Shoe Hare
Hug MW 24

Two Songs of a Fool (W. B. Yeats)
A speckled cat and a tame hare
Foot 36; Rat 443

HATE

Hate Poem (Adrian Mitchell)
Rounders – it's a girls' game
Mit N 28

HAWKS

The Hawk (George Mackay
Brown)
On Sunday the hawk fell on Bigging
Rat 184

The Hawk (Robert Sund)
Afternoon / with just enough of a
breeze
King 226

The Hawk (W. B. Yeats)
Call down the hawk from the air
Floc 92

Hawk Roosting (Ted Hughes)
I sit in the top of the wood, my eyes
closed

Cam II 124; Fire 125; Poem IV 192;
Wind 78

Hurt Hawks (Robinson Jeffers)
The broken pillar of the wing jags
from the clotted shoulder
Rat 204; Voi III 143; Wind 77

The Sparrow Hawk (Russell Hoban)
Wings like pistols flashing at his sides
Six 189; Walk 87; Zoo 71

HAY

Cut Grass (Philip Larkin)
Cut grass lies frail
Cal 61; Foc 73; NTP 123; Poem IV
128; Rat 119

HEADMASTERS

Distracted the Mother Said to her Boy (Gregory Harrison)
Distracted the mother said to her
boy
Bell 124; King 11; Mes 46

The Head's Hideout (Kit Wright)
The Head crouched in his hideout
Wri C 50

Don't Want to Go into School (Colin McNaughton)
I don't want to go into school today,
Mum
McN 113

HEALTH

Health Fanatic (John Cooper Clarke)
around the block against the clock
Life 12

HEAVEN

Going to Heaven (Emily Dickinson)
Going to heaven !
Ring 109

Heaven on High (George Herbert)
O who will show me these delights
on high?
Ring 108; Talk 74

Peace (Henry Vaughan)
My Soul, there is a Country
Fab CV 368

HEDGEHOGS

The Composition (Jean Kenward)
'A hedgehog is a creature with four
legs, and thorns'
CCC 209, Pets 42

Hedgehog (Ahmet Hasim)
Suddenly a dark amorphous
Stuf II 62

Hedgehog (Anthony Thwaite)
Twitching the leaves just where the
drainpipe clogs
Ax 57; CCC 208

Hedgehog (Chu Chen Po)
He ambles along like a walking
pincushion
Ani 30

from *The Hedgehog* (Ian Serraillier)
There's a hedgehog in the garden
– come and see
RT 138

Hedgehog (Miles Gibson)
no one / remembers it
Zoo 42

HELICOPTERS

Flight Plan (Jane Merchant)
Of all the ways of travelling in earth
and air and sea
Walk 223

Helicopter (Gregory Harrison)
Heli, Heli, Heli, / Copter
Name 30; Open 116

The Helicopter (Ian Serraillier)
Along the rim of sea and sky
Open 117

HENS

The Clucking Hen (A. Hawkshawe)
Pray will you take a walk with me
Puf V 35

The Hen (Christian Morgenstern)
In the waiting room of the railway
Rat 187

Musings of a Battery Hen (David Money, aged 14)
One day / While eating my 37.43
grams
Rab 35

The New Pullets (John Walsh)
Strangers inside their netted run
CCC 65

Song of the Battery Hen (Edwin Brock)
We can't grumble about accommodation
Ax 66; CCC 68; Earth 22

HERBS

from *The Land* (Vita Sackville West)
But for this summer's quick delight
Abi 16

HERMITS

The Hermit (Hsu Pen, China, 18th cent., trans. Henry H. Hart)
I dwell apart
Floc 85

The Three Hermits (W. B. Yeats)
Three old hermits took the air
Floc 86

HEROD

Innocent's Song (Charles Causley)
Who's that knocking on the window
Ox CP 63; Quin 58; Star 88; Stoc 120; Sun 112; Ting 38

HERONS

Heron (Edwin Morgan)
A gawky stilt / ed fossicker
Touch IV 203

Heron (John Normanton)
Flaps a way north
Sun 27

The Heron (Ted Hughes)
The Sun's an iceberg
Hug MW 28

The Heron (Vernon Watkins)
The cloud-backed heron will not move
Wind 80

Night Herons (Judith Wright)
It was after a day's rain
Aus R 55; Occ 124

HIAWATHA

Blessing the Cornfields (H. W. Longfellow)
Sing, O Song of Hiawatha
Rhy 21

Hiawatha and the King of the Fishes (H. W. Longfellow)
On the white sand of the bottom
KCP 122

Hiawatha's Canoe (H. W. Longfellow)
Give me of your bark, O Birch-tree!
Mes 65

Hiawatha's Childhood (H. W. Longfellow)
Then the little Hiawatha
Pets 67; Puf V 57

Westward! Westward! (H. W. Longfellow)
On the shore stood Hiawatha
O & A 163

HIDE AND SEEK

Hide and Seek (A. B. Shiffrin)
When I am alone and quite alone
Read 8

Hide-and-seek (Allan Ahlberg)
When we play hide-and-seek
Ahl H 41

Hide-and-Seek (Eleanor Farjeon)
Tiptoe away! tiptoe away!
Far R 56

Hide and Seek (Mick Gowar)
Hiding here / on the floor of the shed
Gow T 53

Hide and Seek (Richard Edwards)
Looking for Daisy
Edw W 50

Hide and Seek (Robert Graves)
The trees are tall, but the moon small
PG 16

Hide and Seek (Roger McGough)
When I played as a kid
McG S 82

Hide and Seek (Vernon Scannell)
Call out. Call loud: 'I'm ready! Come and find me!'

Gang 60; KWP 184; ND 99; PG 23;
Quin 158; Story 3

Hide and Seek (Walter de la Mare)
Hide and seek, says the Wind
WAS 63

In the Wood (Sheila Simmons)
One, two, three, four
AFP 41

HIGHWAYMEN

Dick Turpin and the Lawyer
(anon.)
As Turpin was riding across the
moor
KWP 225

The Female Highwayman (anon.)
Priscilla on one summer's day
KCP 220

The Highwayman (Alfred Noyes)
The wind was a torrent of darkness
among the gusty trees
*Cam I 31; Fav 69; GTP 131; Like 145;
ND 140; NTP 178; Ox SP 158; Ten
101*

Highwayman's Hollow (Gilbert V.
Yonge)
Where the cliff hangs hollow, where
the gloom falls chill
KCP 216; Story 119

My Bonny Black Bess (anon.)
Dick Turpin bold! Dick, hie away
Poem I 80

*William Brennan or Brennan on the
Moor* (anon.)
It's of a fearless highwayman a story
I will tell
Nar 89; Story 20

HIPPOPOTAMI

The Hippopotamus (Jack
Prelutsky)
The huge hippopotamus hasn't a
hair
OTR 87, Zoo 46

The Hippopotamus (Ogden Nash)
Behold the hippopotamus!
Nas C 33, Once 27

The Hippopotamus's Birthday
(E. V. Rieu)
He has opened all his parcels
Like 48, Mes 40

I Had a Hippopotamus (Patrick
Barrington)
I had a hippopotamus; I kept him in
a shed
Fab NV 181; Pets 24

HIROSHIMA

Ghosts, Fire, Water (James
Kirkup)
These are the ghosts of the unwilling
dead
PW 141

Hieronymus Bosch, We Can Do It
(Paul Coltman)
Now we can burn a gesture into
stone
PW 141

Monuments of Hiroshima (D. J.
Enright)
The roughly estimated ones, who do
not sort well
PW 144

No More Hiroshimas (James
Kirkup)
At the station exit, my bundle in
hand
Touch V 88; Wind 35

HOBOES

The Big Rock Candy Mountains
(anon.)
One evenin' as the sun went down
*Iron 38; ND 112; Poem IV 158; Talk
53*

The Dying Hobo (anon.)
Beside a western tank
O & A 124

HOLIDAYS

Holidays at Home (Elizabeth
Jennings)
There was a family who, every year
Quin 116; World 63

*How a Car-journey . . . Made a Liar
out of an Honest Woman* (Ian
Whybrow)
Mum, what are we going camping
for?
World 25

HOMELESSNESS

Ballad of the Landlord (Langston Hughes)
Landlord, landlord
Speak 54

The Hunchback in the Park (Dylan Thomas)
The hunchback in the park
Cam I 128; Fire 174

An Old Woman of the Roads (Padraic Colum)
Oh, to have a little house!
Gold 74; Irish 37; Like 131; O & A 115; Puf V 135

HOMESICKNESS

Blows the Wind (Robert Louis Stevenson)
Blows the wind today and the sun and the rain are flying
O & A 94

from *Brumana* (James Elroy Flecker)
Oh, shall I never, never be home again?
WAS 128

Home Thoughts, from Abroad (Robert Browning)
Oh, to be in England
Fav 15; ND 7; Puf V 177
(part) Cal 41

Lament of Hsi-Chun (trans. Arthur Waley)
My people have married me
Iron 28

The Oak and the Ash (anon.)
A north-country maid up to London had strayed
Fab CV 131

The Tropics in New York (Claude McKay)
Bananas ripe and green, and ginger-root
Afr II 74

HOMEWORK

Homework (Russell Hoban)
Homework sits on top of Sunday
Sk 139

Homework! Oh, Homework! (Jack Prelutsky)
I hate you! You stink!
Pre 54

The Song of the Homeworkers (Trevor Millum)
Homework moanwork
Mill 69

HONEY

Honey for Tea (Eleanor Farjeon)
Buzzing bee, / Buzz away, bee
Far M 26

Sing a Song of Honey (Barbara Euphan Todd)
Honey from the white rose, honey from the red
Pic 26; Puf V 143

HOOPOES

The Hoopoe (John Heath-Stubbs)
A rare one with us
Sun 72

HORATIUS

Horatius (Lord Macaulay)
Lars Porsena of Clusium
Fab CV 159; ND 164

HORRIBLE THINGS

Horrible (Michael Rosen)
I was starving
Ros H 7

Horrible Things (Roy Fuller)
What's the horriblest thing you've seen?
KWP 73; Once 28; Poem I 52; RT 97; Sort 109

HORROR

Alternative Endings to an Unwritten Ballad (Paul Dehn)
I stole through the dungeons while everyone slept
Pro III 80

HORSES (L AND D)

See also Colts, Foals, Ponies, Racehorses

from *Henry V* (William Shakespeare)
I will not change my horse with any that treads
GTP 28

The Horse (The Bible, Job 39)
Hast thou given the horse strength?
GTP 28; Rhy 78

Horses (Edwin Muir)
Those lumbering horses in the steady plough
Fab CV 78; Fire 147

Horses on the Camargue (Roy Campbell)
In the grey wastes of dread
Open 84

The Trotting-Horses (Gregory Harrison)
Grandpa smoothed down the thin grey hair
Trio 33

War God's Horse Song (from Navajo, Louis Watchman)
I am the Turquoise Woman's Son
Rat 455; Talk 58

The Wild, the Free (Lord Byron)
With flowing tail and flying mane
Like 145; Walk 63

HORSES (N)

The Cavalier's Escape (G. W. Thornbury)
Trample! trample! went the roan
Brave 118

Horse (Alan Brownjohn)
The picnickers were sleeping when I
CCC 130; WZ 28

The Horse (William Carlos Williams)
The horse moves / independently
CCC 130

The Horses (Edwin Muir)
Barely a twelvemoth after
Cam II 83; Foc 172; PW 173; Rat 191; Scot 3; Touch V 94

The Horses (Ted Hughes)
I climbed through woods in the hour-before-dawn dark
Touch V 178

How they brought the Good News from Ghent to Aix (Robert Browning)
I sprang to the stirrup and Joris and he
Ox SP 155

Poor Old Horse (anon.)
Once I was a young horse all in my youthful prime
NTP 108

The Runaway (Robert Frost)
Once when the snow of the year was beginning to fall
Fab CV 79; GTP 29

HOSPITALS

After Visiting Hours (U. A. Fanthorpe)
Like gulls they are still calling
Fan 17

Children Imagining a Hospital (U. A. Fanthorpe)
I would like kindness, assurance
Mea 80

Hospital (Brian Geary, aged 15)
The white walls, echoing, lonely corridors
Mea 81

Night Star (Robert Sparrow)
I woke up coughing in the night
Mea 84

Ten Types of Hospital Visitor (Charles Causley)
The first enters wearing the neon armouur
Touch IV 103

Ward F4 (Phoebe Hesketh)
There is no weather in my room
Six 143

HOUSE-PLANTS

How to Treat the House-Plants (Mick Gowar)
All she ever thinks aboout are house-plants
Gow T 42

HOUSES

The Finished House (George Mackay Brown)

In the finished house, a flame is
brought to the hearth
Scot 104

HOUSES, LONELY

At One Thousand Feet (Gillian
Clarke)
Nobody comes but the postman
Five 60

The Deserted House ((Mary
Coleridge)
There's no smoke in the chimney
Tick 18, This W 110

House Fear (Robert Frost)
Always – I tell you this they learned
NTP 72

The House on the Hill (Wes
Magee)
It was built years ago
Shad 64

The Shepherd's Hut (Andrew
Young)
The smear of blue peat smoke
Gh P 14; ND 213

HOUSEWIVES

Dainty Dottie Dee (Jack Prelutsky)
There's no one so immaculate
Pre 44

The Housewife's Lament (anon.)
One day I was walking I heard a
complaining
WP 78

*On a Tired Housewife or Poor
Woman* (anon.)
Here lies a poor woman who always
was tired
CBC 65; Face 65; Gh P 15; Open 55

Sall Scratch (Charles Causley)
Sall Scratch
Cau F 21

from *A Serving Maid* (Thomas
Churchyard)
With merry lark this maiden rose
Face 51

Spring Song of the Poet-Housewife
(Anne Stevenson)
The sun is warm / and the house ... is
filthy
Wind 90

Woman Enough (Erica Jong)
Because my grandmother's hours
Ang II 32

Woman Work (Maya Angelou)
I've got the children to tend
Face 63

HUMMING-BIRDS

Humming-Bird (D. H. Lawrence)
I can imagine in some other world
*Jung 90; ND 66; Rat 197; Touch V
169*

Humming- Bird (Odette Thomas)
Humming-bird, humming-bird, why
don't you hum?
Howl 14

HUMP, THE

The Hump (Rudyard Kipling)
The camel's hump is an ugly lump
Ox CV 319; Young 70

HUNTING

See also Foxes

Before the Hunt (Lari Williams,
Nigeria)
Howling wind, / hear me
Stuf II 60

Foxhunt (Ted Hughes)
Two days after Xmas, near noon, as
I listen
Ang I 66; Hug MT 8

from *Fox-Trot, Funeral March*
(John Fuller)
Here come the hounds alive from
the kennels
Quin 72; YD 55

Hunter Poems of the Yoruba
(anon.)
Baboon : So proud in his furry robe
Rat 197

Hunting Song (Gabon)
On the weeping forest, under the
wing of the evening
Afr II 23

The Sailor and the Seal (Rumer
Godden)
When the seal saw the sailor
Zoo 88

The Three Jolly Welshmen (anon.)
There were three jovial Welshmen

Block City (Robert Louis Stevenson)
What are you able to build with your blocks?
KCP 192; Ste 81

The Castle (Richard Edwards)
There's a castle under the table in the lounge
TG 38

The Centaur (May Swenson)
The summer that I was ten
Nar 34; NTP 34

Control Calling (Max Fatchen)
Just when I am conducting
Fat W 37

Cowboy (Richard Hill)
I remember, on a long
Strict 150

Den to Let (Gareth Owen)
To let / one self-contained
Bright 35

The Dinosaur (Stewart Lackie)
I sit in class / And imagine
WZ 81

A Dog's Life (Gareth Owen)
Waking up last Friday and dressing for school
Owe C 51

A Good Play (Robert Louis Stevenson)
We built a ship upon the stairs
All 77; NV 46; Ox T 26; Ste 29

Halfway Down (A. A. Milne)
Halfway down the stairs
Read 15

'I am Cherry Alive' (Delmore Schwartz)
'I am cherry alive' the little girl sang
Occ 12; Talk 54

I Can be a Tiger (M. L. Anderson)
I can't go walking
Read 17; S Sun 51

In Daylight Strange (Alan Brownjohn)
It was last Friday at ten to four I
Six 55

Invisible (Gareth Owen)
It wasn't a sudden thing
Owe C 63

Knight Errant (Richard Edwards)
With courage in my heart and a saucepan on my head
Edw M 39

The Land of Counterpane (Robert Louis Stevenson)
When I was sick and lay a-bed
Mea 56; Ox CV 295; Ste 31; WAS 62

The Land of Story Books (Robert Louis Stevenson)
At evening when the lamp is lit
GTP 12; KCP 194; NV 145

Manco the Peruvian Chief (Redmond Phillips)
I looked down at my stomach
Aus B 11

Monstrous Imagination (Colin West)
Mummy, can't you see the monster
West 66

Mrs Brown (Rose Fyleman)
As soon as I'm in bed at night
Ox CV 338

Pirate Story (Robert Louis Stevenson)
Three of us afloat in the meadow by the swing
GTP 10; NV 66; Ste 21

The Ships of Yule (Bliss Carman)
When I was just a little boy
Can 12

The Toaster (William Jay Smith)
A silver-scaled dragon with jaws flaming red
All 13; Fab NV 173; Ox T 36; Read 35; Tim 4; Walk 217; Zoo 57

Too Much Story (Brian Morse)
For today's story
Mor 29

Transformations (Tadeusz Rozewicz)
My little son enters
All 102; KCP 165

The Tree in the Garden (Christine Chaundler)
There's a tree in our garden which is very nice to climb
Ox T 31

When I Was a Bird (Katherine Mansfield)
I climbed up the karaka tree
Occ 151

The Wilderness (Tony Bradman)
Sometimes when I'm / In the park
Bra A 88

You Can't Be That (Brian Patten)
I told them / When I grow up
Pat T 84

IMMIGRATION

Questionnaired (Tessa Stiven)
Tell me again – the name of your wife
Ang II 75; Speak 51

Terminal (D. J. Enright)
A small boy, four years
Ang II 76

INDEPENDENCE

Doing Things for Myself (Hiawyn Oram)
They come to do my buttons up
Ora 14

Speaking for Ourselves (Hiawyn Oram)
There's one thing I don't like about mothers
Ora 39

INDIANS, AMERICAN

See Hiawatha

Alabama (Kho-tha-a-hi, Eagle Wing)
My brethren, among the legends of my people
World 74

INFERIORITY

Also Ran (Mick Gowar)
Your chest hurts twice as bad
Gow F 44

Arthur the Fat Boy (Gareth Owen)
They said about Arthur
Owe C 54

Fat Boy (Mick Gowar)
I know it / I know it
Gow S 18

Picking Teams (Allan Ahlberg)
When we pick teams in the playground
Ahl P 35; Day 23; King 25; SO 49

The Question (Allan Ahlberg)
The child stands facing the teacher
Ahl H 19; IC 34

Things (Fleur Adcock)
There are worse things than having behaved foolishly in public
Moon 110

Tich Miller (Wendy Cope)
Tich Miller wore glasses
Face 39; YD 11

INGRATITUDE

Blow, Blow, thou Winter Wind (William Shakespeare)
Blow, blow, thou winter wind
Puf V 30

INSECTS AND RELATED CREATURES

See Bees, Butterflies, Caterpillars, Dragonflies, Fireflies, Flies, Ladybirds, Locusts, Mosquitoes, Scorpions, Spiders

An August Midnight (Thomas Hardy)
A shaded lamp and a waving blind
Cam II 33; Choice 133

The Butterfly's Ball (William Roscoe)
Come take up your hats and away let us haste
Once 35; Ox CV 131; Walk 172

Hurt No Living Thing (Christina Rossetti)
Hurt no living thing
Ox T 86; Pop 78; Rab 26; Tick 132; Walk 72

Insec' Lesson (Valerie Bloom)
Todder nite mi a watch one program
Ang II 84, Stuf 26
(part) *Show I 50*

The Locust (from Africa)
What is a locust?
Pro III 36

Millipede (Roy Bennett)
A column's on the move. Like this
Show II 60

The Wasp (Mark Burgess)
The humble wasp is much maligned
Bur F 21

INSOMNIA

The City of Sleep (Rudyard Kipling)
Over the edge of the purple down
NTP 245

INSULTS

You! (Igbo)
Your head is like a hollow drum
Afr I 9; HH 11

INTERROGATION

Interrogation (Edwin Muir)
We could have crossed the road but hesitated
Show III 38; Wind 27

Questionnaired (Tessa Stiven)
Tell me again – the name of your wife
Ang II 75; Speak 51

You Will be Hearing from us Shortly (U. A. Fanthorpe)
You feel adequate to the demands of this position?
Fan 64

IRELAND

The Rose Tree (W. B. Yeats)
O words are lightly spoken
Show III 71

'J'

Jargon (James Reeves)
Jerusalem, Joppa, Jericho
Pro I 62

JACKDAWS

The Jackdaw of Rheims (Richard Harris Barham)
The Jackdaw sat on the Cardinal's chair!
ND 67; Ox SP 116

JAGUARS

The Jaguar (Ted Hughes)
The apes yawn and adore their fleas in the sun
Cam II 25; Foc 57

Second Glance at a Jaguar (Ted Hughes)
Skinful of bowls, he bowls them
Cam II 27

JAMAICA

Jamaica Market (Agnes Maxwell-Hall)
Honey, pepper, leaf-green limes
PG 18; Wheel 51; World 62

The Lament of the Banana Man (Evan Jones)
Gal, I'm tellin' you, I'm tired fo' true
Bab 91

Mais of Jamaica (Ian Macdonald)
His own life died but he has not truly died
FS 8

Song of the Banana Man (Evan Jones)
Tourist, white man wiping his face
Afr II 52; Bab 92; Blac 78

JANUARY

January (John Updike)
The days are short
PG 12

JAZZ

Jazz Fantasia (Carl Sandburg)
Drum on your drums, batter on your banjoes
Voi III 79

Jazz-Man (Eleanor Farjeon)
Crash and CLANG! Bash and BANG!
Noisy 18; Pro I 56

JERUSALEM

Jerusalem (William Blake)
And did those feet in ancient time

Fab CV 126; Fav 14; ND 5; Puf V 247; Rat 221

Jerusalem (anon.)
Jerusalem, my happy home
Fab CV 370; Ring 104; Voi II 149

JEWELS

Flint (Christina Rossetti)
An emerald is green as grass
GTP 306; Ox CV 277; PG 52; Walk 23

JONAH

Jonah (Aldous Huxley)
A cream of phosphorescent light
Sea 163

Jonah (Gareth Owen)
Well to start with / It was dark
King 153; Nar 20; Owe K 41; Ox SP 114

Jonah (Judith Nicholls)
Jonah was a later one
Nic M 17

Jonah (Thomas Blackburn)
He stands in rags upon the heaving prow
Sun 76

Jonah's Lament (Judith Nicholls)
Dark, only dark
Nic F 37

JOSEPH

Into Egypt (Karen Gershon)
Trading in spices, once they bought a slave
Sun 64

JOURNALISM

Gutter Press (Paul Dehn)
Peer Confesses / Bishop Undresses
Wind 110

JUDAS ISCARIOT

Jack o' Lent (Charles Causley)
Where are you running to, Jack o' Lent
WAS 28

Judas (anon.)
It was upon a Maundy Thursday that our Lord arose
Floc 160

Judas Iscariot (Robert William Buchanan)
'Twas the soul of Judas Iscariot
Sun 168

JUMBLE SALES

The Jungle Sale (June Crebbin)
Once, before I went to school
Cre 9

JUNE

Adlestrop (Edward Thomas)
Yes. I remember Adlestrop
Cal 60; Choice 169; Fire 114; Floc 115; Foc 72; Like 171; Out 42; Ox PC 141; World 17

KANGAROOS

The Kangaroo (anon.)
Old Jumpety-Bumpety-Hop-and-Go-One
Cow 86; WZ 25

Kangaroo (D. H. Lawrence)
In the northern hemisphere
Touch IV 194
(part) *Ark 57*

KEATS, JOHN

John Keats Eats his Porridge (Adrian Mitchell)
It was hot enough to blister
King 97; Mit N 36

KESTRELS

The Defence (Geoffrey Summerfield)
A silent murderer
CBC 90

K is for Kestrel (Eleanor Farjeon)
Still hangs the Kestrel there
CCC 99; Far M 13

The Windhover (Gerard Manley Hopkins)
I caught this morning morning's minion, king
Cam I 55

KEW GARDENS

'Come down to Kew —' (Reginald Arkell)
You know, of course, that pleasant rhyme
Occ 42

Kew in Lilac-Time (Alfred Noyes)
Go down to Kew in lilac-time
Occ 40

KIDD, CAPTAIN

Captain Kidd (R. and S. V. Benet)
This person in the gaudy clothes
Fab NV 40

KILLING

5 Ways to Kill a Man (Edwin Brock)
There are many cumbersome ways to kill a man
Touch V 20

KINDNESS

A Simple Story of Accrington Stanley (Kit Wright)
A nasty old woman once lived in Accrington Town
Wri C 10

KINGFISHERS

The Kingfisher (John Heath-Stubbs)
When Noah left the Ark the animals
Ark 56; Sun 55

Kingfisher (Phoebe Hesketh)
Brown as nettle-beer, the stream
Ang I 72

The Kingfisher (W. H. Davies)
It was the Rainbow gave thee birth
Like 94

KINGS AND QUEENS

See also Fab NV 258-72, Ox NR 113, Sk 52 for mnemonics for order and dates of English rulers
See also Arthur, Charles I, Charles II, Elizabeth I

First William the Norman (anon.)
First William the Norman
Ox NR 113

William I (Eleanor and Herbert Farjeon)
William the First was the first of our kings
NTP 52

With her Head Tucked Underneath her Arm (R. P. Weston and Bert Lee)
In the Tower of London, large as life
Gho 32

KITES

The Kite (Adelaide O'Keeffe)
My kite is three feet broad and six feet long
Ox CV 124

Mama Dot Warns Against an Easter Rising (Frederick D'Aguiar)
Doan raise no kite is good-friday
Bab 30

KITTENS

The Bad Kittens (Elizabeth Coatsworth)
You may call, you may call
Ox A 233

Choosing their Names (Thomas Hood)
Our old cat has kittens three
All 24; NV 84; Pets 13

Familiarity Dangerous (William Cowper)
As in her ancient mistress' lap
CCC 168

Five Little Pussy Cats (anon.)
Five little pussy cats
Voa 94

The Kitten and the Falling Leaves (William Wordsworth)
See the Kitten on the wall
GTP 52; Puf V 48; YD 61

Miss Tibbles (Ian Serraillier)
Miss Tibbles is my kitten; white
Pos 54; Puf Q 155

Three Little Kittens (Eliza Lee Follen)
Three little kittens lost their mittens
Ox A 18

Tiffany: a Burmese Kitten (Elizabeth Jennings)
My friends keep mice – white ones and patched
Quin 120

Two Little Kittens (Jane Taylor)
Two little kittens one stormy night
Fab NV 166; NV 94; Ox A 155

KLEPTOMANIACS

The Kleptomaniac (Roger McGough)
Beware the Kleptomaniac
McG PT 70

KNIGHTS AND LADIES (L AND D)

All in green went my love (e. e. cummings)
all in green went my love riding
Floc 202; This W 149

Advice to a Knight (T. H. Jones)
Wear modest armour; and walk quietly
Floc 245; O & A 147

from *The Canterbury Tales* (Chaucer, trans. L. Untermeyer)
A knight there was and that a worthy man
GTP 86

Eldorado (Edgar Allan Poe)
Gaily bedight / A gallant knight
KCP 156; Like 117; MT 123; NTP 207; O & A 146; Puf V 86; Stuf 80; Ten 173

KNIGHTS AND LADIES (N)

Bad Sir Brian Botany (A. A. Milne)
Sir Brian had a battleaxe with great big knobs on

Mil VY 92; PoWo I 10; Ten 162; Young 78

from *Gawain and the Green Knight* (anon.)
Be brisk, man, by your faith, and bring me to the point
Brave 83
Then Gawain knelt before the king, took hold
Pro III 47

A Knight Came Riding (anon.)
A knight came riding from the East
Ox PC 39

La Belle Dame Sans Merci (John Keats)
O what can ail thee, knight at arms
Cam I 94; Fab CV 202; Fire 86; GTP 126; MT 61; NTP 186; Ox SP 14; Puf M 62; Puf V 107; Rat 71; Ten 119; This W 164

The Lady of Shalott (Lord Tennyson)
On either side the river lie
Cam I 87; ND 204; Ox SP 87
(part) On either side the river lie
Like 155; Puf V 197; Show II 40
(part) There she weaves by night and day
Fav 84

Marmaduke the Noisy Knight (Colin West)
In Arthur's reign or thereabouts
West 164

Sir Eglamore (Samuel Rowlands)
Sir Eglamore that valiant knight
Fab CV 170; MT 130; Ox PC 25

THE KRAKEN

The Kraken (Lord Tennyson)
Below the thunders of the upper deep
AM 51; Mons 31; MT 86; ND 191; This W 119

LADYBIRDS

Clock-a-Clay (John Clare)
In the cowslip pips I lie
Cla J 38; Foot 62; Ox PC 119

Ladybird! Ladybird! (Emily Brontë)
Ladybird! ladybird! Fly away home
Once 56

LAKES

The Great Lakes Suite (James Reaney)
Lakes Superior, Michigan, etc.
I am Lake Superior
Can 48

LAMBS

A Child's Voice (Andrew Young)
On winter nights shepherd and I
CCC 24; O & A 102

First Sight (Philip Larkin)
Lambs that learn to walk in snow
CCC 23

The Lamb (William Blake)
Little lamb, who made thee?
Fab CV 353; GTP 34; Ox CV 85; Ring 18; Ten 41; WAS 49

Young Lambs (John Clare)
The spring is coming by a-many signs
WAS 48

LAMENTS

See Dirges

LANDSCAPES

All the Way to Alfriston (Eleanor Farjeon)
From Chichester to Alfriston
Far R 112

Harrow-on-the-Hill (John Betjeman)
When melancholy Autumn comes to Wembley
Like 55

The Land's End (Sir Humphry Davy)
On the sea /The sunbeams tremble
Sea 92

Rocky Acres (Robert Graves)
This is a wild land, country of my choice
Choice 258

Up on the Downs (Wes Magee)
Up on the Downs
Cal 76; AVF 67

The Welsh Hill Country (R. S. Thomas)
Too far for you to see
ND 20

Wiltshire Downs (Andrew Young)
The cuckoo's double note
NTP 98; O & A 89

LAPWINGS

Landscape with Lapwings (James Aitchison)
It's another April, and a day
Scot 131

Lapwings (Laurence Smith)
Here come the squealing / clowns
Trio 8

LARKS

See Skylarks

LATCHKEY KIDS

Coming Home (Mick Gowar)
It's not really scary
Brave 58

Empty House (Gareth Owen)
There is nothing / Quite so dismal
Owe K 57

The Keys (Brian Morse)
When I was ten years old
Mor 32

No One In (Michael Rosen)
Sometimes you come home
Ros H 90

Platform (Michael Rosen)
I'm standing on platform one
Ros Q 80
(part) Five 88

LAUGHTER

See also Aga L

A Child's Laughter (Algernon Charles Swinburne)
All the bells of heaven may ring
NTP 50

Laughing Song (William Blake)
When the green woods laugh with the voice of joy
GTP 11; Howl 42; Ox CV 87; Talk 48

Laughing Time (William Jay Smith)
It was laughing time and the tall Giraffe
DS 26; Fab NV 12; Pud 96

Laughter and the Elements (John Agard)
Fire and Water / Wind and Earth
Aga L 29

Laughter's Boast (John Agard))
Not a box in the world
Aga L 27

Mrs Reece Laughs (Martin Armstrong)
Laughter, with us, is no great undertaking
Face 95

LAVATORY ATTENDANTS

The Lavatory Attendant (Wendy Cope)
Slumped on a chair, his body is an S
Face 58

LAZINESS

Can't be Bothered to Think of a Title
When they make slouching in the chair
Ang I 61; WS 75

Lazy Man's Song (Po Chu-I, 772-846, trans. Arthur Waley)
I could have a job but am too lazy to choose it
WS 74

Right Now (Michael Rosen)
Right now / I'd like best of all not to be here
Ros M 11

The Sloth, That's Me (Mark Burgess)
I love to do just nothing
Bur F 46

The Sluggard (Isaac Watts)
'Tis the voice of the Sluggard: I heard him complain
Mes 206; Ox CV 51; Puf V 147

Tired Tim (Walter de la Mare)
Poor tired Tim! It's sad for him
de la M P 13; Walk 109

LEAFLETS

Leaflets (Colin West)
Leaflets, leaflets, I like leaflets
West 181

LEAR, EDWARD

Self-Portrait (Edward Lear)
How plesant to know Mr Lear!
Chat 265; Fab CV 124; NTP 66

LEEKS

Leeks (anon., ancient MS, BM)
I like the leeke above all herbes and flowers
Pic 17

LEOPARDS

Leopard (Alan Brownjohn)
I am one / of the great cats
WZ 56

Leopard (from Yoruba, Ulli Beier)
Gentle hunter
KCP 217; Rat 203; Rhy 77; WS 33

Leopard (Sotho)
See the golden leopard with the spots!
Afr I 25

The Snow Leopard (Gavin Ewart)
All Snow Leopards are whitish grey
Ewar 37

LEPANTO

from *Lepanto* (G. K. Chesterton)
White founts falling in the courts of the sun
ND 36; Rat 236

LESSONS

After English Class (Jean Little)
I used to like 'Stopping by Woods on a Snowy Evening . . .'
YD 14

Bad News (Trevor Millum)
I knew it was no good
Mill 23

Drama Lesson (Gareth Owen)
Let's see some super shapes you Blue Group
Bright 45; SO 24; YD 14

Fear (Jean Kenward)
I was afraid of the wall bars
SO 29

Geography Lesson (Zulfikar Ghose)
When the jet sprang into the sky
Bell 38; Foc 164

The Lesson (Roger McGough)
Chaos ruled OK in the classroom
Ax 6; Bell 27; McG G 14; McRo 19; Sk 38; SO 80; Ten 20

Miss Creedle Teaches Creative Writing (Gareth Owen)
'This morninng,' cries Miss Creedle
Owe C 16

Scoo-wool – the Hippiest Time of your Life (Philip Gross)
In the art class I happened to mention
SO 23

Swimming Lesson (Gregory Harrison)
I hate Wednesdays
SO 31

LETTERS

I Can't Say That (Brian Morse)
Dear Auntie Beryl
Mor 11

A Letter of Application (Anita Harbottle)
Dear Sir / (de dah, de dah)
Speak 97

My Brother gets Letters (Michael Rosen)
My brother gets letters – not many but some
Ros W 17

The Postman (J. and G. Curry)
I don't deliver letters
Down 62

LEVIATHAN

The Huge Leviathan (Edmund Spenser)
Toward the sea turning my troubled eye
Mons 23

Leviathan (Edward Lowbury)
Some say Leviathan is just a whale
Mons 24

LIFTS

The Haunted Lift (James Kirkup)
On the ground floor
Shad 86

The Lift Man (John Betjeman)
In uniform behold me stand
Face 56

The Ups and Downs of the Elevator Car (Caroline D. Emerson)
The elevator car in the elevator shaft
King 160; Young 83

LIMERICKS

See *CBC, Chat, Cow, Fab NV, Fat S, Fat W, FF, Fun, Gho, GTP, HH, KCP, King, KWP, Lea B, Lea C, Once, Ox CV, PG, Pop, Puf V, RMP, Walk, Young*

LINNETS

The Burial of the Linnet (Juliana Horatia Ewing)
Found in the garden – dead in his beauty
CCC 109

The Linnet (Walter de la Mare)
Upon this leafy bush
CCC 108

LIONS

Circus (Margaret Stanley-Wrench)
Saucer of sand, the circus ring
Open 90

Lion (Roald Dahl)
The lion just adores to eat
Open 91

Lion (William Jay Smith)
The lion, ruler over all the beasts
Walk 61

The Lion and Albert (Marriott Edgar)
There's a famous seaside place called Blackpool
Ten 157

Lion Tamer (John Mole)
Between the eyes
Mol 56

96

Pride of Lions (Julian Ennis)
They can swipe a tree dead with one
paw
Jung 12

Riverdale Lion (John Robert
Colombo)
Bound lion, almost blind from
meeting their gaze and popcorn
Jung 15

LISTS

Don't (Robert Edwards)
Why do people say 'Don't' so much
Edw P 16

the electric household (Wes Magee)
cooker blanket
Pro I 35

In the Greenhouse (Paul Higgins)
Car exhaust fumes / Oil in the sea
Pro I 38

Mr Marrumpeter's Shop (Richard
Edwards)
In Mr Marrumpeter's junk shop
Edw P 20

My Christmas List (Gyles
Brandreth)
A police car
Pro I 34

LIZARDS

Lizard (D. H. Lawrence)
A lizard ran out on a rock and
looked up
NTP 103

LOCUSTS

The Locust (from Malagasy, A.
Marre and W. R. Trask)
What is a locust?
Rat 249

LONDON

Composed upon Westminster Bridge
(William Wordsworth)
Earth has not anything to show more
fair

*Choice 28; Earth 10; Fab CV 128; Fire
144; ND 11; Puf V 249; Rab 50*

The Fire of London (John Dryden)
Such was the rise of this prodigioous
fire
KWP 63

London (William Blake)
I wander thro' each chartered street
Choice 47; Fire 67 Rat 251

London Bridge (anon.)
London Bridge is broken down
*Chat 148; Lob 72; Ox Dic 270; Ox NR
76; Puf NR 49; Puf V 188*

London Mourning in Ashes (anon.)
Of fire, fire, fire I sing
Nar 135

Trip to London (Leonard Clark)
By seven o'clock we were on our way
Cla C 54

LONELINESS

Alone in the Grange (Gregory
Harrison)
Strange/ Strange
FF 44; Pos 83; RT 92

Desert Places (Robert Frost)
Snow falling and night falling fast,
oh, fast
Rat 125; Voi III 140

The Darkest and Dingiest Dungeon
(Colin West)
Down in the darkest and dingiest
dungeon
West 105

First and Last (June Crebbin)
I like to be first in the playground
Cre 10

I'm Alone in the Evening (Michael
Rosen)
I'm alone in the evening
Ros M 95

In this City (Alan Brownjohn)
In this city, perhaps a street
Nine 181

The Lamplighter (Robert Louis
Stevenson)
My tea is nearly ready and the sun
has left the sky
Ox CV 297; Ste 50

Librarian (Eric Millward)
Girl in the library, with mousy hair
Face 57

Loneliness (Vivian Underwood,
aged 12)
My friends just left me
Life 28

The Loner (Julie Holder)
He leans against the playground wall
Bell 105

Missing (John Fuller)
Lonely in London is an endless story
Face 125

'My Heart is Broken' (George
Barker)
'My heart is broken,' cried the Owl
Six 27

Not-Loving (Sylvia Kantaris)
The spine doesn't give or arch to it
Wind 83

Not Waving but Drowning (Stevie
Smith)
Nobody heard him, the dead man
Like 105; ND 235

Pets' Day (Brian Morse)
Pets' day / Let's sit on the carpet and
discuss
Mor 15

The River-Merchant's Wife: a Letter
(Ezra Pound)
While my hair was still cut straight
across my forehead
Cam I 84; Rat 357; Talk 34; Wind 106

*A Sad Song about Greenwich
Village* (Frances Park)
She lives in a garret
Walk 96

Self-Love (Vernon Scannell)
I love me very much
Sca L 24

Spinster (Sylvia Plath)
Now this particular girl
Cam II 37

LOONS

The Loon (Ted Hughes)
The Loon, the Loon? Hatched from
the Moon
Hug MW 12

LOSING THINGS

Anyone Seen My . . .? (Max
Fatchen)
The people who keep losing things
Fat S 20

LOT'S WIFE

Lot's Wife (Karen Gershon)
My home, my lovely home, she wept
Sun 59

LOVE

See also Courtship, Lovers,
Marriage

Amo Ergo Sum (Kathleen Raine)
Because I love
Show II 6

As you Came from the Holy Land
(Sir Walter Ralegh)
As you came from the holy land
Fab CV 336; Iron 4; NTP 157; Rat 43

The Clod and the Pebble (William
Blake)
Love seeketh not itself to please
*Choice 44; Rat 108; Touch V 190; Voi
III 97*

The Confirmation (Edwin Muir)
Yes. yours, my love, is the right
human face
Love 41

Go Spread Wings (John Agard)
If I be the rain / you the earth
FS 96

Hawthorn White (Charles
Causley)
Hawthorn white, Hawthorn red
YD 79

In a Bath Teashop (John
Betjeman)
'Let us not speak, for the love we
bear one another . . .'
Love 159

Keep True to Me: A Valentine
(Eleanor Farjeon, aged 7)
My heart has never beat before
Occ 29

Like a Flame (Grace Nichols)
Raising up / from my weeding
Moon 66

Love (Philip Larkin)
The difficult part of love
Touch V 191

Love (Vernon Scannell)
Is it like a carnival with spangles and
balloons
Sca L 10

Love (George Herbert)
Love bade me welcome, yet my soul
drew back
ND 231; Sun 78; Touch IV 117

Love is . . . (Adrian Henri)
Love is feeling cold in the back of
vans
*Cam II 39; Love 13; Pro III 18; Strict
108*

Love Poem (Mick Gowar)
If I can get from here to the pillar
box
Gow T 8

Sonnet (William Shakespeare)
Let me not to the marriage of true
minds
*Cam II 59; Fire 50; Love 105; Touch V
55*

XII (W. H. Auden)
Some say that love's a little boy
PW 28

LOVE, FIRST

See Love 15-34

First Love (Brian Patten)
Sarah's my girl friend
Pat T 122

First Love (John Clare)
I ne'er was struck before that hour
Touch V 62

First Love (Mick Gowar)
Both waiting for the bus, a 102
Gow F 72

Freak (Brian Moses)
Why do I start walking
Side 11B

Girl's Song (Wilfrid Gibson)
I was so happy that I hardly knew it
Foc 87

King of the Kurzel (Mick Gowar)
The Kurzel, Southend
Gow F 9

A New World (Vernon Scannell)
When I awoke this morning
Sca L 70

The Picnic (John Logan)
It is the picnic with Ruth in the
spring
Voi III 71; Touch V 57

Plucking the Rushes (Chinese,
trans. Arthur Waley)
Green rushes with red shoots

*Mes 187; O & A 97; Touch V 56; Voi
III 73; World 68*

Studup (Barrie Wade)
'Owaryer' / 'Imokay' / 'Gladtwearit'
Wad 9

A True Story (Michael Rosen)
First love / when I was ten
McRo 64

What's Best (June Crebbin)
Funny how it's all right for me
Side 17G

LOVERS

As I Walked Out One Night (anon.)
As I walked out one night, it being
dark all over
Mes 175

A Blade of Grass (Brian Patten)
You ask for a poem
Love 77; Strict 121

Famous Lovers (Vernon Scannell)
Everyone has heard about
Sca L 42

The Good Morrow (John Donne)
I wonder by my troth, what thou,
and I
Cam II 57; Fire 185; Love 74

She Tells her Love while Half Asleep
(Robert Graves)
She tells her love while half asleep
Love 71

Teach the Making of Summer
(James Berry)
Dave. Dear Dave./ I could write a
letter
Ber 19

The Sunne Rising (John Donne)
Busie old foole, unruly sunne
Touch V 71

*A Valediction: Forbidding
Mourning* (John Donne)
As virtuous men passe mildly away
Fire 32

When (Yansan Agard)
When tigers don't roar
Life 33

Without You (Adrian Henri)
Without you every morning would
be like going back to work after a
holiday
Cam II 39

LOVERS: FAITHLESS

Donal Og (from the Irish, Lady Augusta Gregory)
It is late last night the dog was speaking of you
Rat 132

First Frost (Andrei Voznesensky)
A girl is freezing in a telephone booth
Love 122

Frankie and Johnny (anon.)
Frankie and Johnny were lovers
KCP 224; NTP 189; Rat 167; Voi III 88

Hornpipe (C. Day Lewis)
Now the peak of summer's past, the sky is overcast
Love 127

My Cat and I (Roger McGough)
Girls are simply the prettiest things
Love 129

My Version (Kit Wright)
I hear that since you left me
Strict 124

Ou Phrontis [I don't care] (Charles Causley)
The bells assault the maiden air
Voi III 90

The Ruined Maid (Thomas Hardy)
O 'Melia my dear, this does everything crown!
Ax 53

Sea Love (Charlotte Mew)
Tide be runnin' the great world over
KWP 141

She was Poor but She was Honest (anon.)
She was poor but she was honest
Ax 52; Story 68

from *A Shropshire Lad* (A. E. Housman)
Oh, when I was in love with you
Love 137, Talk 44

from *Waiting at the Church* (Fred W. Leigh)
I'm in a nice bit of trouble I confess
Love 101

The Water is Wide (anon.)
The water is wide I cannot get o'er
NTP 62

A Year's Spinning (Elizabeth Barrett Browning)
He listened at the porch that day
Show III 31

LOVERS: REUNITED

The Bailiff's Daughter of Islington (anon.)
There was a youth and a well-loved youth
GTP 114

Johnny Come Over the Water (Charles Causley)
Johnny come over the water
Cau E 46

Lady Clare (Alfred Lord Tennyson)
It was the time when lilies blow
Nar 66

Lochinvar (Sir Walter Scott)
O young Lochinvar is come out of the west
Brave 131; GTP 134; ND 133; NTP 192; Puf V 92

Meeting at Night (Robert Browning)
The grey sea and the long black land
Foc 89; KWP 46; Sea 196; Show II 67

LOVERS: UNHAPPY (L AND D)

Absence (Elizabeth Jennings)
I visited the place where we last met
Ang I 31; Love 148; Strict 123

Beyond the Last Lamp (Thomas Hardy)
While rain, with eve in partnership
Foc 91

Being-in-love (Roger McGough)
you are so very beautiful
Strict 107

A Chinese Poem (anon.)
White clouds are in the sky
O & A 43

First Boy Friend (Mick Gowar)
Every wheel you can hear
Gow S 46

from *First Love* (Mick Gowar)
I don't know why, but something's going wrong
Gow F 78; Love 124

The Gardener (anon.)
The gardener stood at the garden gate
WS 6

If You Don't Come (Marguerite Mack)
The sun will get
Til 60

Lost Love (Robert Graves)
His eyes are quickened so with grief
Fab CV 346; Love 142; Mes 183

Love Without Hope (Robert Graves)
Love without hope, as when the young bird-catcher
Choice 256; Iron 100; NTP 70

Mariana (Alfred Lord Tennyson)
With blackest moss the flower-pots
Cam II 49; Choice 84; Fire 52; Nar 79

Miss Blues'es Child (Langston Hughes)
If the blues would let me
Talk 28

Neutral Tones (Thomas Hardy)
We stood by a pond that winter day
Cam II 131; Choice 138

O, This Estrangement (Mervyn Peake)
O this estrangement forms a distance vaster
Show III 87

Our Love Now (Martyn Lowery)
I said / observe how the wound heals in time
Strict 112

Simple Lyric (Brian Patten)
When I think of her sparkling face
Love 150

Sonnet (William Shakespeare)
Being your slave, what should I do but tend
Love 48

Sounds of the Day (Norman MacCaig)
When a clatter came
Rat 404

This is to Let You Know (Noel Coward)
This is to let you know
Love 93

Warning to Gloria (A. S. J. Tessimond)
I wait for you whose half past six is seven
Love 47

White in the Moon (A. E. Housman)
White in the moon the long road lies
NTP 144

You Make Me So Nervous (Fran Landesman)
You make me so nervous
Ang I 26

LOVERS: UNHAPPPY (N)

La Belle Dame Sans Merci (John Keats)
O, what can ail thee, Knight-at-arms
CAM 194; Fab CV 202; Fire 86; GTP 126; MT 61; NTP 186; Ox SP 14; Puf M 62; Puf V 107; Rat 71; Ten 119; This W 164

Bredon Hill (A. E. Housman)
In summertime on Bredon
Love 154

Cushie Butterfield (George Ridley)
I's a broken-hearted keelman, and I's over head in love
Iron 18; NTP 61

The Despairing Lover (William Walsh)
Distracted with care
Fab CV 345

The Douglas Tragedy (anon.)
'Rise up, rise up, now, Lord Douglas' she says
Kist 84; NTP 190

Down by the Salley Gardens (W. B. Yeats)
Down by the Salley Gardens my love and I did meet
Iron 10

Hair Today, No Her Tomorrow (Brian Patten)
'I've been upstairs' she said
Love 132

In the Orchard (Muriel Stuart)
'I thought you loved me.' 'No, it was only fun.'
Love 130

The Letter (Elizabeth Riddell)
I take my pen in hand
Love 92

Lord Thomas and Fair Eleanor
(trad.)
Lord Thomas he was a bold forester
Nar 69

Message (Wendy Cope)
Pick up the phone before it is too late
Love 46

Noble Sisters (anon.)
Now did you mark a falcon
Puf M 67

The Puzzle (Vernon Scannell)
I didn't used to think that I was vain
Sca L 44

The Unquiet Grave (anon.)
The wind doth blow today, my love
Rat 446; Story 36

from *Why Doesn't She Come?*
(A. P. Herbert)
Why doesn't she come?
Love 49

LOVE SONGS

The Baite (John Donne)
Come live with mee and bee my love
Rat 338

Go Lovely Rose (Edmund Waller)
Go, lovely rose
Love 81

I Get a Kick Out of You (Cole
Porter)
I get no kick from champagne
Fire 157

I Know Where I'm Going (anon.)
I know where I'm going
NTP 26

John Anderson, My Jo (Robert
Burns)
John Anderson, my Jo, John
Love 160

Love will Find out the Way (anon.)
Over the mountains
Fab CV 332; Voi III 74

The Passionate Shepherd to his Love
(Christopher Marlowe)
Come live with me and be my Love
*KCP 132; Rat 336; Talk 33, This W
55; Touch V 70*

The Nymph's Reply to the Shepherd
(Sir Walter Ralegh)
If all the world and love were young
Rat 337

O My Love is Like a Red Red Rose
(Robert Burns)
O my love is like a red red rose
*Fab CV 335; Fav 87; Love 84; NTP
62; Show II 14*

Reasons Why (Langston Hughes)
Just because I loves you
Blac 18

from *Song* (W. H. Auden)
Some say that love's a little boy
Love 12

from *The Song of Solomon* (The
Bible)
The voice of my beloved! behold he
cometh
KWP 38

Why (Vernon Scannell)
They ask me why I love my love. I
say
Sca L 8

LOVE SONGS: HAPPY

A Birthday (Christina Rossetti)
My heart is like a singing bird
Love 6; Talk 41; This W 62

It Was a Lover and his Lass
(William Shakespeare)
It was a lover and his lass
Rat 218; Talk 38

Juke Box Love Song (Langston
Hughes)
I could take the Harlem night
Talk 46

The Man in the Opera Sings (Gavin
Ewart)
You're like the jolliest picnic in a
children's book
Love 38

My True Love hath my Heart (Sir
Philip Sidney)
My true love hath my heart, and I
have his
Love 52

To my Valentine (Ogden Nash)
More than a catbird hates a cat
Love 39

LOVE SONGS: UNHAPPY

*Adrian Henri's Talking After
Christmas Blues* (Adrian
Henri)

Well I woke up this mornin' it was
Christmas Day
Love 146

Greensleeves (anon.)
Greensleeves was all my joy
Fab CV 338

Tonight at Noon (Adrian Henri)
Tonight at noon
Pro III 90

The Voice (Thomas Hardy)
Woman much missed, how you call
to me
Choice 136; Love 148

Western Wind (anon.)
Western wind, when wilt thou blow
Fab CV 351; Fire 126; Love 67

LULLABIES

See also Bed 58-72, Ox NR 18-20

Benue Lullaby (modern African)
The fishing boats sway
Bed 60

Can Ye Sew Cushions? (anon.)
O can ye sew cushions?
Fab CV 93

Golden Slumbers (Thomas
Dekker)
Golden slumbers kiss your eyes
Ox PC 161; This W 89

Hushabye Lullaby (Brian Patten)
Listen. Hush / Don't be hasty
Pat T 42

Kentucky Babe (anon.)
Skeeters are a-humming on the
honeysuckle vine
Bed 70

Lullaby (Akan people, Africa)
Someone would like to have you for
her child
Talk 23

Lullaby (anon.)
Hush, little baby, don't say a word
*Bed 65; Fab NV 126; Lob 119; Tick
154; Voa 99; Young 52*

Lullaby (Elizabeth Jennings)
Sleep, my baby, the night is coming
soon
Quin 139; Star 42

Lullaby (Gilles Vigneault, trans.
John Glassco)
Sleep, sleep beneath the old wind's
eye
Can 35

Lullaby for a Naughty Girl (E. V.
Rieu)
Oh peace, my Penelope; slaps are the
fate
Fab NV 271; Puf V 148

Lully, Lulla (anon., 15th cent.)
Lully, lulla, thou little tiny child
Talk 24

Nurse's Song (anon., German)
Sleep, baby, sleep!
*Bed 55; GTP 301; Lob 76; Ox T 157;
This W 88; WP 90*

Seal Lullaby (Rudyard Kipling)
Oh! hush thee my baby the night is
behind us
WS 24; Zoo 82

Sweet and Low (Alfred Lord
Tennyson)
Sweet and low, sweet and low
*GTP 300; Ox CV 212; Ox PC 160; Spi
106; This W 86*

*Welsh Lullaby or All Through the
Night* (anon.)
Sleep my babe lie still and slumber
GTP 301; NV 147

Wynken, Blynken and Nod
(Eugene Field)
Wynken, Blynken and Nod one
night
*Fab NV 244; GTP 302; NV 126; Ox A
160; Ox CV 303; Ox T 160; Rat 52;
RMP 58*

You Spotted Snakes (William
Shakespeare)
You spotted snakes with double
tongue
*Gold 107; GTP 297; Ox PC 160; This
W 37*

LYCHEES

The Lychee (Wang I, trans Arthur
Waley)
Fruit white and lustrous as a pearl
Fab CV 110; Pic 139

MACHINES

See also Motor cars, Steam
shovels, Tractors

Automatic Pilot Answers Back (Leo
Aylen)
The pilot of Gulf Alpha Tango
Ang I 77

Concrete Mixers (Patricia Hubbell)
The drivers are washing the
concrete mixers
Pro I 67; Walk 94

The Dinosaurs are not all Dead
(Charles Malam)
The dinosaurs are not all dead
King 207

Engineers (Jimmy Garthwaite)
Pistons, valves and wheels and gears
Noisy 21; Tick 288

The Toaster (William Jay Smith)
A silver-scaled dragon with jaws
flaming red
*All 13; Fab NV 173; Ox T 36; Read 35;
Tim 4; Walk 217; Zoo 57*

MADNESS

Counting the Mad (Donald
Justice)
This one was put in a jacket
Face 128

The Mad Maid's Song (Robert
Herrick)
Good morrow to the day so fair
Face 149; Puf V 202

Snipers (Roger McGough)
When I was kneehigh to a tabletop
McRo 34

MAGDALEN

Magdalen at Michael's Gate
(Henry Kingsley)
Magdalen at Michael's gate
Sun 185

THE MAGI

See Epiphany

MAGIC

See *Hug MW* throughout

Bill's Eraser (Terry Jones)
Bill had an eraser
Jon 44

A Bit of a Devil (Brian Morse)
The headmaster rubbed his hands in
glee
Mor 25

The Collarbone of a Hare (W. B.
Yeats)
Would I could cast a sail on the water
Chat 340

The Cunjah Man (James Edwin
Campbell)
O children, run, the Cunjah Man
Afr I 51

*James had a Magic Set for
Christmas* (Brian Morse)
James had practised the tricks for
days
Mor 26

Kemp Owyne (anon.)
Her mother died when she was
young
MT 23

Kiph (Walter de la Mare)
My Uncle Ben, who's been
Chat 353

Laughter and the Magician (John
Agard)
The magician tried
Aga L 21

The Magic Show (Vernon
Scannell)
After a feast of sausage rolls
Stoc 94

The Magic Wood (Henry Treece)
The wood is full of shining eyes
Gho 38

Merlin and the Snake's Egg (Leslie
Norris)
All night the tall young man
Ox SP 124

Moon-Mirror (Ted Hughes)
In every moon-mirror lurks a
danger
Hug MW 16

The Song of Wandering Aengus
(W. B. Yeats)
I went out to the hazel wood
*Gold 11; GTP 127; Irish 174; Iron 94;
KWP 218; MT 120; NTP 205; Ox T
129; Story 42; Talk 89; Ten 171; This
W 38; Wind 66; YD 90*

Three (Peter Fallon)
Where three fields meet
Strict 38

Tillie (Walter de la Mare)
Old Tillie Turveycombe
Gh P 18

104

Up a Hundred-Mile-High Pine Tree with You (Adrian Mitchell)
Glabber is my name and round is my shape
Mit N 47

The Woman of Water (Adrian Mitchell)
There once was a woman of water
Five 27; Mit N 14

MAGPIES

Magpies (W. H. Davies)
I have an orchard near my house
CCC 92

Magpies in Picardy (T. P. Cameron Wilson)
The magpies in Picardy
FWW 64; PW 162; War 48

A Shot Magpie (Andrew Young)
Though on your long-tailed flight
CCC 92

MALE VERSUS FEMALE

See Side throughout

Behaviour of Fish in an Egyptian Tea-Garden (Keith Douglas)
As a white stone draws down the fish
Show III 68

Boys will be Boys (Leon Rosselson)
Look at little Peter. Isn't he a terror?
Side 43B

The Buddha's Wife (Ruth Silcock)
It can't have been fun for the Buddha's wife
Moon 21

Get Up and Bar the Door (anon.)
It fell about the Martinmas time
GTP 123

Get Up and Shut the Door (Ian Serraillier)
It happened one December night
KCP 176

Hate Poem (Adrian Mitchell)
Rounders – it's a girls' game
Mit N 28

Listn Big Brodda Dread, Na! (James Berry)
My sista is younga than me
KWP 34

he and she (R. D. Laing)
she: it's the same thing
Speak 62

Lizzie (or) Unfair (Michael Rosen)
When we went over the park
Cham 21; Ros Q 103; SS 55; Wheel 21

Men Talk (Liz Lochhead)
Women / Rabbit rabbit rabbit women
Pro III 87

The New Kid on the Block (Jack Prelutsky)
There's a new kid on the block
KWP 169; Pre 7

Not Me! (Adrian Henri)
Every little girl would like to be
Hen 65

The Old Man who Lived in the Woods (anon.)
There was an old man who lived in the woods
Once 78

Paper Matches (Paulette Jiles)
My aunts washed dishes while the uncles
Mes 226

Three Brothers (Joyce Grenfell)
I had three brothers
Face 107

To Iva, Two-and-a-Half (Marilyn Hacker)
Litttle fat baby, as we
Moon 111

A Touch of Class (John Kitching)
When Miss asks a question
Side 12G

Trio (Mike Rosen)
Once I went out with a girl in my class
Ros F 16

War (Mike Rosen)
A group of eight-year-olds
Ros F 69

Wash up the Dishes (Lorraine Simeon)
'Wash up the dishes', my mum says
Side 22G

MANDELA

My Country (Zinziswa, daughter of Nelson Mandela, aged 12)
I stand by the gate
Blac 70

MANGOES

Mango (Grace Nichols)
Have a mango
Pic 140; Stuf II 34

Mango, Little Mango (anon. trans,
Chris Searle)
The mango stands for Africa
Pic 38; Wheel 27

MANNERS

See also Table manners

Hot and Cold (Brian Lee)
Everybody all excited and hot
All 97

Manners (1918) (Elizabeth
Bishop)
My grandfather said to me
Rat 268

Politeness (A. A. Milne)
If people ask me
Pop 97

Riding (William Allingham)
His lordship's steed
Ox CV 216

To the Gentleman in Row E
(Virginia Graham)
Dear Sir, We in Row E are well aware
Face 124

To the Lady behind Me (A. P.
Herbert)
Dear Madam, you have seen this
play
Face 123

A Thank-you can Break no Bone
(John Agard)
When I forget my manners
Gran 14

Whole Duty of Children (Robert
Louis Stevenson)
A child should always say what's true
Ox CV 293

MARBLES

Marbles in my Pocket (Lydia
Pender)
Marbles in my pocket
DS 44

MARCH

Jolly March Wind (Eleanor
Farjeon)
Jolly March Wind / Blows in the
street
Far M 47

March (Emily Dickinson)
Dear March – Come in
Occ 30

March Morning Unlike Others
(Ted Hughes)
Blue haze. Bees hanging in air at the
hive-mouth
Ang II 30; Out 26

Written in March (William
Wordsworth)
The cock is crowing
*GTP 270; NV 16; O & A 81; P Sev
126; RMP 28; This W 103*

MARKETS

Granny in de Market Place (Amryl
Johnson)
Yuh fish fresh?
Wind 96

The Hausa Trader (J. H. Sackey)
Beneath the trees along the highway
Afr II 17

Jamaica Market (Agnew Maxwell-
Hall)
Honey, pepper, leaf-green limes
PG 18; Wheel 51; World 62

Market Women (Daisy Myrie)
Down from the hills they come
Blac 76

Sunny Market Song (James Berry)
Coffee / Spiced chocolate / Ackee
Ber 91; Stuf 56

MARRIAGE

An Arundel Tomb (Philip Larkin)
Side by side, their faces blurred
Love 164

*Hardly Believable Horace and
Hattie in Hell* (Kit Wright)
Horace and Hattie, in cacophonous
concert
Love 114

The Honeymoon is Over (Judith
Viorst)
The honeymoon is over
Love 113

106

My Old Dutch (Albert Chevalier)
We've been together now for forty years
Love 120

Nervous Prostration (Anna Wickham)
I married a man of the Croydon class
Wind 91

On Giles and Joan (Ben Jonson)
Who says that Giles and Joan at discord be?
Love 117

One Flesh (Elizabeth Jennings)
Lying apart now, each in a separate bed
Fire 156; Love 116; Strict 72; Touch V 68

Les Sylphides (Louis MacNeice)
Life in a day: he took his girl to the ballet
Love 112; Touch V 67

The Sailor's Song (Vernon Scannell)
The north wind howls, the swollen seas
Sca L 32

The Sailor's Wife (William Julius Mickle)
And are ye sure the news is true?
Scot 34; Sea 192

A Slice of Wedding Cake (Robert Graves)
Why have such scores of lovely, gifted girls
Love 106

To His Wife (Samuel Bishop)
Thee, Mary, with this ring I wed
WAS 122

To My Dear and Loving Husband (Anne Bradstreet)
If ever two were one, then surely we
Voi III 87

Wedding-Wind (Philip Larkin)
The wind blew all my wedding-day
Foc 95

40—Love (Roger McGough)
middle .... aged
Mot 164

MASSACRE OF THE INNOCENTS

The Miraculous Harvest (anon.)
Rise up, rise up, you merry men all
Chris 19

MATHS

Exercise Book (Jacques Prevert, trans. Paul Dehn)
Two and two four
Gang 64; Sk 42; Stuf II 53

Maths (Deepak Kalha)
What do you minus
Blac 142; Stuf II 50

Summing Up (Nigel Gray)
A poet came to our school
SO 87

Writing and Sums (Derek Stuart)
When the teacher asks us to write
SO 83

MAY

May (Roger McGough)
Fields of golden rape
McG S 33

MEASLES

Measles (Kaye Starbird)
The few times back in the early fall
Mea 17

MEDICINE

Poor Henry (Walter de la Mare)
Thick in its glass
de la M P 41

MERMAIDS AND MERMEN

The Eddystone Light (anon.)
Me father was the keeper of the Eddystone Light
MT 83; Puf M 195; Voi II 25

Fishy (Shirley Hughes)
Great Uncle Morissey, Dad and Mum
TG 29

The Forsaken Merman (Matthew Arnold)
Come, dear children, let us away

Fab CV 325; ND 197; NTP 105; Ox
PC 59; Ox SP 48; (part) Sea 177

Little Fan (James Reeves)
I don't like the look of little Fan,
mother
Mes 165; MT 81; Puf Q 87; Ree C 6

The Merrymaid (Charles Causley)
Robert Stephen Hawker
Cau F 68; Quin 44

They Call to One Another (George
Barker)
They call to one another
MT 82; Six 20

MICE

Anne and the Fieldmouse (Ian
Serraillier)
We found a mouse in the chalk
quarry today
Cal 106; Pos 76; WZ 35

Invitation to a Mouse (Eleanor
Farjeon)
There's pudding in the pantry
Far M 9

The Meadow House (Theodore
Roethke)
In a shoebox stuffed in an old nylon
stocking
Foc 63; Gang 22; Pets 49; Pro II 75

Mice (Rose Fyleman)
I think mice/Are rather nice
Gold 31; Pop 71; Pos 75; Read 24; Tim
25

Missing (A.A. Milne)
Has anybody seen my mouse?
Ani 50

The Mouse (Elizabeth
Coatsworth)
I heard a mouse
Fab NV 86; Puf V 45

The Mouse (Laura E. Richards)
I'm only a poor little mouse ma'am!
Ox A 167

The Mouse and the Cake (Eliza
Cook)
A mouse found a beautiful piece of
plum cake
NV 82; Ox CV 209

A Mouse in my Roof (Richard
Edwards)
'There's a mouse in my roof!' cried
Henry
Edw M 35

The Mouse in the Wainscot (Ian
Serraillier)
Hush, Suzanne/Don't lift your cup
Ox T 99

*The Mouse that Gnawed the Oak-
tree Down* (Vachell Lindsay)
The mouse that gnawed the oak-tree
down
WS 88

Mouse's Nest (John Clare)
I found a ball of grass among the hay
Cla J 29; Rat 299

To a Mouse (Robert Burns)
Wee, sleek it, cowrin, tim'rous
beastie
Kist 30

MILKMEN

I've Never Seen the Milkman
(Charles Causley)
I've never seen the Milkman
Cau J 12

MILLERS

The Miller (Chaucer, trans. N.
Coghill)
The Miller was a chap of sixteen
stone
KCP 49; ND 133

The Miller (Chaucer, trans. L.
Untermeyer)
The Miller, stout and sturdy as the
stones
GTP 87

There Was a Jolly Miller Once
(anon.)
There was a jolly miller once
GTP 94; NV 119; Ox Dic 308; Puf NR
98; Voa 19

MINERS

Doon the Pit (Norman
Thompson)
Aa've seen young lads gang doon the
Pit
Wheel 45

The Image o' God (Joe Corrie)
Crawlin' aboot like a snail in the mud
Kist 75

MIRACLES

The Ballad of Father Gilligan
(W.B. Yeats)
The old priest Peter Gilligan
Sun 201

MISCHIEF

Eshu (Yoruba)
Eshu, who muddles men's minds
Afr II 27

MISFITS

The Hunchback in the Park (Dylan
Thomas)
The hunchback in the park
Cam I 128; Fire 174

Left Out Together (Eric Finney)
There's the crowd of them again
Side 33B

Not Waving but Drowning (Stevie
Smith)
Nobody heard him, the dead man
Pro III 81; Touch V 34

MOLES

A Dead Mole (Andrew Young)
Strong-shouldered mole
WZ 110

Mole (Alan Brownjohn)
To have to be a mole?
Ark 61

The Mole (F. W. Harvey)
Small piteous thing in the sun's
yellow blaze
CCC 149

Mole (Robert Sykes, aged 14)
Tapered black barrel with excavator
paws
Rab 68

The Song of a Mole (Richard
Edwards)
All I did this afternoon was
Edw P 64

MONEY

Fantasy of an African Boy (James
Berry)
Such a peculiar lot
NTP 149

Money Moans (Roger McGough)
Money I haven't got enough
Ang II 56

MONKEYS

See Apes and monkeys

MONOPOLY

It's a Bit Rich (Max Fatchen)
Playing Monopoly's
Day 37; Fat W 55; Ox T 29

MONSTERS

See also Dinosaurs, Dragons,
Kraken, Wendigos

Be a Monster (Roy Fuller)
I am a frightful monster
AM 10; Mons 14; Poem I 52

from *Beowulf* (Old English,
trans.)
I have heard it said (Michael Rosen)
KWP 32
Over the misty moor (Ian Seraillier)
Pro III 45

The Black Beast (Ted Hughes)
Where is the Black Beast?
Mons 11

The Bogus-boo (James Reeves)
The Bogus-boo
MT 69

The Demon Manchanda (Mike
Rosen)
The two-headed two-body
Mons 10

Ffangs the Vampire Bat (Ted
Hughes)
Ffangs the vampire landed in
London
Hug V 32

I am Jojo (Mike Rosen)
I am Jojo
FF 41; Mons 60; Ros Y 21

The Invisible Beast (Jack Prelutsky)
The beast that is invisible
ATP 61

The Lambton Worm (Northumberland folk song)
One Sunday morning Lambton went
Brave 50; Mons 36

The Loch Ness Monster (Roger McGough)
Has just been spied
McG M 60

The Loon (Ted Hughes)
The Loon, the Loon
Hug U 12; Mons 25

The Malfeasance (Alan Bold)
It was a dank, dark, dreadful night
AM 26; Bright 13; Mons 38; Ox SP 12

The Marrog (R.C. Scriven)
My desk's at the back of the class
AM 11; Like 85; MCF 60; Mons 8; Nine 158; Spa 77; Sk 60; Walk 125

The Mewlips (J.R.R. Tolkien)
The shadows where the Mewlips dwell
AM 32; KCP 198; MCF 26; MT 149; PG 102; Shad 79

The Moon-Oak (Ted Hughes)
The Moon-oak/Is a sort of vegetable hawk
Hug MW 21

Nessie (Ted Hughes)
No, it is not an elephant or any such grasshopper
AM 52; HH 106; WZ 84

Pantomime Poem (Roger McGough)
'HE'S BEHIND YER'
Howl 57; MCF 64; Mons 15; Strict 33; WP 19

The Snitterjipe (James Reeves)
In mellow orchards, rich and ripe
MCF 16

The Spangled Pandemonium (Palmer Brown)
The spangled pandemonium is missing from the zoo
AM 18; OTR 26

The White Monster (W. H. Davies)
Last night I saw the monster near; the big
AM 30; MCF 10

The Worst (Shel Silverstein)
When singing songs of scariness
WZ 80

MONTHS

See also April, August, February, June, March, May, November, October

A Cautionary Calendar (Roger McGough)
Beware January
McG F 64

A Child's Calendar (George Mackay Brown)
No visitors in January
Gold 46; Occ 21; Sun 126

Days in the Month (anon.)
Thirty days hath September
Ox Dic 380; Ox NR 112

The Garden Year or *The Months* (Sara Coleridge)
January brings the snow,
Fab NV 227; Fav 102; GTP 268; NV 21; Ox CV 169; Ox T 137; PoWo I 96; Puf V 15; Walk 36; WP 28

A Haiku Yearbook (Anthony Thwaite)
Snow in January
Pro II 70

January Jumps About (George Barker)
January jumps about
Six 32

January to December (Patricia Beer)
The warm cows have gone
WP 29

Married When the Year is New (anon.)
Married when the year is new
Lob 125

Martha's Hair (Colin West)
In January Martha's hair
West 158

The Months (Christina Rossetti)
January cold desolate
Like 37

The School Year (Wes Magee)
September stars a fresh school year
Mag W 24

110

MOON

Above the Dock (T. E. Hulme)
Above the quiet dock in midnight
All 124; NTP 30; Sea 94; WP 12

Autumn (T. E. Hulme)
A touch of cold in the Autumn
night
All 103; Cal 95; NTP 124; Rhy 58;
Show I 55; WP 12

Cat in Moonlight (Douglas
Gibson)
Through moonlight's milk
Bed 31

Flying (J. M. Westrup)
I saw the moon
Once 57; Pos 146; Shad 90; SS 34;
S Sun 83

Full Moon (William Bealby-
Wright)
A Cannon ball/A lost balloon
Rhy 26

Full Moon (Walter de la Mare)
One night as Dick lay fast asleep
de la M P 42; Pos 144

The Harvest Moon (Ted Hughes)
The flame-red moon, the harvest
moon
O & A 100; Shad 95; Strict 133

Is the Moon Tired? (Christina
Rossetti)
Is the moon tired? She looks so pale
Ox T 148; YD 127

Mad Ad (Roger McGough)
A Madison Avenue whizzkid
Rab 93

*The Man in the Moon stayed up Too
Late* (J. R. R. Tolkien)
There is an inn, a merry old inn
Ox SP 164

Moon (Alan Bold)
At its fullest the moon
Spa 20

The Moon (Robert Louis
Stevenson)
The moon has a face like the clock in
the hall
Puf V 225; Ste 53

The Moon and a Cloud (W. H.
Davies)
Sometimes I watch the moon at
night
Rat 291

The Moon's the North Wind's Cooky
(Vachell Lindsay)
The Moon's the North Wind's cooky
Bed 30; GTP 258; Ox A 220; Read 51;
Walk 32

Moths and Moonshine (James
Reeves)
Moths and moonshine mean to me
HH 64; Ree 'M'

Rags (Judith Thurman)
The night wind/rips a cloud sheet
Shad 94

Silver (Walter de la Mare)
Slowly, silently, now the moon
de la M P 106; Fav 83; Gold 108; GTP
262; Like 144; MT 105; PG 44; Pos
145; RMP 55; Talk 73; Walk 33; WP
52

Silverly (Dennis Lee)
Silverly, silverly
Read 87; Til 47

The Wind and the Moon (George
Macdonald)
Said the Wind to the Moon, 'I will
blow you out; . . .'
Fab NV 127; GTP 258; (part) *Read 51*

MOON FANTASY

See Hug MW throughout

*'Jump Over the Moon?' the Cow
Declared* (Max Fatchen)
'Jump over the moon?' the cow
declared
Fat S 30; King 60; Spa 42

The Man in the Moon (J. W. Riley)
And the Man in the Moon has a boil
on his ear
CBC 114

Moon-transport (Ted Hughes)
Some people on the moon are so idle
Hug MW 78; Spa 41

Moon-Whales (Ted Hughes)
They plough through the mooon-
stuff
MT 105

Moon-wind (Ted Hughes)
There is no wind on the moon at all
Poem I 56; Spa 40; YD 140

A Moon-Witch (Ted Hughes)
A moon-witch is no joke
Pud 34

Picnic on the Moon (Brian Morse)
A picnic on the moon
Mor 110

Surprise! or the Escapologist (Carey Blyton)
At the foot of the Apennine Mountains
Shad 100

MOON LANDING

Burning Burning Moonward (Adrian Rumble)
Burning burning moonward
Shad 101; WP 103

The Eagle has Landed (Adrian Rumble)
The airlock swings open
Shad 102; Spa 27; WP 97

MOOR-HENS

Moor-Hens (Charles Causley)
Living by Bate's Pond, they
Cau J 34

MOOSES

The Bull Moose (Alden Nowlan)
Down from the purple mist of trees on the mountain
NTP 104

Mooses (Ted Hughes)
The goofy Moose, the walking house-frame
Hug U 36

MORTALITY

As I Walked Out One Evening (W. H. Auden)
As I walked out one evening
Chat 427; Rat 39

Dockery and Son (Philip Larkin)
Dockery was junior to you
Fire 113

Even Such is Time (Sir Walter Ralegh)
Even such is time, which takes in trust
Brave 90; NTP 148; Rat 143

Gone (Walter de la Mare)
Where's the Queen of Sheba?
Fab NV 263

Last Lauch (Douglas Young)
The Minister said it wald dee
Scot 55

My Busconductor (Roger McGough)
My busconductor tells me
Fire 165

Nothing Gold Can Stay (Robert Frost)
Nature's first green is gold
Show II 17

The Old Familiar Faces (Charles Lamb)
I have had playmates, I have had companions
Face 157

Rising Five (Norman Nicholson)
'I'm rising five' he said
Fire 15

Sic Vita (Henry King)
Like to the falling of a star
Show III 68

Sonnet 60 (William Shakespeare)
Like as the waves make towards the pebbled shore
Show III 93

To Daffodils (Robert Herrick)
Fair daffodils
NTP 120; Puf V 22; Talk 17; YD 121

Upon His Departure Hence (Robert Herrick)
Thus I/Pass by/And die
Show II 20

MOSES

The Burning Bush (Norman Nicholson)
When Moses, musing in the desert, found
Sun 65

MOSQUITOES

Mosquito (D. H. Lawrence)
When did you start your tricks
Cam I 44; Choice 191; Rat 294; Vol II 42

Mosquito (John Updike)
On the fine wire of her whine she walked
Floc 206

A Mosquito in the Cabin (Myra Stilborn)
Although you bash her
Til 26

Mosquitoes (J.E. Pacheco, Mexico, trans. A. Reid)
They are born in the swamps of sleeplessness
Stuf II 64

MOTHERS

Always Right Always Wrong (Leonard Clark)
Why, O why, does mother chatter and chatter
Cla C 27

Amanda! (Robin Klein)
Don't bite your nails, Amanda!
Ox T 56

Disobedience (A. A. Milne)
James James/Morrison Morrison
Fun 110; Mil VY 30; Nine 90; Ox T 62

Fanfare (U.A. Fanthorpe)
You, in the old photographs, are always
Fan 36

from *The Forsaken* (Duncan Campbell Scott)
Once in the winter
Can 62

Happy Birthday from Bennigans, (Julie O'Callaghan)
Why did you do it, Mother?
O'Ca 17; Occ 80

I Love me Mudder . . . (Benjamin Zephaniah)
I love me mudder and me mudder love me
Blac 17; Life 18

The Irreplaceable Mum (Brian Patten)
If you were a crack in a mirror
Pat T 86

The Kite (Alexander Blok, trans. F. Cornford and E. P. Salamon)
Over the empty fields a black kite hovers
PW 128

Mother to Son (Langston Hughes)
Well, son, I'll tell you
Ox A 247

Mothering Sunday (George Hare Leonard)
It is the day of all the year
Sun 130; WAS 34

The Mother's Song (Eskimo, trans. Peter Freuchen)
It is so still in the house
Ox CP 31

Mum (Mike Rosen)
When Mum was dying
Ros F 68

Mum'll be Coming Home Today (Michael Rosen)
Mum'll be coming home today
Ros M 73; Ros W 36

My Mother (Ted Hughes)
All mothers can serve up a bit of buttered toast
Hug F 53

Our Mother (Allan Ahlberg)
Our mother is a detective
Mad 23

Rock my Baby (Jean Goulbourne)
Sittin/upon the stool
FS 90

Sang (Robert McLellan)
There's a red lowe in yer cheek
Scot 26

Swinging (Gillian Clarke)
At the end of the hot day it rains
Five 70

To My Mother (George Barker)
Most near, most dear, most loved and most far
Flock 63; Six 17

Together (Carolyn Mamchur)
Lying in bed/Next to my mother
Til 66

A War Film (Teresa Hooley)
I saw/With a catch of the breath
PW 128

Wha Me Mudder Do (Grace Nichols)
Mek me tell you wah me Mudder do
Blac 34; Nic 14; Pro III 61

MOTORBIKES

Fifteen (William Stafford)
South of the bridge on Seventeenth
Face 42

A Motorbike (Ted Hughes)
We had a motorbike all through the war
Gang 16

Oh, Brother! (Max Fatchen)
My brother's a motorbike freak
Fat W 36

MOTOR CARS

See also Accidents: transport

Autobahnmotorwayautoroute
(Adrian Mitchell)
Around the gleaming map of Europe
Cam I 125; Rat 52

Car Breakers (Marian Lines)
There's a graveyard in our street
Pos 34; Tick 25

The Car Trip (Michael Rosen)
Mum says:/'Right, you two . . .'
PG 54; Ros H 20

Uncle Joe's Jalopy (Kit Wright)
When you're riding in my Uncle Joe's jalopy
DS 50: WriR 46

Southbound on the Freeway (May Swenson)
A tourist came in from Orbitville
Pro I 61

Who They Are (Charlotte Harvey)
Wife and husband,/brother and sister
CCC 124

Why Did they Knock Down the Trees, Daddy? (Colin Thiele)
It's a question of standards, boy
Rab 18

Windshield Wipers (Dennis Lee)
Windshield wipers/Wipe away the rain
Can 78

MOUNTAIN LIONS

Mountain Lion (D. H. Lawrence)
Climbing through the January snow
Fire 40; Mes 119; Pro III 84; Rat 297

MOUNTAINEERING

See Cham 77-83

Breathless (written at 21,200 feet) (Wilfred Noyce)
Heartaches/Lungs pant
KWP 159

from *Burning: John Muir on Mt Ritter* (Gary Snyder)
After scanning its face again and again
Floc 140

De Gustibus (St. J. E. C. Hankin)
I am an unadventurous man
Cham 80

Everest Climbed: The Icefall (Ian Seraillier)
It was April when they came to the Icefall
Puf Q 183

Everest Climbed: The Summit (Ian Seraillier)
Their steps were weary, keen was the wind
Open 6

A Prayer for Everest (Wilfred Noyce)
That I may endure
Cham 79

MOVEMENTS

from *Movements* (Norman MacCaig)
Lark drives invisible pitons in the air
Touch IV 11

MOVING HOUSE

How You Move House (Alan Brownjohn)
Your mum or dad brings a huge box
TG 36

MOWING

Mowing (Robert Frost)
There was never a sound beside the wood but one
Choice 277

MUD

Mandy Likes the Mud (Gareth Owen)
Polly likes to play with toys
Name 57; Owe C 69

Mud (John Smith)
I like mud
Nine 58; Tick 83

Mud (Polly Chase Boyden)
Mud is very nice to feel
Fun 78; Read 13; Walk 28

The Muddy Puddle (Dennis Lee)
I am sitting/In the middle
Gold 78; PG 67; Til 14; Walk 28

MUMPS

Feeling Great! (Robert Sparrow)
I've been waiting for today
Mea 20

Mumps (Nicola Jane Field, aged 9)
I'm down in the dumps
Mea 23

Sickness Does Come on Horseback (John Agard)
Yesterday I was jumping
Mea 21

MURDER

Angel Boley (Stevie Smith)
There was a wicked woman called Malady Festing
Nar 15

The Ballad of Charlotte Dymond (Charles Causley)
It was a Sunday evening
Pro III 4; Voi II 112

The Bread-Knife Ballad (Robert Service)
A little child was sitting
OTR 88

Childe Maurice (trad.)
Childe Maurice hunted the Silver Wood
Ox SP 141

The Cruel Mother (anon.)
She sat down below a thorn
Ten 122

The Dorking Thigh (William Plomer)
About to marry and invest
Story 78

The Fair (Vernon Scannell)
Music and yellow steam, the fizz
Cam II 19

The Inquest (W. H. Davies)
I took my oath I would inquire
Rat 213; Story 62

Notting Hill Polka (W. Bridges-Adam)
We've – had – A Body in the house
Ax 43; King 192; Story 141

The Sorrowful Lamentation . . . of John Lomas (anon.)
Good people all I pray attend
Voi II 118

MUSHROOMS

Mushrooms (Sylvia Plath)
Overnight, very
Cam I 59; Fav 135; Fire 12; Foot 58; Gold 104; Rat 299; Voi II 52

Phew or Into the Frying-pan of Eternity (Roger McGough)
On the floor of the universe
McG S 38; Spa 84

Picking Mushrooms (Boris Pasternak)
Road and milestones
Pic 19

MUSIC

See Banjos, Bugles, Drums, Guitars, Singing, Trumpets

Charlie Strong (F. Knowles and B. Thompson)
Charlie Strong had a favourite song
DS 36

The Choirmaster's Burial (Thomas Hardy)
He often would ask us
Voi II 154; WAS 120

Embrionic Megastars (Brian Patten)
We can play reggae music, funk and skiffle too
King 162; Name 82; Pat 31

Heaven's in the Basement (Miles Davis Landesman)
Heaven's in the basement
Life 19

I Wish I Were a Crochet (Roger McGough)
I'd sing and dance and play
McG G 22

Interruption at the Opera House (Brian Patten)
At the very beginning of an important symphony
Nar 41

Lewis has a Trumpet (Karla Kuskin)
A trumpet/A trumpet
Name 52

Man the Musicmaker (Roger McGough)
In the beginning was the word
McG P 54

The Money Came in, Came in (Charles Causley)
My son Sam was a banjo man
Cau E 55

Musical Chairs (John Mole)
Father, weighty as a minim
Mol 40

A Musical Family (John Mole)
I can play the piano
Mol 39

Music Makers (Grace Ebon)
My Auntie plays the piccolo
Howl 116; Mad 27

Narnian Suite (C. S. Lewis)
March for Strings, Kettledrums and 63 Dwarfs
MT 97
March for Drum, Trumpet and 21 Giants
MT 97

Orpheus with his Lute (John Fletcher?)
Orpheus with his lute made trees
Fab CV 36

Ourchestra (Shel Silverstein)
So you haven't got a drum, just beat your belly
Sil 23

Russian Dance (Ogden Nash)
The Russian moujik is made for music
World 36

Tout Ensemble (Colin West)
Paula pounds the grand piano
West 25

Way Down in the Music (Eloise Greenfield)
I get way down in the music
Black 84

MYSTERY (L AND D)

At the Keyhole (Walter de la Mare)
'Grill me some bones,' said the Cobbler
de la M P 89; Ox PC 88; Shad 69

The Door (Miroslav Holub, trans. I. Milner & G. Theiner)
Go and open the door
Ten 13

The Lurkers (Adrian Henri)
On our Estate/When it's getting late
Hen 16

Mystery (ancient Irish, trans. Douglas Hyde)
I am the wind which breathes upon the sea
Irish 17; Sun 22

Mystery (John Kitching)
Was it really?
ATP 50

The Mystery (Ralph Hodgson)
He came and took me by the hand
Like 34

The Rainflower (Richard Edwards)
Down in the forest where light never falls
Edw P 22; Rab 20

The Riddle (Louis MacNeice)
What is that goes round and round the house?
Gho 20

The Way Through the Woods (Rudyard Kipling)
They shut the road through the woods
Fab CV 377; Gold 62; Like 96; MT 110; ND 18; NTP 183; Ox CV 323; Shad 82; Show I 5; Ten 37; This W 163; Ting 8

Who's That? (James Kirkup)
Who's that/stopping at
Gho 14

MYSTERY (N)

The Ballad of Longwood Glen
(Vladimir Nabokov)
That Sunday morning at half-past
ten
Wind 44

The Combat (Edwin Muir)
It was not meant for human eyes
Show I 2

Flannan Isle (Wilfrid W. Gibson)
Though three men dwell on Flannan
Isle
Cam I 64; Nar 104; Ox PC 78; Ten 77

The Huntsman (Edward
Lowbury)
Kagwa hunted the lion
*King 65; Nar 36; Ox SP 140; Story 54;
Ten 152*

In the Bathroom (Roy Fuller)
What is that blood-stained thing
Gold 95

The Listeners (Walter de la Mare)
'Is there anybody there?' said the
Traveller
*Fav 66; Gold 84; Like 176; MT 19; ND
209; NTP 182; Open 106; Ox SP 9;
Show I 8; Story 74; Ten 38; This W 147*

Lollocks (Robert Graves)
By sloth on sorrow fathered
Choice 262; Floc 196; Rat 249

The Mistletoe Bough (Thomas
Haynes Bayley)
The mistletoe hung in the castle hall
KCP 31; Stoc 124; Story 86

Prince Kano (Edward Lowbury)
In a dark wood Prince Kano lost his
way
Gho 35; MCF 15; Story 2

The Terrible Path (Brian Patten)
While playing at the woodland's
edge
Ox T 124; Pat 72; YD 81

The Trap (Jon Stallworthy)
The first night that the monster
lurched
MT 151; ND 210; Voi III 142

Welsh Incident (Robert Graves)
But that was nothing to what things
came out
*Chat 391; MCF 30; ND 212; Story 92;
Voi II 11; Wind 32*

What has Happened to Lulu?
(Charles Causley)
What has happened to Lulu,
Mother?
*All 17; Cau F 16; Fav 35; Foc 127;
Gold 49; KCP 47; Ox SP 13; Strick 34;
Wind 43*

MYTHOLOGICAL CREATURES

The Centaurs (James Stephens)
Playing upon the hill three centaurs
were!
AM 81

Minotaur (Robert Fisher)
in the middle of the sea lies an island
AM 85

NAMES

An ABC of Shopshire Field Names
(Michael Richards)
Ant Trump Piece
WP 24

from *Adam's Apple* (John Fuller)
All creation's got to have a name
Quin 92

Boys' Names (Eleanor Farjeon)
What splendid names for boys
there are!
Far R 73

Choosing a Name (Charles and
Mary Lamb)
I have got a new-born sister
Name 19

Choosing their Names (Thomas
Hood)
Our old cat has kittens three
All 24; NV 84; Pets 13

The Christening (A. A. Milne)
What shall I call
Like 98; Mil VY 5; Young 28

Girls' Names (Eleanor Farjeon)
What lovely names for girls there
are!
Far R 73

istri (Trevor Millum)
I like istri/Think I know why
Mill 28

My Baby Has No Name Yet (Kin-
Nam-Jo, trans. Ko Won)
My baby has no name yet
Face 17

My Name is . . . (Pauline Clarke)
My name is Sluggery-wuggery
FF 71; Like 33; Pop 8; Walk 118

Picnic (Hugh Lofting)
Ella, fell a/Maple tree
*Fun 112; Name 27; Ox T 20; Pic 93;
P Sev 50*

Sweet Herbs (Eleanor Farjeon)
What shall I plant in my little herb
border/
Far M 51

Sweet Maiden of Passamaquoddy
(James de Mille)
Sweet maiden of Passamaquoddy
Can 31

Too Many Daves (Dr Seuss
[Theodore Geisel])
Did I ever tell you that Mrs McCave
Ox A 254; Spi 40

NAPOLEON

Napoleon (Miroslav Holub)
Children, when was/Napoleon
Bonaparte born
Brave 96; Speak 26

Napoleon (Walter de la Mare)
What is the world, O soldiers?
Fab CV 147; Rat 307

A St Helena Lullaby (Rudyard
Kipling)
How far is St Helena from a little
child at play?
Fab CV 147

THE NATIVITY (L AND D)

All in Tune to William's Flute
(anon.)
All in tune to William's flute
Sun 99

The Angels for the Nativity
(William Drummond)
Run, shepherds, run where Bethlem
blest appears
Sun 94

Angels' Song (Charles Causley)
Fear not, shepherds, for I bring
Ox CP 39

The Barn (Elizabeth Coatsworth)
'I am tired of this barn,' said the colt
GTP 228; Ox CP 37; Stoc 106

BC: AD (U.A. Fanthorpe)
This was the moment when Before
Fan 66; Ox CP 29

A Carol for Christmas Eve (Eleanor
Farjeon)
We come to your doorstep
Far R 146

Carol of the Field Mice (Kenneth
Grahame)
Villagers all, this frosty tide
Star 24

Christmas Star (Boris Pasternak)
It was winter
Floc 282

The Friendly Beasts (anon.)
Jesus our brother, kind and good
Chris 9

Hail the King of Glory (Christina
Rossetti)
Before the paling of the stars
Ring 19

How Far to Bethlehem? (Frances
Chesterton)
How far is it to Bethlehem?
Star 34

In Freezing Winter Night (Robert
Southwell)
Behold, a silly tender babe
Floc 281; GTP 287

Legend of the Raven (Charles
Causley)
Raven, hill-scavenging, was first to
see
Cau V 40

Mice in the Hay (Leslie Norris)
out of the lamplight
CCC 219

New Prince, New Pomp (Robert
Southwell)
Behold a silly tender babe
This W 94

O Jesu Parvule (Hugh
MacDiarmid)
His mither sings to the bairnie Christ
Scot 6

An Ode on the Birth of our Saviour
(Robert Herrick)
In numbers, and but these few
Star 37

On the Morning of Christ's Nativity
(John Milton)
But peaceful was the night
Fab CV 355

A Peculiar Christmas (Roy Fuller)
Snow? Absolutely not
Gold 41

Song for a Winter Birth (Vernon
Scannell)
Under the watchful lights
Sun 104

Stable Song (Judith Nicholls)
She lies, a stillness in the crumpled
straw
Nic M 39

THE NATIVITY (N)

In the Town (anon.)
Joseph: Take heart, the journey's
ended
Ox CP 22

Nativity Play Plan (James Berry)
Sistas and broddas and everybody
Ber 102

Never Again (Harri Webb)
You never saw such a stupid mess
Ax 92

Our Nativity Play (Eric Finney)
It went pretty well, our Nativity play
Stoc 56

The Starry Night (John Masefield)
That starry night when Christ was
born
Sun 96

St Joseph and God's Mother
(Spanish, trans. E. C. Batho)
St Joseph and God's Mother
Sun 92

NEIGHBOURS

Mending Wall (Robert Frost)
Something there is that does not love
a wall
Choice 278; Fire 105; Touch V 154

The People Upstairs (Ogden Nash)
The people upstairs all practice
ballet
*KWP 150, Nas C 105; Walk 93; WP
117*

NELSON

See also Trafalgar

from *Nationality in Drinks*
(Robert Browning)
Here's to Nelson's memory!
Sea 140

What a Life! (Raymond Barnett,
aged 9)
What a life!
Brave 140

1805 (Robert Graves)
At Viscount Nelson's lavish funeral
Brave 140; Fab CV 146

NETTLES

Nettles (Vernon Scannell)
My son aged three fell in the nettle
bed
Quin 147; Ten 36

Tall Nettles (Edward Thomas)
Tall nettles cover up, as they have
done
*Choice 169; Fire 11; Iron 43; Out 44;
PG 13; Ten 35*

NEW YEAR

Dragon Dance (Max Fatchen)
A Chinese dragon's in the street
Cele 10

Good Riddance But Now What?
(Ogden Nash)
Come children, gather round my
knee
Occ 23

My New Year's Resolutions (Robert
Fisher)
I will not throw the cat out the
window
ATP 82; Cele 9

The New Year (Edward Thomas)
He was the one man I met up in
the woods
Occ 24

New Year Exhilaration (Ted
Hughes)
On the third day
Hug MT 10

New Year Song (Ted Hughes)
Now there comes
Ox CP 146; Sun 108

Ring Out Wild Bells (Alfred Lord
Tennyson)
Ring out, wild bells, to the wild sky
Cal 121; Fav 106; Ring 49

NEWTS

NIGHT: INDOORS

NIGHT: OUT OF DOORS

NIGHTINGALES

NIGHTMARES

NOAH

Captain Noah and his Floating Zoo
(Michael Flanders)
The Lord looked down on the earth
and it made him sad
Ark 25; 92, 103, 113

The History of the Flood (John
Heath-Stubbs)
Bang Bang Bang/Said the nails in
the Ark
Floc 38: NTP 80; Sun 51

Japheth's Notes: a Fragment
(Judith Nicholls)
Blue wash/drifting to grey
Nic M 37

Measles in the Ark (Susan
Coolidge)
The night it was horribly dark
Ox CV 282

Noah (Miracle Play)
I, God, that all the world hath
wrought
Ark 19, 91, 102

Noah (James Reeves)
Noah was an Admiral
Ox T 79; Ree C 162; Ree 'N'; YD 42

Noah (Roy Daniells)
They gathered around and told him
not to do it
Ark 31; Can 45; Mes 195

Noah and the Rabbit (Hugh
Chesterman)
'No land' said Noah
Ark 34; Earth 15

Noah's Ark (Mark Burgess)
One stormy night when all was dark
Bur 32

Noah's Ark (Roger McGough)
It began/When God popped His
head
Ox SP 131; YD 91

Noah's Journey (George MacBeth)
oak/is the keel. He is aged and
PoWo I 15

from The Legends of Evil (Rudyard
Kipling)
'Twas when the rain fell steady an'
the Ark was pitched an' ready
Ark 32; Sea 121

The Unicorn (Shel Silverstein)
A long time ago when the earth was
green
Sil 76

*When the Animals were Let Out of
the Ark* (anon., 14th cent.)
There was scurrying and scrimmage
Ark 116

NOISES

Cries of London (Wes Magee)
the busker and his echo in the
subway
Show I 82

Ears Hear (Lucia and James L.
Hymes, Jr)
Flies buzz/Motors roar
Read 84

In the Kitchen (John Cotton)
In the Kitchen
Crys 11; WP 61

Noise (James Parker)
Billy is blowing his trumpet
Howl 15; Tick 73; Tim 10

Noise (J. Pope)
I like noise.
DS 38; Pro I 56

Pleasant Sounds (John Clare)
The rustling of leaves under the feet
in woods
Like 89; NTP 247; Rhy 46

The Sound Collector (Roger
McGough)
A stranger called this morning
McG PT 44

Whisper Whisper (Kit Wright)
Whisper whisper
Wri R 9

NONSENSE

See Cow, Edw Ph, McG M
throughout

Aerobics (Richard Edwards)
Bend and stretch / Stretch and bend
Edw M 31

The African Lion (A. E.
Housman)
To meet a bad lad on the African
waste
Chat 335

At the Sign of the Prancing Pony
(J. R. R. Tolkien)
There is an inn, a merry old inn
Like 16

Brian O'Linn or *Tam o' the Linn* (anon.)
Brian O'Linn had no breeches to wear
Chat 364
Brian O'Linn was a gentleman born
Rat 85
Tam o' the linn cam up the gait
Fab CV 280; Kist 1
Tommy O'Linn was a Scotsman born
Ox NR 202
Tommy o'Lin, and his wife and wife's mother
Ox Dix 413; Puf NR 102

The Centipede's Song (Roald Dahl)
I've eaten many strange and scrumptious dishes
Like 59

The Chickamungus (James Reeves)
All in the groves of dragon-fungus
GTP 222; Ree C 130

The Contrary Waiter (Edgar Parker)
A tarsier worked as a waiter
OWN 26

Eletelephony (Laura Richards)
Once there was an elephant
CBC 36; CCV 80; Fab NV 56; Howl 52; Once 142; Ox A 165; Ox CV 289; Pop 108; PoWo I 59; P Sev 145; Pud 101; RMP 17; Walk 192; WZ 64; Young 22

Frank Carew MacGraw (Terry Jones)
The name of Frank Carew MacGraw
Jon 22; King 56

It's Dark in Here (Shel Silverstein)
I am writing these lines
HH 85; PoWo I 9; Sil 21

It Was a Stormy Night (Michael Rosen)
It was a stormy night
Corn 70

I've Had this Shirt (Michael Rosen)
Like 99

Jim Jay (Walter de la Mare)
Do diddle di do / Poor Jim Jay
Chat 354

The Land of the Bumbley Boo (Spike Milligan)
In the land of the Bumbley Boo
OSF 30

Mr Kartoffel (James Reeves)
Mr Kartoffel's a whimsical man
FF 22; OWN 64; Ree C 31

O Such Silliness (William Cole)
O such silliness
Corn 84; OSF 11

On the Ning Nang Nong (Spike Milligan)
On the Ning Nang Nong
CCV 22; Howl 51; Like 10; Nine 168; Noisy 4; OWN 69; RT 30; Walk 171

Phoot Signs (Richard Edwards)
If you find a beech leaf balanced on a stinkhorn
Edw Ph 29

Phoot Superstitions (Richard Edwards)
For Phoots it is unlucky
Edw Ph 43

Sally Simplin's Lament (Thomas Hood)
He left his body to the sea
Chat 209

There Was an Old Woman (Charles Causley)
. . . of Chester-le-Street
S Sun 74

The Towers of Phoots (Richard Edwards)
The Towers of Phoots, or Phoot-Towers
Edw Ph 25

Uncle Ted's Tea (Richard Edwards)
The table was laid and ready
Edw P 26

NONSENSE: EDWARD LEAR

See also Lea B, Lea C throughout

The Akond of Swat (Edward Lear)
Who or why, or which, or what
CBC 72; Chat 261; FAB CV 121; GTP 226; Lea C 257

Chalico Pie (Edward Lear)
Calico Pie
Cow 26; Fab CV 85; Fab NV 88; GTP 225; Lea C 78; NTP 219; Ox Pc 12; RMP 26

The Courtship of the Yonghy-Bonghy-Bo (Edward Lear)
On the coast of Coromandel
GTP 213; Lea B 180; Lea C 237

The Dong with a Luminous Nose (Edward Lear)
When awful darkness and silence reign
AM 34; Chat 255; KWP 122; Lea B 170; Lea C 225; Mons 54; Ten 96

The Duck and the Kangaroo (Edward Lear)
Said the Duck to the Kangaroo
Fun 84; Lea B 70; Lea C 64; Ox CV 186

Incidents in the Life of My Uncle Arly (Edward Lear)
O my aged Uncle Arly
CBC 38; Chat 263; Lea B 185; Lea C 275

The Jumblies (Edward Lear)
They went to Sea in a Sieve, they did
Chat 247; Fab NV 248; Fun 100; KCP 114; Lea B 167; Lea C 71; Nine 74; Ox CV 187; Ox PC 54; Pop 51; Pos 40; Puf V 77

Mr and Mrs Spikky Sparrow (Edward Lear)
On a little piece of wood
Lea C 81; Ox CV 190

The New Vestments (Edward Lear)
There lived an old man in the kingdom of Tess
CCV 20; Ten 164

The Owl and the Pussy-Cat (Edward Lear)
The Owl and the Pussy-Cat went to see
CBC 83; Chat 243; Cow 8; Fab CV 87; Fab NV 250; Fav 56; GTP 224; Lea B 65; Lea C 61; Like 11; NIP 223; Ox CV 185; Ox PC 117; OX SP 112; OX T 98; Pos 36; P Sev 76; Puf V 167; RMP 12; Talk 54; Walk 175

The Pellican Chorus (Edward Lear)
King and Queen of the Pelicans we
Ox SP 137

The Pobble Who Has No Toes (Edward Lear)
The Pobble who has no Toes
AM 56; Chat 258; Fab CV 91; Fab NV 153; GIP 212; Lea B 97; Lea C 242; Mons 26; Nine 154; Ox CV 198; Ox PC 16; Ox T 82; Pos 37; Puf V 80

The Quangle Wangle's Hat (Edward Lear)
On the top of the Crumpetty Tree
AM 69; Chat 259; Cow 66; Fab NV 59; Once 126; Ox T 84

The Scroobious Pip (Edward Lear)
The Scroobious Pip went out one day
Chat 267

The Table and the Chair (Edward Lear)
Said the Table to the Chair
Fab NV 235; GTP 215

NONSENSE: LEWIS CARROLL

Beautiful Soup! (Lewis Carroll)
Beautiful Soup, so rich and green
Nine 106; Ox PC 12; Pac 31; Walk 145

How Doth the Little Crocodile (Lewis Carroll)
How doth the little crocodile
Fab CV 89; GTP 70; Ox PC 116; Rat 194; Ten 52

Humpty Dumpty's Song (Lewis Carroll)
In winter when the fields are white
Chat 290; Fab NV 130; GTP 209; Mes 207; Ox PC 14; Ox SP 110; Puf V 75; Talk 52; Ten 141

The Hunting of the Snark (Lewis Carroll)
'Just the place for a Snark!' the Bellman cried
Chat 295
(part) There was one who was famed for the number of things
Fab NV 209

Jabberwocky (Lewis Carroll)
'Twas brillig and the slithy toves
AM 44; Chat 286; GTP 208; KWP 48; Like 51; Mons 19; MT 124; ND 191; Ox SP 10; Pos 39; Rat 219; Show I 43; Story 150; Talk 53; Ten 92; Walk 170

The Knight's Song (Lewis Carroll)
I'll tell thee everything I can
Chat 292; Fab NV 142; GTP 210

The Lobster Quadrille (Lewis Carroll)
'Will you walk a little faster?' said a whiting to a snail
CBC 130; Chat 284; Ten 62

The Mad Gardener's Song (Lewis Carroll)
He thought he saw an elephant
Chat 315; Fab NV 144; King 196; Once 140; Puf V 169; Rat 256

They Told Me You Had Been to Her (Lewis Carroll)
They told me you had been to her
Chat 282; Ten 143

'Tis the Voice of the Lobster (Lewis Carroll)
'Tis the voice of the lobster
Chat 285; Fab NV 146

The Walrus and the Carpenter (Lewis Carroll)
The sun was shining on the sea
CBC 56; Chat 287; Fab NV 245; Ox PC 125; Ox SP 34; Ox T 110; Ten 63

The White Knight's Song (Lewis Carroll)
I'll tell thee everything I can
Fab CV 277; Ten 111

You Are Old, Father William (Lewis Carroll)
'You are old, Father William,' the young man said
CBC 142; Chat 281; FF 62; GTP 106; Iron 62; ND 150; Ox CV 239; P Sev 42; RMP 34; Ten 26; Walk 182

NONSENSE: TED HUGHES

See also Hug F throughout

Folks (Ted Hughes)
I've heard so much about other folks' folks
Hug F 11

My Aunt (Ted Hughes)
You've heard how a green thumb
Hug F 37

My Brother Bert (Ted Hughes)
Pets are the Hobby of my Brother Bert
Ani 52; BBGG 27; FF 10; Hug F 33; Walk 158

My Father (Ted Hughes)
Some fathers work at the office, others work at the store
Ten 114

My Grandpa (Ted Hughes)
The truth of the matter, the truth of the matter
Hug F 21

My Sister Jane (Ted Hughes)
And I say nothing – not a word
All 18; CCV 12; Fav 44; Floc 95; Hug F 13; Once 70

NOVEMBER

No! (Thomas Hood)
No sun – no moon!
Cal 112; CBC 24; GTP 280; Ox PC 99; Poem I 43

November (Elizabeth Coatsworth)
November comes
Tick 118

November (John Clare)
The shepherds almost wonder where they dwell
GTP 282

NUCLEAR POWER

The Experts (Terry Jones)
Give three cheers for experts
Jon 92

Windscale (Norman Nicholson)
The toadstool towers infest the shore
Earth 50; Show III 13

NUCLEAR WAR

See also Hiroshima

The Children's Fall-Out Shelter (Brian Patten)
Deep in their underground shelter
Pat 23

Requirements in the Shelter (Adrian Mitchell)
Clothing . . . . . . Shrouds
Ax 86

The Responsibility (Peter Appleton)
I am the man who gives the word
Cam I 115; Touch IV 183

They Dared Him (Kevin Myhill)
Tommy has dropped his Atom Bomb
PW 145

The War Game (Gavin Ewart)
Watching rugger, you see the bodies piling up
Show II 74

Your Attention Please (Peter Porter)
The Polar DEW has just warned that
Foc 37; PW 168; Touch V 90

NUMBERS

Child Margaret (Carl Sandburg)
The Child Margaret begins to write
numbers
Floc 74

OBSTINACY

Get Up and Bar the Door (anon.)
It fell about the Martinmas time
Nar 23; Ox PC 19

Get Up and Shut the Door (Ian
Serraillier)
It happened one December night
KCP 176

OCCUPATIONS

See also Bakers, Barbers,
Blacksmiths, Burglars, Butchers,
Chimney sweeps, Clowns,
Cowboys, Dentists, Dowsers,
Drovers, Dustbin men, Engine
drivers, Engineers, Farmers,
Farm workers, Ferrymen,
Fishermen, Fishmongers,
Gardeners, Gipsies,
Highwaymen, Lavatory
attendants, Liftmen, Milkmen,
Millers, Miners, Painters,
Pedlars, Pipers, Poachers,
Riveters, Sailors, Salesmen,
Smugglers, Thieves, Tramps,
Wagon drivers, Watchmen,
Woodmen

Hay for the Horses (Gary Snyder)
He had driven half the night
Foc 147; Voi III 15

What My Lady Did (Roger
McGough)
I asked my lady what she did
WS 12

OCTOBER

Poem in October (Dylan Thomas)
It was my thirtieth year to heaven
Rat 347

OGRES

Song of the Ogres (W. H. Auden)
Little fellow, you're amusing
Walk 205

OLD AGE

Good (R. S. Thomas)
The old man comes out on the hill
Foc 129

In Oak Terrace (Tony Connor)
Old and alone, she sits at nights
Ax 26; Touch V 192

Lore (R. S. Thomas)
Job Davies, eighty-five
Choice 311; Rat 253

Love Songs in Age (Philip Larkin)
She kept her songs, they took so little
space
Foc 96; Touch V 193

Note for the Future (Jim Burns)
When I get old / don't dress me in
Speak 119; Strict 70

Old Age Report (Adrian Mitchell)
When a man's too old or ill to work
Ax 24

The Old Man (Leonard Clark)
He sits there all day
Cla C 44

The Old Man at the Window
(Anthony Harvey, aged 8)
Oh how black the night is
Mes 235

The Old Man's Comforts (Robert
Southey)
'You are old, Father William,' the
young man cried
Ox CV 93

Old People (Elizabeth Jennings)
Why are people impatient when they
are old?
Quin 119

Old Woman (Iain Crichton
Smith)
'The Old Age Pensioners,' she said
Ang II 23
And she, being old, fed from a
mashed plate
Scot 112

Transitional Object (U. A.
Fanthorpe)
Sits, holding nurse's hard reassuring
hand
Crys 43

Warning (Jenny Joseph)
When I am an old woman I shall
wear purple
Face 138; Moon 120; Open 54

Yew Tree Guest House (Phoebe Hesketh)
In guest-house lounges
Six 149

OLD AND YOUNG

My Gramp (Derek Stuart)
My gramp has got a medal
Gold 54

When I Was Your Age (Michael Frayn)
When I was your age, child
Sort 14; Ten 16

ONE-PARENT FAMILIES

One Parent Family (Moira Andrew)
My mum says she's clueless
SS 10

OPTIMISTS

Say Not the Struggle Naught Availeth (Arthur Hugh Clough)
Say not the struggle naught availeth
ND 231

OTTERBOURNE

The Battle of Otterbourne (anon.)
It fell upon the Lammas tide
Fab CV 232

OTTERS

An Otter (Ted Hughes)
Underwater eyes, an eel's
Talk 65; Zoo 31

OVER-FED AND UNDER-FED

The Banquet (Vernon Scannell)

Two hundred guests have come to see who wins
Sca 58

The Commission (Roger McGough)
In this poem there is a table
McG G 36

Mrs Middleditch (William Plomer)
Fitting a thin glove
Foc 160

Punishment Diet (Vernon Scannell)
'A solitary cell for you'
Sca 60

Third World Hunger (Vernon Scannell)
Two thousand years ago Christ fed
Sca 62

OWLS

The Bird of Night (Randall Jarrell)
A shadow is floating through the moonlight
Open 70; PoWo II 75; Voi III 136

The Cat-Eyed Owl (Edward Kamau Braithwaite)
The cat-eyed owl, although so fierce
Blac 51; Stuf 48

Elegy on the Death of Juliet's Owl (Maurice Baring)
Juliet has lost her little downy owl
CCC 170

The Owl (Edward Thomas)
Downhill I came, hungry and yet not starved
Iron 70; Rat 330

Owl (Barbara Juster Esbensen)
What a moonstruck / word OWL
Esb 22

The Owl (Alfred Lord Tennyson)
When cats run home and light is come
Choice 87; Fab CV 87; Fab NV 23; GTP 65; NV 81; Ox PC 65; Ten 46; This W 31

The Owl and the Pussycat (Edward Lear)
(*See* Nonsense: Edward Lear)

The Owl Looked out of the Ivy Bush (Charles Causley)
The Owl looked out of the ivy bush
Cau E 19

126

Owl of the Greenwood (Patricia Hubbell)
Owl / Who? / Who are you?
Ox T 103; Poem I 122

The Owls (John Mole)
The owls take a broad view
Mol 24

Owls (Leonard Clark)
They stare at you
Six 112

Sweet Suffolk Owl (Thomas Vautor)
Sweet Suffolk owl, so trimly dight
Rat 413

Town Owl (Laurie Lee)
On eves of cold when slow coal fires
Ang I 73; ND 65; Touch IV 200

OXEN

Black Harry's Team (A. B. Paterson)
No soft-skinned Durham steers are they
Pat A 50

The Herd Boy's Song (Chen Shan-Shih)
Splashing water
Stuf 82

The Oxen (Thomas Hardy)
Christmas Eve and twelve of the clock
Chris 92; NTP 111; Ox CP 36; Rat 331; WAS 159; Wind 10

The Ox-Tamer (Walt Whitman)
In a far-away northern county
Rat 332; Voi II 47

The Peasant's Address to his Ox: Egyptian Peasant's Song 1400 B.C. (Bertolt Brecht)
O Ox our goodly puller of the plough
Stuf 49

PAINTERS

The Painter (Mick Gowar)
She has a hidden eye
Gow F 71; SS 17; WS 11

PAINTING

See also Colours

Crayoning (Stanley Cook)
The sheet of paper is white
AVF 14

First Art Lesson (James Kirkup)
My new paintbox's shining black lacquer lid
SO 22

Now You See It (Richard Edwards)
I found a pot of paint
Edw M 34

The Paint Box (E. V. Rieu)
'Cobalt and umber and ultramarine...'
MT 9; Ox T 4; PG 17; Puf Q 106

Painting the Gate (May Swenson)
I painted the mailbox. That was fun
Occ 152; Stuf 31

There's More Than One Way (Trevor Millum)
I'm no good at Art
Mill 31

Uncle and Auntie (John Hegley)
My auntie gives me a colouring book and crayons
King 148

PAINTING: POEMS ABOUT PICTURES

The Boyhood of Raleigh (Roger McGough)
Entranced, he listens to salty tales
McG F 33

The Bystander (Rosemary Dobson)
I am the one who looks the other way
Mes 29

Don't Let that Horse (Lawrence Ferlinghetti)
Don't let that horse / eat that violin
Chat 442; Rat 134

Fall of Icarus: Brueghel (Joseph Langland)
Flashing through falling sunlight
Touch V 203

Landscape with the Fall of Icarus (William Carlos Williams)
According to Brueghel
Touch V 204

Musée des Beaux Arts
(W. H. Auden)
About suffering they were never
wrong
(Fall of Icarus)
Fire 42; Touch V 202; Voi III 135

Not My Best Side (U. A.
Fanthorpe)
Not my best side; I'm afraid
(Uccello, St George and the
Dragon)
Fan 28

Paint (Walter de la Mare)
A dumpy plain-faced child stands
gazing there
(Velasquez, The Infanta)
Face 89

*Samuel Palmer's Coming from
Evening Church* (Charles
Causley)
The heaven-reflecting usual moon
Cau V 36; NTP 233

Sheep Meadow (Samuel Menashe)
French spoken / across the snow
Mes 28

PAINTING: POEMS FOR
PICTURE-MAKING

from *Goblin Market* (Christina
Rossetti)
Evening by evening
Puf M 217

Good Taste (Christopher Logue)
Travelling, a man met a tiger, so
O & A 137; Ox SP 109

Hector the Collector (Shel
Silverstein)
Hector the Collector
Gang 32

Quack! (Walter de la Mare)
The duck is whiter than whey is
CCC 76; RT 156

*Stopping by Woods on a Snowy
Evening* (Robert Frost)
Whose woods these are I think I
know
(*See* Snow (N))

PAN

Pan With Us (Robert Frost)
Pan came out of the woods one day
Puf M 227

PANDAS

Bei-Shung (Gerard Benson)
I am Bei-shung, they call me the
white bear
Jung 96

Grandfather, Grandfather (George
Barker)
Grandfather, grandfather
Jung 98

PANTHERS

The Panther (R. M. Rilke, German
trans. J. B. Leishman)
His gaze, going past those bars, has
got so misted
Floc 61

PARABLES

Dives and Lazarus (anon.)
As it fell out upon a day
Sun 163

The Good Samaritan (Langland,
trans. R. Tamplin)
I walked the road, deep in
conversation
Sun 162

The Prodigal Son (Charles
Causley)
I could remember nothing of the
village
Cau V 39

PARENTS

Clarence (Shel Silverstein)
Clarence Lee from Tennessee
Ox A 276

Just Fancy That (Max Fatchen)
'Just fancy that!' my parents say
Mad 34

PARODY

Christmas Bills (Joseph Hatton)
(Original: *The Bells* [Edgar Allen
Poe])
See dear Pater with the bills
Ox CP 136

How Doth the Little Crocodile
(Lewis Carroll)
(Original: *How Doth the Little Busy
Bee, see* Bees)
How doth the Little Crocodile
GTP 70

Lewis Carroll (Eleanor Farjeon)
(Original: *You are old, Father William*,
below)
'You are wise, Mr Dodgson,' the
young child said
Ox CV 331

The Owl and the Astronaut (Gareth
Owen)
(Original: *The Owl and the Pussycat* [E.
Lear])
The owl and the astronaut sailed
through space
Spa 44

Ruinous Rhymes (Max Fatchen)
(Original: *Nursery rhymes*)
Pussycat, pussycat, where have you
been?
Fat W 21

'You are old,' Father William
(Lewis Carroll)
(Original: *see* Old age, *The Old Man's
Comforts*)
'You are old, Father William,' the
young man said
*CBC 142; Chat 281; FF 62; GTP 106;
Iron 62; ND 150; Ox CV 239; P Sev
42; RMP 34; Ten 26; Walk 182*

PARROTS

Galàhs (Gavin Ewart)
The most beautiful grey and pink
parrots
Ewar 55

Gran's Green Parrot (Wes Magee)
It was high summer
Pets 68

Parakeet (Leonard Clark)
They always put a large crimson
sheet
Cla C 41; Mes 112

Parrot (Alan Brownjohn)
Sometimes I sit with both eyes closed
All 31; PG 42; Six 78

The Parrot (Grace Nichols)
I'm a parrot
AFP 70; Five 8; Nic 34; Stuf 38

The Parrot (Edward Lucie-Smith)
The parrot is a thief
Stuf 39

Sergeant Brown's Parrot (Kit
Wright)
Many policemen wear upon their
shoulders
KCP 214; Strict 157; Wri R 35-8

*When George the Fifth was a
Midshipman* (Charles Causley)
When George the Fifth was a
Midshipman
Cau J 29

PARTIES

See Children's parties

PEACE

Peace (Henry Vaughan)
My soul, there is a country
Fav 12; Sun 211

Peace (Walter de la Mare)
Night is o'er England, and the winds
are still
PW 190

The Peace-pipe (Henry W.
Longfellow)
Gitche Manito, the mighty
Like 65

Road of Peace (Paul Robeson)
Build a road of peace before us
Wheel 54

PEDLARS

The Pedlar (Eleanor Farjeon)
There was an old Pedlar
Fab NV 39

The Pedlar's Caravan (W. B.
Rands)
I wish I lived in a caravan
Ox CV 233; Ox PC 145

There Was a Little Woman (anon.)
There was a little woman , as I've
heard tell
*Fab NV 150; GTP 103; Ox Dic 427;
Ox NR 169; Puf NR 142*

PENGUINS (N)

Peter and Percival (E. V. Rieu)
Peter and Percival lived in a place
Puf Q 125

PESSIMISTS

The Pessimist (Ben King)
Nothing to do but work
FF 68; KWP 113; Ox PC 14

PETS

See Pets throughout

See also Beetles, Cats, Dogs, Dormice, Gerbils, Hamsters, Mice

The Barkday Party (James Berry)
For my dog's birthday party
Ber 67

Erica Thirl's Dog (Richard Stilgoe)
My nose is wet and shiny and I never clean my teeth
CCC 163

Mary's Lamb (Sarah Josepha Hale, 1788-1879)
Mary had a little lamb
Ox A 19; Ox CV 166
(part) *Lob 30; Puf NR 95; Ox Dic 299; Ox NR 36*

Mother Doesn't Want a Dog (Judith Viorst)
Mother doesn't want a dog
Walk 133

Mum Won't Let Me Keep a Rabbit (Brian Patten)
Mum won't let me keep a rabbit
Pat 14; Pets 34

My Brother Bert (Ted Hughes)
Pets are the Hobby of my Brother Bert
Ani 52; BBGG 27; FF 10; Hug F 33; Walk 158

One Day at a Perranporth Pet-shop (Charles Causley)
One day at a Perranporth pet-shop
Fun 26; Pets 70; Sort 44

Pet Shop (Louis MacNeice)
Cold blood or warm, crawling or fluttering
Pets 81

Scribbled Notes Picked Up by Owners (James Berry)
Letter is signed – YOUR ONE BABY PERSON
Ber 25

Take One Home for the Kiddies (Philip Larkin)
On shallow straw, in shadeless glass
Earth 74; King 87; Pets 82; Poem I 29; Sort 57

PHEASANTS

Cock Pheasant (Leonard Clark)
Halfway to school a pheasant flew overhead
CCC 106

Pheasant (Sylvia Plath)
You said you would kill it this morning
Rat 342

from *Windsor Forest* (Alexander Pope)
See! from the brake the whirring pheasant springs
Floc 127; GTP 64; O & A 58

PHYSICAL ACTIVITIES

See also Bicycling, Boxing, Dancing, Diving, Football, Games, Mountaineering, Roller Skating, Skating, Skipping, Sliding *see* Snow, Swinging, Trampolining, Tree-climbing

Health Fanatic (John Cooper Clarke)
around the block against the clock
Pro II 60

The High Jump (anon.)
He slowly paced his distance off and turned
Mot 166

Skateboarder (Charles Connell)
I can soar. I can swoop
CCV 30

Somersaults (Jack Prelutsky)
It's fun turning somersaults
S Sun 12

PICNICS

Eating Out of Doors (Vernon Scannell)
I'm really not a picnic person
Sca 16

PIGEONS

Doves (John Clare)
Roaming the little path neath dotterel trees
Cla J 20

Pigeons (Patricia Beer)
Pigeons perch on the Holy Family
CCC 104

Pigeons (Richard Kell)
They paddle with staccato feet
Ang I 70; ND 73; WZ 102

Mrs Peck Pigeon (Eleanor Farjeon)
Mrs Peck Pigeon
Far M 10; Once 32; Pop 122; Rog 32

PIGS

Ode to the Pig: His Tail (Walter R. Brooks)
My tail is not impressive
Walk 64

Poor Jane Higgins (James Reeves)
She had five piggins
Tim 13

The Poor Man's Pig (Edmund Blunden)
Already fallen plum-bloom stars the green
CCC 81

Robert Herrick's Pig (John Heath-Stubbs)
'A runt, a diddler, that is what you are'
CCC 177

View of a Pig (Ted Hughes)
The pig lay on a barrow dead
Floc 229

The Wicked Pig (L. A. G. Strong)
Merciful powers, will ye look at this villain
Sun 28

PIKE

Pike (Ted Hughes)
Pike, three inches long, perfect
Fire 78; ND 60; Touch V 196;
(part) *Zoo 86*

PILATE

Pilate at Fortingall (Edwin Morgan)
A Latin harsh with Aramaicisms
Scot 90

PILGRIMS

'Prologue' from *The Canterbury Tales* (Geoffrey Chaucer)

Whan that Aprill with his shoures soote
Floc 17
(trans. Nevill Coghill)
When the sweet showers of April fall and shoot
Floc 16

The Passionate Man's Pilgrimage (Sir Walter Ralegh)
Give me my scallop-shell of quiet
Rat 334

The Pilgrim (John Bunyan)
Who would true valour see
Fav 11; ND 232

from *The Path to Rome* (Hilaire Belloc)
In these boots and with this staff
O & A 46; Puf V 179

PIPERS

The Pied Piper of Hamelin (Robert Browning)
Hamelin Town's in Brunswick
Fab CV 160; GTP 153; ND 101; Ox CV 173; Ox SP 63
(part) Once more he stept into the street
KCP 40
Rats! They fought the dogs and killed the cats
P Sev 133

A Piper (Seamus O'Sullivan)
A piper in the streets today
Irish 135; Like 115; Ten 177

The Piper (William Blake)
Piping down the valleys wild
Fab CV 32; Fav 21; GTP 11; Like 181; Once 149; Ox CV 84; This W 51; Walk 216

The Piper o' Dundee (anon.)
The piper came to our town
Fab NV 41; Scot 17

Over the Hills and Far Away (anon.)
Tom he was a piper's son
Fab NV 31; Lob 40; Ox Dic 408; Ox NR 164; Puf NR 168

PIRATES

Captain Kidd, 1650-1701 (Rosemary and Stephen Vincent Benet)
This person in the gaudy clothes
KCP 34

131

The Coasts of High Barbary (anon.)
Look ahead, look astern, look the
weather and the lee
Ox PC 50

Pirate Don Durk of Dowdee
(Mildred Meigs)
Ho, for the Pirate Don Durk of
Dowdee!
Once 99; Pos 88

The Reformed Pirate (T. G.
Roberts)
His proper name was Peter Sweet
Ox T 20

PLANETS

The Planets Turn in Stately Dance
(John Kitching)
The planets turn in stately dance
Spa 61

PLANTS

See Nettles

PLATYPUSES

Old Man Platypus (A. B.
Paterson)
Far from the trouble and toil of town
Pat A 23

PLOUGHING

Ploughing on Sunday (Wallace
Stevens)
The white cock's tail
Rat 346; Talk 100; This W 19

As the Team's Head-brass (Edward
Thomas)
As the team's head-brass flashed out
Choice 171; FWW 40; Rat 42

POACHERS

The Lincolnshire Poacher (anon.)
When I was bound apprentice in
famous Lincolnshire
Fav 122

The Poacher (R. S. Thomas)
Turning aside, never meeting
Choice 307

Poaching in Excelsis (G. K.
Menzies)
I've poached a pickel paitricks
Kist 60; Open 94

A Poaching Song (Donagh
MacDonagh)
When God created water He must
have thought of fish
Irish 103

POEMS, POETS AND
POETRY

Digging (Seamus Heaney)
Between my finger and my thumb
Fire 183; Foc 117; Touch IV 59

The Dis-satisfied Poem (Grace
Nichols)
I'm a dissatisfied poem
Five 20

A Good Poem (Roger McGough)
I like a good poem
McG G 24; McRo 11; ND 245; Sk 49

Here I Am (Roger McGough)
Here I am / forty-seven years of age
McG F 15

Homework (Margaret Porter)
I have to write an autumn poem
Occ 58

How to Eat a Poem (Eve Merriam,
USA)
Don't be polite.
Stuf II 96

Jordan II (George Herbert)
When first my lines of heavenly joys
made mention
Touch IV 71

Listen Mr Oxford Don (John
Agard)
Me not no Oxford don
Touch IV 72

Poem about Writing a Poem (Eric
Finney)
'Write a poem,' she says
Fifth 25

Poem for a Dead Poet (Roger
McGough)
He was a poet he was
NTP 68; Strict 169; Touch V 207

Poem on Bread (Vernon Scannell)
The poet is about to write a poem
Nine 105; Sca 54; Sort 121

Poetry (Peter, aged 9)
Poetry is poetry
Mes 20

Poetry for Supper (R. S. Thomas)
Listen, now, verse should be as natural
Touch IV 73

Poetry Jump-Up (John Agard)
Tell me if ah seeing right
Blac 88; Five 114; Pro I 77; Stuf II 102

The Poet's Prayer (Philip Gross)
The poet in the garret is
Gro 40

Shallow Poem (Gerda Mayer)
I've thought of a poem
WP 124

The Robin (June Crebbin)
I tried to write a poem today
Cre 24

There are Not Enough of Us (Adrian Mitchell)
There are not enough of us
King 30

Verse (O. St. J. Gogarty)
What should we know
Fab CV 29

What the Chairman Told Tom (Basil Bunting)
POETRY? It's a hobby
Strict 172, Touch IV 82

Word (Stephen Spender)
The word bites like a fish
WP 124

The Writer of this Poem (Roger McGough)
Is taller than a tree
Pro II 18; WP 60

POETS

See also Carroll, Chaucer, Hardy, Keats, Lear, Vaughan, Yeats

Madly Singing in the Mountains (Po Chu-I, trans. A. Waley)
There is no one among men that has not a special failing
Mes 21; O & A 117; Voi III 7

POLICEMEN

The Policeman's [Love] Song (Vernon Scannell)
I am the guardian of the law
Sca L 28

POLLUTION

Countdown (Judith Nicholls)
Hurry, cried Progress
Earth 16

Country Matters (Christopher Mann)
How gaily glows the gliding foam
Rab 29

The Day the Bulldozers Came (David Orme)
The day the bulldozers came
Earth 67

Going, Going (Philip Larkin)
I thought it would last my time
Earth 64

Harvest Hymn (Judith Nicholls)
We plough the fields and scatter
Earth 86

In the Greenhouse (Paul Higgins)
Car exhaust fumes / Oil in the sea
Pro I 38

The Inheritor (Gerda Mayer)
I the unsophisticated primate
Earth 14

It's Poisoning Down (Brian Patten)
Grannie keeps telling stories
Pat T 29

Kinlochbervie (Alexander Hodson, aged 17)
The land here is dying
Rab 31

The Lake (Roger McGough)
For years there have been no fish in the lake
Rab 46

A Message to the Moon (Millicent L. Pettit)
You're not as dead as you look
Rab 92

'Mummy, Oh Mummy' (anon.)
'Mummy, Oh Mummy, what's this pollution . . .'
Earth 84; PG 46

Poisoned Talk (Raymond Williams)
Who killed cock robin?
Earth 69

The River's Story (Brian Patten)
I remember when life was good
Pat T 110

POLTERGEISTS

Peter Poulter (Philip Gross)
Peter's such a good boy, isn't he?
Gro 19

PONDS

Our Pond (Richard Edwards)
The pond in our garden
ASP 8; Edw P 14

PONIES

Hunter Trials (John Betjeman)
It's awf'lly bad luck on Diana
*Cham 92; Fav 42; Gold 12; Name 24;
Ten 60*

POOLS

The Rock Pool (Peter Skrzynecki)
The rock pool / is a magic circle
Aus B 28

POPLARS

Binsey Poplars (Gerard Manley
Hopkins)
My aspens dear, whose airy cages
quelled
*Choice 116; Earth 43; Floc 104; Mes
109; Rat 77*

Poplar (Gerda Mayer)
propped up / against the pale
Candy 9

The Poplar Field (William
Cowper)
The poplars are felled; farewell to
the shade
Earth 20; Floc 105

PORTRAITS: FEMALE

See also Face throughout

Aunt Julia (Norman McCaig)
Aunt Julia spoke Gaelic
Gold 18; Rat 51; WS 66

from *The Girl in the Baker's* (John
Moore)
We call her the girl in the baker's,
though she's a girl no longer
Face 52

Maggie Dooley (Charles Causley)
Old Maggie Dooley
Cau J 16

Maude Ruggy (John Skelton)
Maude Ruggy thither skipped
Face 96

Mrs Malone (Eleanor Farjeon)
Mrs Malone / Lived hard by a wood
*Far M 90; Ox CV 332; Puf Q 32; Sun
194*

Mrs McHingy (Diana Harland)
Old Mrs McHingy so drab and so
dingy
Sort 25

Phenomenal Woman (Maya
Angelou)
Pretty women wonder where my
secret lies
Touch V 36

Sally (Phoebe Hesketh)
She was a dog-rose kind of girl
Bell 64

To a Peevish Woman (Stanley
Roger Green)
You occupied the royal suite of my
soul
Scot 142

PORTRAITS: MALE

See also Face throughout

Business (Victor Hernandez
Cruz)
Don Arturo says:there was a man
CCV 37

He Man (Michelene Wandor)
Jumbo jets / never spit flame
Life 31

Hot Dog (Kit Wright)
My Dad can't stand my sister's latest
boyfriend
Wri H 11

John Mouldy (Walter de la Mare)
I spied John Mouldy in his cellar
Ox CV 326; Rat 226

The Love Song of J. Alfred Prufrock
(T. S. Eliot)
Let us go then, you and I
Cam II 147; Fire 169

Miniver Cheevy (Edwin Arlington
Robinson)
Miniver Cheevy, child of scorn
Fab CV 120

Mr Bleaney (Philip Larkin)
This was Mr Bleaney's room. He stayed
Touch V 28

Mr Kartoffel (James Reeves)
Mr Kartoffel's a whimsical man
FF 22; OWN 64; Ree C 31

Mr Strugnell (Wendy Cope)
'This was Mr Strugnell's room,' she'll say
Touch V 29

from *Spoon River Anthology* (Edgar Lee Masters)
Where are Elmer, Herman, Bert, Tom and Charley
Cam I 132

Who's Who (W. H. Auden)
A shilling life will give you all the facts
Choice 241

POSSUMS

Hist! (C. J. Dennis)
Hist! . . . Hark! The night is very dark
Aus B 88

If You Go Softly (Jenifer Kelly)
If you go softly out to the gum trees
Aus B 109

Possums (Ann Coleridge)
We've possums in our roof – how very sweet
Aus R 69

POTATOES

The Clever Potato (Vernon Scannell)
Over sixty years ago
Sca 9

The Singing Spud (Kit Wright)
This is the story of Chinese Li
Wri C 53

Versatile Murphy (Vernon Scannell)
The plain potato, you might think
Sca 11

POVERTY

The Ballad of Hollis Brown (Bob Dylan)
Hollis Brown
KWP 221

from *Piers Plowman* (William Langland)
The neediest are our neighbours if we give heed to them
KWP 120

PRAISES

All Things Bright and Beautiful (Cecil Frances Alexander)
All things bright and beautiful
Ox CV 200; Walk 22

from *Benedicite, Omnia Opera*
O All ye Works of the Lord, Bless Ye the Lord
Earth 87

For All the Saints (Bishop W. W. How)
For all the saints who from their labours rest
WAS 131

Glorious the Sun in Mid-career (Christopher Smart)
Glorious the sun in mid-career
Sun 36

Glory be (Hindu, from the Svetasvatara Upanishad)
Glory be to that God who is in the fire
PPP 8

God's Grandeur (Gerard Manley Hopkins)
The world is charged with the grandeur of God
Earth 33; PW 10; Touch V 104

I Like that Stuff (Adrian Mitchell)
Lovers lie around in it
Pro II 67; Touch IV 160

I thank You God (e. e. cummings)
i thank You God for most this amazing
ND 4; NTP 146; PW 15; Wind 8

Lauds (W. H. Auden)
Among the leaves the small birds sing
Ten 183

Pied Beauty (Gerard Manley Hopkins)
Glory be to God for dappled things
Choice 116; GTP 246; Iron 75; Floc 101; Like 72; ND 224; NTP 146;

Rab 3; Rat 344; Talk 101; This W 112; Touch IV 117

Pleasure It Is (William Cornish)
Pleasure it is / To hear, iwis
Earth 2

Praise Ye the Lord (Psalm 150)
Praise ye the Lord
Ring 34

Stufferation (Adrian Mitchell)
Lovers lie around in it
Mit N 11

PRAYERS

An Evening Prayer (Thomas Ken)
Glory to thee, my God, this night
Ring 43

God Be In My Head (anon.)
God be in my head
Puf V 129; Ring 121

Morning Prayer (Ogden Nash)
Now another day is breaking
Ox CV 349; PPP 5; Ring 44; WAS 64

Prayer Before Birth (Louis MacNeice)
I am not yet born: O hear me
Fire 139; PW 171

Prayer to Laughter (John Agard)
O Laughter / giver of relaxed mouths
Aga L 37

PRIDE

Every Day in Every Way (Kit Wright)
When I got up this morning
Face 133

Me (Kit Wright)
My Mum is on a diet
All 16; Wri R 8

Observation on a Cockerel About to Crow, for a Young Man
He's got a crow in his throat
Afr II 37

Pride (Kit Wright)
Two birds sat in a Big White Bra
Ten 160; Wri H 52

A Song of Toad (Kenneth Grahame)
The world has held great heroes
Nine 52

PROHIBITIONS

Don't (Michael Rosen)
Don't do / Don't do / Don't do that
Ros D 4

Don't (Richard Edwards)
Why do people say 'Don't' so much
Edw P 16

PROJECTS

Do a Project (Allan Ahlberg)
Do a project on dinosaurs
Ahl P 76

The Project (Michael Rosen)
At school / we were doing a project
Ros H 74

PROVERBS

See Gran throughout

Caribbean Proverb Poems (James Berry)
Dog mornin prayer is, Laard
Bab 181

Don't Call Alligator Long-mouth til you Cross River (John Agard)
Call alligator long-mouth
Gran 7; KWP 7

PUCK

See Robin Goodfellow

PUDDLES

Puddle Splashing (Frank Flynn)
I'm fed up / with dry sunny days
Candy 25

Puddles (J. Stickells)
There are large puddles, small puddles
Pud 68

The Muddy Puddle (Dennis Lee)
I am sitting / In the middle
Gold 78; PG 67; Til 14; Walk 28

Watch Your Step – I'm Drenched (Adrian Mitchell)
In Manchester there are a thousand puddles
Ang I 35; Rat 457; Strict 168; World 77

PUMPKINS

The Pumpkin (Robert Graves)
You may not believe it, for hardly
could I
Tick 15

Pumpkin Pie Song (anon.)
In the West there lived a maid
Pic 72

PUPPIES

My Puppy (Aileen Fisher)
It's funny / my puppy
Pos 65

Puppy and I (A. A. Milne)
I met a man as I went walking
Tick 68

QUARRELS

Flame and Water (James Berry)
She steams him up
Life 44

Incident in Hyde Park, 1803
(Edmund Blunden)
The impulses of April, the rain-gems
Wind 54

My Hard Repair Job (James
Berry)
In the awful quarrel
Ber 32

The Quarrel (Brian Morse)
When Dad and our next-door
neighbour quarrelled
Mor 40

The Quarrel (Eleanor Farjeon)
I quarrelled with my brother
Nine 95; YD 7

The Quarrel (Mark Winyard,
aged 11)
It was a joint partnership
Wheel 22

You Were the Mother Last Time
(Mary Ann Hoberman)
You were the mother last time
AVF 16; CCV 10; Mad 24

QUEENS

See also Kings and queens

Lullaby for a Naughty Girl (E. V.
Rieu)
Oh peace my Penelope; slaps are the
fate
Fab NV 271

The Queen of Hearts (anon.)
The Queen of Hearts she made
some tarts
Puf NR 126

QUESTIONS

The Akond of Swat (Edward Lear)
Who, or why, or which, or what
*CBC 72; Chat 261; Fab CV 12; GTP
226; Lea C 257*

I'm Just Going Out for a Moment
(Michael Rosen)
I'm just going out for a moment
*DS 17; HH 12; Poem I 16; Ros W 46;
S Sun 66*

*An Interview with Someone who has
Seen a Phoot* (Richard Edwards)
Did it squeak? Did it talk?
Edw Ph 19

Rabbiting On (Kit Wright)
Where did you go?
Poem I 17

Tell Me Why? (Roger McGough)
Daddy will you tell me why
McG P 16

Thoughts Like an Ocean (Gareth
Owen)
The sea comes to me on the shore
Owe C 10

What if (Shel Silverstein)
Last night while I lay thinking here
Ox T 153; YD 135

Who? Why? Where? What?
(Michael Rosen)
Who invented spoons?
Ros D 25

QUESTIONS AND ANSWERS

After Dark (Michael Rosen)
Where are you going? ROUND
THE PARK
TG 44

Edward, Edward (anon.)
Why dois your brand sae drap wi'
bluid,
Kist 91; Mes 54

The False Knight and the Wee Boy
(anon.)
'O whare are ye gaun?
Fab CV 105
O where are you going?
Bell 14

The Lesson (Marin Sorescu,
Romania)
Every time I'm called to the front
Life 56

Lord Randal (anon.)
O where hae ye been, Lord Randal,
my son
*NTP 188; Ox Dic 76; Story 53; Voi III
133*

Meet-on-the-Road (anon.)
Now, pray, where are you going?
*Ox PC 84; Ox SP 8; Ox T 42; Puf V
205; Sk 11; Talk 50*

Overheard on a Saltmarsh (Harold
Monro)
Nymph, nymph, what are your
beads?
*Gold 102; HH 71; KCP 143; Like 104;
Mes 158; MT 64; Puf M 207; This W
33*

O What Is That Sound? (W. H.
Auden)
O what is that sound that so thrills
the ear?
*Choice 237; Floc 254; KCP 27; Story
94; Wind 30*
(part) *Howl 29*

O Where Are You Going? (W. H.
Auden)
'O where are you going?' said
reader to rider
Choice 238; Fab CV 294

Waiting for the Barbarians (C. V.
Cavafy, Greek)
What are we waiting for, assembled
in the forum?
Wind 31

QUINCES

Q is for Quince (Eleanor Farjeon)
The Quince tree has a silken flower
Pic 33

RABBITS

Master Rabbit (Walter de la Mare)
As I was walking
CCC 215

Rabbits (Ray Fabrizio)
Rabbits have fur / And also more
rabbits
CCC 127

The Snare (James Stephens)
I hear a sudden cry of pain!
Irish 162; ND 84; Ox PC 130; WS 54

We are Going to See the Rabbit
(Alan Brownjohn)
We are going to see the rabbit
*Earth 55; Gold 58; KCP 42; ND 85;
Open 76; Rab 70; Six 76; Ten 56; WAS
98; WZ 116*

The White Rabbit (E. V. Rieu)
He is white as Helvellyn when winter
is well in
Puf Q 136

The White Rabbit (John Walsh)
One white ear up
CCC 167; Pets 32

RACEHORSES

At Grass (Philip Larkin)
The eye can hardly pick them out
CCC 131; Foc 59; Rat 45

RACE RELATIONS

See also Being black

The Ballad of Rudolph Reed
(Gwendolyn Brooks)
Rudolph Reed was oaken
PoWo II 54; Rat 62

Ballad of the Landlord (Langston
Hughes)
Landlord, landlord
Speak 54

The Cage (Savitri Hensman)
The racist / Sweats to build a cage
Life 49

A Country Club Romance (Derek
Walcott)
The summer slams the tropic sun
Wind 100

*The Fat Black Woman Goes
Shopping* (Grace Nichols)
Shopping in London winter
Touch IV 88

Georgetown Children (Ian
McDonald)
Under the soursop silver-leaf tree
Blac 31

Harassment (Frederick Williams)
One evening, me a com from wok
Speak 56

Hiccups (Leon Damas)
I gulp down seven drinks of water
FS 14

If My Right Hand (Zinzi Mandela, aged 12)
If my right hand was white
Life 48

Palm Tree King (John Agard)
Because I come from the West Indies
Bab 173

Playground (Mike Rosen)
I'm in the house
Ros F 22

A Mugger's Game (E. A. Markham)
Chase him down the alley
Bab 37

Questionnaired (Tessa Stiven)
Tell me again – the name of your wife
Ang II 75; Speak 51

When I Went to the New School (Mike Rosen)
When I went to the new school
Ros F 20

RAILWAY STATIONS

Adlestrop (Edward Thomas)
Yes. I remember Adlestrop
Cal 60; Fire 114; Floc 115; Foc 72; Like 171; Out 42; Ox PC 141; Puf V 180; World 17

At the Railway Station, Upway (Thomas Hardy)
There is not much that I can do
Floc 71

A Lunatic's London (Gavin Ewart)
Edgware Rumpkin to Euston Squeaker
King 45

Victoria (Eleanor Farjeon)
From Victoria I can go
Ox PC 142; Puf Q 26; World 16

RAIN

Cloudburst (Richard Edwards)
There was a young cloud
Edw P 28; S Sun 78

Down the Road (Michael Rosen)
Down the road
RT 38

Happiness (A. A. Milne)
John had / Great Big
Mil VY 4; RT 107; S Sun 72

Like Rain it Sounded till it Curved (Emily Dickinson)
Like rain it sounded till it curved
Rat 243

Miss Peacock (Gregory Harrison)
You shut that umbrella, my girl, in this gale
Trio 23

Monsoon (Savitri Hensman)
Rain, rain, monsoon rain
Stuf II 78

Rain (Brian Lee)
The lights are all on, though it's just past midday
Open 19; Poem I 68; Pos 119; Six 217; Sort 37

Rain (James Reeves)
Rain and rain is all I see
Ree 'R'

Rain (Marc Matthews, Guyana)
When / on a schoolday
Stuf II 74

The Rain (Richard Edwards)
I don't care what you say
Edw W 10

Rain (Shel Silverstein)
I opened my eyes
Day 8; OTR 15

Rain (Ted Hughes)
Rain. Floods. Frost. And after frost, rain
Cam II 34; Hug MT 1

Rain (Walter de la Mare)
I woke in the swimming dark
de la Mare V 2

Rain in Summer (Henry Wadsworth Longfellow)
How beautiful is the rain!
Sing 12

Rain Sizes (John Ciardi)
Rain comes in various sizes
RT 40

Rainy Nights (Irene Thompson)
I like the town on rainy nights
Out 58; Pos 116; Shad 26; Walk 97

A Soft Day (W. M. Letts)
A soft day, thank God!
Irish 100; Like 113

from *A Song of Rain* (C. J. Dennis)
Mile on mile from Mallacoota
Aus B 105

Spring Rain (Marchette Chute)
The storm came up so very quick
Walk 42

RAINBOWS

My Heart Leaps Up (William
Wordsworth)
My heart leaps up when I behold
NTP 162

Rainbow (Leonard Clark)
Rain still drizzling down
Cla C 39

The Rainbow (Walter de la Mare)
I saw the lovely arch
NTP 162

RAINFOREST

A Poem for the Rainforest (Judith
Nicholls)
Song of the Xingu Indian
Earth 40

RAMS

The Wonderful Derby Ram (anon.)
As I was going to Derby
*Chat 362; Fab NV 70; Iron 2; Nine
102; NTP 216; Ox Dic 145; Ox NR
205; Pud 20*

RATS

An Advancement of Learning
(Seamus Heaney)
I took the embankment path
Cam I 42

Bishop Hatto (Robert Southey)
The summer and the autumn had
been so wet
*KWP 194; MT 146; ND 128; Ox SP
77*

He Was a Rat (anon.)
He was a rat and she was a rat
KCP 20; Nine 131

The Pied Piper of Hamelin (Robert
Browning)
Hamelin Town's in Brunswick
*Fab CV 160; GTP 153; ND 101;
Ox CV 173; Ox SP 63*
(part) Once more he stept into the
street
KCP 40

(part) Rats! They fought the dogs
and killed the cats
P Sev 133

The Rat (Andrew Young)
Strange that you let me come so near
CCC 144

RATTLESNAKES

The Rattlesnake (Alfred Purdy)
An ominous length uncoiling and
thin
Can 99

Rattlesnake Ceremony Song
(Yokuts Indians, USA)
The king snake said to the
rattlesnake
Puf M 291

RAVENS

Moon-Ravens (Ted Hughes)
Are silver white
Hug MW 64

The Raven (Edgar Allan Poe)
Once upon a midnight dreary
Fab CV 190

The Three Ravens (anon.)
There were three ravens sat on a
tree
Mes 53; Voi III 160

The Twa Corbies (anon.)
As I was walking all alane
*Fab CV 266; Kist 49; Puf V 98; Rat
440; Voi III 159*

REFUGEES

*Algerian Refugee Camp Ain-
Khemouda* (Alan Ross)
You have black eyes
Touch V 123

The Companion (Yevgeny
Yevtushenko, trans. Milner-
Gulland and Levi)
She was sitting on the rough
embankment
Cam II 78; Floc 252

For This Relief (Virginia Graham)
Because your husband was killed in
concentration camp
War 88

140

The Little Cart (Ch'en Tsu-Lung,
trans. Arthur Waley)
The little cart jolting and banging
through the yellow haze of dusk
Iron 47; Floc 89; O & A 122

Refugee Mother and Child (Chinua
Achebe)
No Madonna and Child could touch
Fire 138

Say This City Has Ten Million Souls
(W. H. Auden)
Say this city has ten million souls
Foc 26; ND 174; Touch V 120

REHEARSALS

The Harvest Festival Rehearsal
(Wes Magee)
Miss Monkhouse, our teacher
Mag M 46

RELIGIOUS THEMES

All But Blind (Walter de la Mare)
All but blind
de la M P 80

The Call (George Herbert)
Come my Way, my Truth, my Light
Show I 25

The Destruction of Sennacherib
(Lord Byron)
The Assyrian came down like the
wolf on the fold
*Fab CV 254; GTP 143; KCP 45; ND
176; Rat 126*

Diary of a Church Mouse (John
Betjeman)
Here among long-discarded cassocks
ND 75

Vertue (George Herbert)
Sweet day. so cool, so calm, so bright
Touch IV 116

Vision of Belshazzar (Lord Byron)
The king was on his throne
Puf M 177

RELIGIOUS THEMES: NEW
TESTAMENT

See Christ, Christmas: Religious,
Crucifixion, Easter, Epiphany,
Flight into Egypt, Harrowing of
Hell, Herod, Judas Iscariot,
Magdalen, Massacre of the
Innocents, Nativity, Pilate,
Virgin Mary

RELIGIOUS THEMES: OLD
TESTAMENT

See Abraham and Isaac, Adam
and Eve, Babel, Creation,
Daniel, David and Goliath,
Jonah, Joseph, Lot's Wife,
Moses, Samson, Ten
Commandments

REPTILES

See also Crocodiles, Lizards,
Snakes

Iguana Memory (Grace Nichols)
Saw an iguana once
Jung 35

REVENGE

Green (J. and G. Curry)
Sitting in the launderette
Down 16

Heriot's Ford (Rudyard Kipling)
What's that that hirples at my side?
Story 88

Moonrise (Mabel Forrest)
The Barley creek was running high,
the Narrows were abrim
Story 142

THE REVENGE

The Revenge (Lord Tennyson)
At Flores in the Azores Sir Richard
Grenville lay
ND 38; Puf V 87; Show I 33; Ten 129

RHYMES

*Katherine's and Jane's Poem about
Rhyme* (Peter Porter)

141

Dear girls, the English language, which you speak
Sort 122

Rhymes (Y. Y. Segal, trans. Miriam Waddington)
Two respectable rhymes
Ox T 6

Rhyme-Time (Vernon Scannell)
I know that poems do not have to rhyme
Pro I 72; Trio 48; WP 74

Some Rhymes are a Sight . . . (Brian Patten)
It's a pity the sound of cough
Pat T 66

RICE

Pudding Time (anon.)
Pudding-time comes once a day
Pic 120

Rice-Planting (Tokiyo Yamada)
From early morning the cultivator
Pic 11

Rice Pudding (A. A. Milne)
What is the matter with Mary Jane?
Pic 121

RIDDLES

See *Ber 98-100; Fab NV 48-54; Fun 66, 71; HH 81, 88; KCP 230-3; KWP 229-31; McG S 58-9; Mol 17-20, 44-6; Ox NR 147-54; Poem I 8-9, 22-4; Pro III 50, 51; Puf NR 72-5, 118-9, 159, 182; PG 92-3; Pud 104, 105; Rat 206, 428; Rhy 90-3; Voa 26-7; Young 40-1*

I Saw a Strange Creature (Anglo-Saxon, trans. K. Crossley-Holland)
I saw a strange creature
Puf M 183

Anglo-Saxon Riddles (trans. Crossley-Holland)
Pro III 50; Sea 118, 128, 168

Riddle (U. A. Fanthorpe)
Awash in the watery airway, I drift
Crys 33

Totleigh Riddles (John Cotton)
Insubstantial I can fill lives
Crys 7-10

RIDDLES (N)

King John and the Abbot of Canterbury (anon.)
An ancient story I'll tell you anon
GTP 120; Puf V 103

The Riddling Knight (anon.)
There were three sisters fair and bright
Fab CV 281

RIVERS

The River God (Stevie Smith)
I may be smelly and I may be old
Wind 117

The Tide River or *The River's Song* (Charles Kingsley)
Clear and cool, clear and cool
NV 68; Ox CV 227

Tweed and Till (anon.)
Tweed said to Till
Fab CV 268

RIVETERS

The Riveter (Mabel Watts)
This worker is a fearless one
Walk 90

ROADS

Moon-Ways (Ted Hughes)
The moon's roads are treacherous
Hug MW 44

The Road Not Taken (Robert Frost)
Two roads diverged in a yellow wood
Fab CV 292

The Rolling English Road (G. K. Chesterton)
Before the Roman came to Rye
Fab CV 292

ROBIN GOODFELLOW

Puck's Speech (William Shakespeare)
Now the hungry lion roars
Puf M 219

Robin Goodfellow (anon.)
From Oberon in fairy land
Fab CV 206; Puf M 221

ROBIN HOOD

The Death of Robin Hood (anon.)
When Robin Hood and Little John
Floc 156

Robin Hood and Allan a Dale (anon.)
Come listen to me, you gallants so free
GTP 115

Robin Hood and the Bishop (anon.)
Come, Gentlemen all, and listen a while
Ox PC 73

Robin Hood and the Bishop (anon.)
Some they will talk of bold Robin Hood
Nar 31

Robin Hood and the Widow's Sons (anon.)
There are twelve months in all the year
GTP 118

ROBINS

Cock Robin and Jenny Wren (anon.)
It was on a merry time
Puf NR 36

Robin (Hal Summers)
With a bonfire throat
CCC 112

Robin (Iain Crichton Smith)
If on a frosty morning
Ani 28; AVF 116; Cal 27

The Robin (John Clare)
Again the robin waxes tame
Cla J 31

Robin Redbreast's Testament (anon.)
Guid-day now, bonnie Robin
NTP 96

Robin's Round (U. A. Fanthorpe)
I am the proper / Bird for this season
CCC 111

Who Killed Cock Robin? (anon.)
Who killed Cock Robin?
Chat 146; Fab NV 114; GTP 62; Lob 138; Ox Dic 130; Ox NR 166; Puf NR 76; Puf V 38; RMP 44; Voa 102
Who killed Cocky Robin?
Iron 60

ROBOTS

Domestic Help (Adrian Henri)
The other day
Hen 18

ROLLER-COASTERS

Flight of the Roller-Coaster (Raymond Souster)
Once more around should do it the man confided . . .
Ox T 40; Touch IV 41

ROLLER SKATING

Rolling Away (Vernon Scannell)
Lots of children must have thought
Sca T 17

We're Racing, Racing down the Walk (Phyllis McGinley)
We're racing racing down the walk
Walk 111

ROMAN BRITAIN

Over the Heather the Wet Wind Blows (W. H. Auden)
Over the heather the wet wind blows
Choice 243; KCP 26; ND 144; NTP 171

ROOKS

The Rooks (Albert Rowe)
The bald-faced rooks
O & A 59

The Rooks (Jane Euphemia Browne)
The rooks are building on the trees
CCC 94

ROUNDABOUTS

The Merry-go-round (Myra C. Livingston)
The merry-go-round
Tick 45

Roundabout (James Reeves)
At midsummer fair on a galloping pony
Ree C 11

Roundabout (Lydia Pender)
The roundabout horses are back at the show
Pos 20

RUGBY FOOTBALL

A Bit of a Ballad (Gavin Ewart)
Oh, broken, broken was the play!
Cham 26

Kitchen Conversation (Pat Cutts)
What've you been doing this afternoon, Son?
Cham 23; Mot 168

SADNESS

Deep Down (Michael Rosen)
deep down / where I don't know
Five 102; Ros H 50

SAILORS (L AND D)

A.B.C. of a Naval Trainee (Roy Fuller)
A is the anger we hide with some danger
PW 7

Ship Ahoy! (A. J. Mills)
All the nice girls love a sailor
Sea 185

from *The Canterbury Pilgrims* (Chaucer, trans. N. Coghill)
There was a Skipper hailing from far west
Sea 137

Follow the Sea (C. Fox-Smith)
What is it makes a man follow the sea?
Sea 132

from *The Seafarer* (anon. Anglo-Saxon, trans. K. Crossley-Holland)
I can sing a true song about myself
Sea 115
Prosperous men / Living on land
O & A 123

SAILORS (N)

The Last Chantey (Rudyard Kipling)
Thus said the Lord in the Vault above the Cherubim
Sea 31

The Old Sailor (A. A. Milne)
There was once an old sailor my grandfather knew
Fab NV 36; Mil NS 36

On a British Submarine (Cyril Tawney)
It happened on a sunny day in nineteen fifty-four
Voi II 140

The Rime of the Ancient Mariner (S. T. Coleridge)
It is an ancient Mariner
Fab CV 301
And I had done a hellish thing
(part) *Show I 26*
And now the Storm-blast came, and he
(part) *Sea 215*
We were the first that ever burst
(part) *Spi 22*

Sailor (Eleanor Farjeon)
My sweetheart's a sailor
Far R 42

The Sailor's Consolation (Charles Dibden)
One night came on a hurricane
Brave 120

A Sailor Sat on the Watery Shore (Charles Causley)
A sailor sat on the watery shore
Quin 46

There's Nae Luck about the House (W. J. Mickle)
And are ye sure the news is true?
Kist 34; Sea 192

SAILORS' SONGS

Count Arnaldos (Spanish, trans. W. S. Merwin)
Who ever will find such fortune
Puf M 197

Spanish Ladies (anon.)
Farewell and adieu to you, Fair Spanish Ladies
Fab CV 300

A Wet Sheet and a Flowing Sea
(Allan Cunningham)
A wet sheet and a flowing sea
Ox PC 46

SAINTS

See also Becket

The Feast o' Saint Stephen (Ruth
Sawyer)
Hearken all ye, 'tis the feast o' Saint
Stephen
Ox CP 49

The Pets (Robert Farren)
Colm had a cat
Irish 48

Rocco (Charles Causley)
I am St Roche's dog. We stand
Cau J 28

St Christopher (Eleanor Farjeon)
'Carry me, ferryman, over the ford.'
Young 50

St Francis and the Birds (Seamus
Heaney)
When Francis preached love to the
birds
*Floc 89; NTP 69; Sun 182; WAS 124;
WS 47*

St George and the Dragon (Alfred
Noyes)
St George he slew the dragon
Brave 49

St George and the Dragon (trad.)
Open your doors and let me in
Chris 124

[St George] *Not my Best Side* (U.
A. Fanthorpe)
Not my best side, I'm afraid
Fan 28

St Godric and the Hart (Charles
Causley)
Out of the river clear
Cau V 37

from *St Jerome and the Lion*
(Rumer Godden)
One February there came an
afternoon
Sun 172

Saint Jerome and his Lion (anon.)
St Jerome in his study kept a great
big cat
Pets 23

St John the Baptist (William
Drummond)
The last and greatest herald of
heaven's king
Sun 192

St Martin and the Beggar (Thom
Gunn)
Martin sat young upon his bed
Mes 69; Nar 63

St Stephen and King Herod (anon.)
Saint Stephen was a clerk
Puf V 258; Sun 183

St Valentine's Day (after Chaucer)
St Valentine, that art full high aloft
WAS 23

SALAD

from *The Chef Has Imagination*
(Ogden Nash)
Hark to a lettuce lover
Pic 110

Recipe for Salad (Sydney Smith,
1771-1845)
To make this condiment your poet
begs
Pic 65

SALAMIS

from *The Persians* (Aeschylus,
trans. G. M. Cookson)
The word was given, and
instantaneously
PW 104

SALESMEN

The Betterwear Man (Phoebe
Hesketh)
The Betterwear man
Face 59

SALT

Salt (Robert Francis)
Salt for white
Pic 78

SAMSON

Angry Samson (Robert Graves)
Are they blind, the lords of Gaza
Voi III 49

from *Samson Agonistes* (John Milton)
Occasions drew me early to this city
Floc 173; Sun 67

SANDPIPERS

The Sandpiper (Celia Thaxter)
Across the lonely beach we flit
Ox A 129; Ox CV 281

The Sandpiper (Robert Frost)
At the edge of tide
Gold 79

SARDINES

A Baby Sardine (Spike Milligan)
A baby Sardine
Once 27; P Sev 83

How to Open Sardines (John Fuller)
You don't have to grope in a
Quin 75; Sort 12

SCARECROWS

Even Before His Majesty (Dansui, Japan, 17th cent., trans. R. H. Blyth)
Even before His Majesty
Floc 130; WS 98

The Lonely Scarecrow (Darren Mackintosh, aged 8)
He stands alone in rags and tatters
WS 97

The Lonely Scarecrow (James Kirkup)
My poor old bones – I've only two –
Fav 133; Ox PC 139; Pos 86; P Sev 117

The Scarecrow (H. L. Doak)
One shoulder up, the other down
Irish 47

The Scarecrow (Walter de la Mare)
All winter through I bow my head
Gold 64

Scarecrow Independence (James Kirkup)
I may look raggy and queer

Pos 87; Tick 83
from *Our Village* (John Yeoman and Quentin Blake)
He stands upon his single leg
Vil 10

SCHOOL

See also Bullying, Dunces, Exams, Homework, Lessons, Maths, Spelling, Teachers, Truancy

Another Assembly (John Cunliffe)
The old man mounts the platform
Straw 8

Another Day (John Cunliffe)
Boys shout / Girls giggle
Howl 9

Back to School (Allan Ahlberg)
In the last week of the holidays
Ahl P 12

Back to School Blues (Eric Finney)
Late August / The miserable countdown starts
ATP 13

The Blackboard (Adrian Mitchell)
Five foot by five foot
Mit N 65; SO 72; YD 17

The Cane (Allan Ahlberg)
The teacher / had some thin springy sticks
KPC 8

Holidays (J. K. Annand)
As I gang up the Castlehill
Kist 16

A Hot Day at the School (Wes Magee)
All day long the sun glared
ATP 15

Look Out (Max Fatchen)
The witches mumble horrid chants
SO 9; YD 2

Monday Assembly (Tony Bradman)
Three hundred children
Bra A 56

Morning Break (Wes Magee)
Andrew Flag plays football
Mag M 3; SO 40

Old School (Mike Rosen)
Last week / I went to my old school
Ros F 34

Our School (Gareth Owen)
I go to Weld Park Primary
All 37; Bell 53; Owe K 20; Sk 5

from *Our Village* (John Yeoman
and Quentin Blake)
Little Miss Thynne gets to school
bright and early
Vil 8

Parents' Evening (Allan Ahlberg)
We're waiting in the corridor
Ahl H 36

Parents' Evening (Shirley
Toulson)
Tonight your mum and dad go off
to school
Bell 147; Sk 138

Progress Report (Eric Finney)
. . . and you can't go
SO 110

School is Great (Allan Ahlberg)
When I'm at home I just can't wait
Day 18

The Schoolboy (William Blake)
I love to rise in a summer morn
*Bell 15; Fab CV 102; Floc 136; ND
116; Sk 20*

Schoolitis (Brian Patten)
You haven't got a cough
Pat T 12

Thug (Raymond Garlick)
School began it.
Bell 153; Strict 29

Today (Jean Little)
Today I will not live up to my
potential
YD 3

The Unhappy Schoolboy (anon. c.
1525)
Hey! Hey! by this day
Ox CV 11; YD 22

Where's Everybody? (Allan
Ahlberg)
In the cloakroom / Wet coats
IC 32

Why Must We Go to School? (Allan
Ahlberg)
Why must we go to school, dad?
Ahl H 21

SCHOOL: THE FIRST DAY

First Day (J. I. Jones)
I am teaching again
Ax 5

First Day at School (Barry Heath)
it wurorribul m'fost
Occ 120; Show I 47

First Day at School (Roger
McGough)
A millionbillionwillion miles from
home
*All 35; HH 13; KPC 129; McG G 8;
McRo 66; Poem I 66; Sk 21; Speak 18;
Strict 15*

Kindergarten (Stanley Martin)
Me dey ya in dis place wid dese
strange faces
Face 26

The New Boy (John Walsh)
The door swung inward. I stood and
breathed
Open 32; Quin 191

The New Girl (Tony Bradman)
A new girl started
Bra A 36

New Scholar (Louise Bennett)
Good mahnin, teacher – ow is yuh?
FS 15

SCHOOL: LATENESS

Coming Late (Barrie Wade)
Isabel comes late to school
Wad 17

*Early Bird Does Catch the Fattest
Worm* (John Agard)
Late again
Gran 9; SO 14

Getting Ready for School (Caryl
Brahms)
Kate, Kate, / I know you'll be late
Bell 12

Late (Judith Nicholls)
You're late, said miss
Nic M 28; SO 19; SS 51; YD 9

Late Comers (John Cunliffe)
There's a special club
Straw 24

Veronica (Charlotte Hough)
Now this is a tale of a child I once
knew
Name 84

SCHOOL MEALS

Dinner Lady (Jane Whittle)
Hold your plate a little nearer, dear
Sk 80

School Dinners (anon.)
If you stay to school dinners
Pac 53

SCHOOL: TO AND FROM

Bus Home (John Walsh)
The school bus now
Bell 139

Bus to School (John Walsh)
Rounding the corner
Bell 19; Sk 18

Crunching Home from School (Julie O'Callaghan)
a paper my mother has to sign in my mitten
O'Ca 18

Down by the School Gate (Wes Magee)
There goes the bell
AFP 28; King 14; Mag W 5

Lollipop Lady (John Agard)
Lollipop lady
Ox T 66

The Lollipop Lady (Pamela Gillilan)
When we come to the busy street
AFP 29

Out of School (Hal Summers)
Four o'clock strikes
Bell 135; ND 118; Sk 132

from *Summoned by Bells* (John Betjeman)
Walking from school is a consummate art
Bell 143; Sk 133

where are you going? (Jenny Boult)
i've put my bus pass in my pocket
Aus R 13

11 Plus (Martyn Wiley)
We spent all afternoon buying the uniform
Face 37

SCHOOL: TRIPS

At the Science and Industry Museum (Julie O'Callaghan)
I'm not joking ya
Bright 30; O'Ca 25

A Day in the Country (Leonard Clark)
That summer Saturday they took us by coach
Bell 47; Cla C 55

Going on the Sunday School Outing (Stewart Henderson)
Duffle bag packed and a shilling to spend
Occ 105

London Trip (Peter Dixon)
When we went up to London
SO 98

School Visit to the Sculpture Park (J. and G. Curry)
'Don't touch! Don't touch!' the grown-ups glare
Down 82

Sunday School Outing (Charles Causley)
They always say
Cau V 10

Trip to London (Leonard Clark)
By seven o'clock we were on our way
Cla C 54

Trips (Ian McMillan and Martyn Wiley)
For our school trip this term
SO 96

Visit to a Graveyard (Eric Finney)
Last Tuesday, instead of sitting at desks in school
Bell 34

A Visit to the Zoo (J. J. Webster)
Now then children, form a queue
SO 97

The Wendella Boat Ride (Julie O'Callaghan)
We ride the school bus first
Bright 32

SCHOOLMASTERS

Schoolmaster (Yevgeny Yevtushenko, USSR, trans. Milner-Gulland & Levi)
The window gives onto the white trees
Bell 117; Floc 137

The Village Schoolmaster (Oliver Goldsmith)
Beside yon straggling fence that skirts the way
Bell 115; Irish 54; KWP 76; ND 114

SCORPIONS

Night of the Scorpion (Nissim Ezekiel)
I remember the night my mother
Blac 130

The Scorpion (Hilaire Belloc)
The Scorpion is as black as soot
Fab NV 75

SCOTLAND

See Kist, Scot throughout
See also Wilderness

Bruce before Bannockburn (Robert Burns)
Scots, wha hae wi' Wallace bled
Brave 128; Fab CV 143

Lourd on my Hert (Hugh MacDiarmid)
Lourd on my hert as winter lies
Scot 14

My Heart's in the Highlands (Robert Burns)
My heart's in the Highlands, my heart is not here
Ox PC 141

Scotland Small? (Hugh MacDiarmid)
Scotland small? Our multiform, our infinite Scotland small
Rat 365

To S. R. Crockett (Robert Louis Stevenson)
Blows the wind today, and the sun and the rain are flying
Puf V 201

SCRATCHING

Taboo to Boot (Ogden Nash)
One bliss for which
Rat 413

SEA (L AND D)

See ND 30-53
See also Bathing, Beachcombing, Beaches, Fishermen, Fishes and Sea Creatures, Fishing, Mermaids and Mermen, Pirates, Sailors, Sea Birds, Sea Monsters, Sea Shanties, Seaside, Shells, Ships, Shipwrecks, Smugglers,

Tides, Waves

The Harp Song of the Dane Women (Rudyard Kipling)
What is a woman that you forsake her
Brave 141; PW 131

Hungry Waters (Hugh MacDiarmid, Scots, trans. G. Summerfield)
The old men of the sea
PoWo I 89

Look, Stranger, on This Island Now (W. H. Auden)
Look, stranger, on this island now
Choice 243; Fire 35; Floc 44; PW 8; Sea 91

Morwenstow (Charles Causley)
Where do you come from, sea?
Cau J 84

Once by the Pacific (Robert Frost)
The shattered water made a misty din
Sea 52

Ramhead and Dodman (Charles Causley)
Said Ramhead to Dodman
Cau F 48

The Rime of the Ancient Mariner (S. T. Coleridge)
It is an ancient Mariner
Fab CV 301
And now the Storm Blast came, and he
(part) *Sea 215*
We were the first that ever burst
(part) *Spi 22*

The Sea (James Reeves)
The sea is a hungry dog
ND 47; NTP 231; Open 10; Pro III 39; Puf Q 82; Ree C 53; Show I 52

The Sea (R. S. Thomas)
They wash their hands in it
Sea 23; YD 123

Sea Fever (John Masefield)
I must go down to the seas again, to the lonely sea and the sky
Like 103; NTP 237

Sea Strain (A. D. Mackie)
I fand a muckle buckie shell
Scot 23

Sea Timeless Song (Grace Nichols)
Hurricane come
KPC 150; Nic 40; Stuf II 90; WS 25

Song of the Galley Slaves (Rudyard Kipling)
We pulled for you when the wind was against us
KWP 114; NTP 199; Ten 135

Tell Me, Tell Me, Sarah Jane (Charles Causley)
Tell me, tell me, Sarah Jane
Cau F 40; Sea 24; WS 22

Thalassa (Louis MacNeice)
Run out the boat, my broken comrades
ND 31

Until I Saw the Sea (Lilian Moore)
Until I saw the sea
Gold 29; Open 7; Pop 115; Walk 29; YD 122

The Waves of the Sea (Eleanor Farjeon)
Don't you go too near the sea
WS 17

SEA (N)

I Started Early (Emily Dickinson)
I started Early – Took my Dog
Fun 98; Sea 25

The Last Chantey (Rudyard Kipling)
Thus said the Lord in the Vault above the Cherubim
Fab CV 323

The Rime of the Ancient Mariner (S. T. Coleridge)
It is an ancient Mariner
Fab CV 301

A Sailor Sat on the Watery Shore (Charles Causley)
A sailor sat on the watery shore
Cau F 56

SEA BATTLES

See also Armada, Lepanto, The Revenge, Salamis, Trafalgar

A Ballad for a Boy (William Cory)
When George the Third was reigning a hundred years ago
Ox CV 290

SEA BIRDS

Great Black-Backed Gulls (John Heath-Stubbs)
Said Cap'n Morgan to Cap'n Kidd
Sea 173

Gulls Playing (P. J. Kavanagh)
The day was so dull
IC 61

Sandpiper (Elizabeth Bishop)
The roaring alongside he takes for granted
Rat 363

Sea-Change (John Masefield)
Goneys an' gullies an' all o' the birds o'the sea
Rat 365; Sea 172

Sea Gull (Elizabeth Coatsworth)
The sea gull curves his wings
Tick 94; Walk 84

Seagulls (Roger McGough)
Seagulls are eagles
McG M 83

The Storm (Walter de la Mare)
First there were two of us, then there were three of us
Foot 44; NTP 128

SEA MONSTERS

See also Kraken, Leviathan
Just Then Another Event (Virgil, trans. C. Day Lewis)
Just then another event, the most alarming yet
Sea 57

The Monster (T. Harri Jones)
When the sea monster came to visit us
Mons 30

The Monster (Walter de la Mare)
There was an Old Man with a net
Mons 32

Sea Monsters (Edmund Spenser)
Eftsoons they saw an hideous host arrayed
Mons 28

The Sea Serpent Chantey (Vachel Lindsay)
There's a snake on the western wave
AM 72; MT 88

SEA SHANTIES

Billy Boy (anon.)
Where have you been all the day,
Billy Boy?
Ox Dic 78; Ox NR 189

Bobby Shaftoe (anon.)
Bobby Shaftoe's gone to sea
Ox Dic 90; Ox NR 185

Donkey Riding (anon.)
Were you ever in Quebec
Can 15; NV 88

SEALS

The Great Silkie of Sule Skerrie
(anon.)
In Norway there sits a maid
Story 58

The Ice Floes (E. J. Pratt)
Dawn from the foretop! Dawn from
the barrel!
Nar 128

The Rhyme of the Three Sealers
(Rudyard Kipling)
Away by the lands of the Japanee
Nar 120

Seal (William Jay Smith)
See how he dives
WZ 91

Seal Lullaby (Rudyard Kipling)
Oh! hush thee my baby, the night is
behind us
WS 24; Zoo 82
(part) *Jung 71*

SEASIDE

See also Bathing

Archie and Tina (Stevie Smith)
Archie and Tina / Where are you
now
Face 147

The Arrival (John Walsh)
Our train steams slowly in, and we
creep to a stop at last
Pro I 74; Quin 207

At the Seaside (Robert Louis
Stevenson)
When I was down beside the sea
Ox CV 293; RT 55; Ste 18

August Outing (Trevor Hardy)
The August Bank Holiday's here
again
Cele 62

The Beach Trail (Julie
O'Callaghan)
That was the most tedious journey
O'Ca 36

Cornish Holiday (John Betjeman)
Then before breakfast down toward
the sea
ND 50

A Day at the Beach (Mick Gowar)
God Almighty! What a trip!
Gow F 23

Down the Sandhills (Lydia
Pender)
A giant I stride
Aus B 7

Holidays (Max Fatchen)
Loading of our caravan
SO 123

I Do Like to be Beside the Seaside
(John A. Glover-Kind)
I do like to be beside the seaside
Occ 101; Sea 73

The Lugubrious, Salubrious Seaside
(Louis MacNeice)
The dogs' tails tick like metronomes
Sea 78

maggie and milly (e. e. cummings)
maggie and milly and molly and may
*KPC 55; ND 53; Poem I 69; P Sev 78;
Rat 260; Walk 112*

Sand (John Foster)
Sand in your finger-nails
AFP 106

Seaside Song (John Rice)
It was a / sunboiled brightlight
Cal 75; DS 10

Trip to the Seashore (Lois Simmie)
We drove to the seashore
Til 87

Work and Play (Ted Hughes)
The swallow of summer she toils all
summer
ND 51

SEASONS

See also Autumn, Spring,
Summer, Winter

The Calendar (Barbara Euphan
Todd)
I knew when Spring was come
Like 75; Occ 65; Puf V 24

A British Garden (Wes Magee)
The Spring garden is Irish green
Mag M 36

SEA-TROUT

The Names of the Sea-trout (Tom Rawling)
He who would seek her in the clear stream
WS 36

SECRETS

Secrets (Augusta Skye)
I swear I'll never tell him
IC 42

Mouth Open, Story Jump Out (John Agard)
Mouth open / story jump out
Gran 13; PG 28

SEDER

Ballad of the Warsaw Seder – Passover 1943 (L. J. Anderson)
How can we keep the feast, mother?
Ang II 96

Seder (Judith Nicholls)
Why celebrate with bitter herbs
Cele 36

SHADOWS

Copycat (Robert Heidbreder)
Copycat, copycat / Shadow's a copycat!
Hei 26

Hide-and-Seek Shadow (Margaret Hillert)
I walked with my shadow
Read 25

Me and My Shadow (Roger McGough)
Me and my sha - dow
McG S 73

My Shadow (Robert Louis Stevenson)
I have a little shadow that goes in and out with me

Fab NV 112; Once 92; Ox CV 295; Ox T 35; Ste 34

The Shadow (Walter de la Mare)
When the last of gloaming's gone
Once 114

Shadow Dance (Ivy O. Eastwick)
O Shadow / Dear Shadow
Shad 12; Tick 176

Shadow March (Robert Louis Stevenson)
All round the house is the jet-black night
Ste 68

SHAKESPEARE'S *HAMLET*

Mother-in-law (U. A. Fanthorpe)
Such a nice girl. Just what I wanted
Fan 31

SHAKESPEARE'S *THE TEMPEST*

The Coiner (circa 1611) (Rudyard Kipling)
Against the Bermudas we foundered, whereby
Sea 213

The Heir (U. A. Fanthorpe)
It was very quiet on the island after
Crys 48

SHARKS

About the Teeth of Sharks (John Ciardi)
The thing about a shark is – teeth
Ox A 263; WS 27

The Flattered Flying-Fish (E. V. Rieu)
Said the Shark to the Flying-Fish over the phone
P Sev 68; Puf Q 122; Walk 77

The Maldive Shark (Herman Melville)
About the Shark, phlegmatical one
Rat 261; Sea 43; Touch IV 193

The Shark (E. J. Pratt)
He seemed to know the harbour
Can 46; Open 102; WZ 90

The Shark (Lalla Ward)
The shark / swims
RT 119

The Shark (Lord Alfred Douglas)
A treacherous monster is the Shark
Like 71; Walk 78

SHEEP

A Child's Pet (W. H. Davies)
When I sailed out of Baltimore
Rat 106

A Poem for Breathing (George MacBeth)
[*see Sheep, Buried* below]
Trudging through drifts along the hedge, we
Show II 84

Shearing with a Hoe (A. B. Paterson)
The track that led to Carmody's is choked and overgrown
Pat A 52

Sheep (Alan Bold)
Stuck in a field, grazing
Bright 10

Sheep (Alan Brownjohn)
There have been times I have been a sheep
CCC 62

The Sheep (Ann and Jane Taylor)
Lazy sheep, pray tell me why
CCC 63

Sheep (Ted Hughes)
The sheep has stopped crying
Foc 60; Hug MT 51
(part) The mothers have come back
CCC 64; ND 77

Sheep (W. H. Davies)
When I was once in Baltimore
NTP 109; Rat 379; Story 26; Ten 49

Sheep, Buried (Wes Magee)
Overnight, an airborne invasion
Show II 61

A Sheep Fair (Thomas Hardy)
The day arrives of the autumn fair
Iron 119; KWP 84; O & A 50; Zoo 40

Sheep in Winter (John Clare)
The sheep get up and make their many tracks
Ani 58; Cal 22; Cla J 25; Floc 280; Stoc 23

SHEEPDOGS

Collie Romance (Alan Ross)
Sometimes at night I remember
IC 31

Full Circle (Ruth Skilling)
When John was ten they gave the boy
CCC 175; Open 83

'Glen' a Sheep-Dog (Hilton Brown)
I ken there isna a p'int in yer heid
Kist 33

Old English Sheep-Dog (George MacBeth)
Eyes / drowned in fur
Gold 68

Praise of a Collie (Norman MacCaig)
She was a small dog, neat and fluid
Gold 106; Rat 351; Strict 138

SHELLS

The Shell (James Stephens)
And then I pressed the shell
Floc 43; Gold 16; MT 79; ND 49; Sea 65
(part) *Open 11*

SHIPS (L AND D)

Cargoes (John Masefield)
Quinquereme of Nineveh from distant Ophir
Like 42; ND 42; Show III 56; World 19

The Cutty Sark (George Barker)
I think of her as she lies there
Floc 51

The Old Ships (James Elroy Flecker)
I have seen old ships sail like swans asleep
ND 42

She is Far from the Land (Thomas Hood)
Cables entangling her
WP 72

The Ship (J. C. Squire)
There was no song or shout of joy
Brave 79

SHIPS (N)

The Golden Vanity (anon.)
A ship I have got in the North Country

Brave 138; Fab CV 171; Iron 54; Ox
PC 57

Mary Celeste (Judith Nicholls)
Only the wind sings
YD 97

The North Ship or **Legend** (Philip
Larkin)
I saw three ships go sailing by
Floc 50; Rat 310; Sea 254; Story 96;
WS 63; YD 96

The Revenge (Alfred Lord
Tennyson)
At Flores in the Azores Sir Richard
Grenville lay
Fab CV 247

from **Windjammer** (Paul Keens-
Douglas, Trinidad)
Boat bow cuttin' water
Stuf II 86

SHIPWRECKS

The Alice Jean (Robert Graves)
One moonlight night a ship drove in
MT 89

Capstan Bars (Capt. Q. Crauford
RN retd)
Come ladies man the capstan bars
Brave 64

A Dirty Night on the Fastnet Rock
(Rev. William
Packenham-Walsh, written aged
12)
Oh Flutes! the night came on
Rhy 38

The Inchcape Rock (Robert
Southey)
No stir in the air, no stir in the sea
Fav 52; GTP 160; KPC 189; Nar 114;
Ox SP 53; Ten 154

**In Memory of the Circus Ship
Euzkera** (Walker Gibson)
The most stupendous show they
ever gave
Sea 160

Pat Cloherty's Version of The Maisie
(Richard Murphy)
I've no tooth to sing you the song
Rat 339; Sea 225

Posted (John Masefield)
Dream after dream I see the wrecks
that lie
MT 80; ND 43

Posted as Missing (John
Masefield)
Under all her topsails she trembled
like a stag
Ox PC 51; Sea 161

from **Richard III** (William
Shakespeare)
As we paced along / Upon the giddy
footing
KPC 182
Methought I saw a thousand fearful
wracks
Sea 160
Methoughts that I had broken from
the Tower
Cam I 76

from **The Odyssey** (Homer, trans.
J. W. Mackail)
Even as he spoke, a monstrous
wave abaft
Sea 207

Sir Patrick Spens (anon.)
The king sits in Dunfermline toun
Fab CV 296; Floc 46; Kist 37; ND 33;
Ox PC 47; Ox SP 59; Puf V 99; Rat
391

from **The White Ship** (Dante
Gabriel Rossetti)
Swifter and swifter the White Ship
sped
Sea 210

The Wreck of the Hesperus (Henry
Wadsworth Longfellow)
It was the schooner Hesperus
Fav 48; Nar 111; Ox A 51

The Yarn of the Nancy Bell (W. S.
Gilbert)
'Twas on the shores that round our
coast
Fab CV 179; GTP 203

SHOES

Choosing Shoes (Ffrida Wolfe)
New shoes, new shoes
RMP 6; RT 163; Tim 2

New Shoes (John Agard)
Buying new shoes / takes so long
Aga 18; Ox T 39

Trainers (Michael Rosen)
See me in my trainers
Ros D 2

SHOOTING

Cock Pheasant (Leonard Clark)
Halfway to school a pheasant flew
overhead
CCC 106

Done For (Walter de la Mare)
Old Ben Bailey
CCC 217

First Blood (Jon Stallworthy)
It was the breech smelling of oil
Wind 71

Hi! (Walter de la Mare)
Hi! handsome hunting man
CCC 216; PoWo I 43; WS 55

I Saw a Jolly Hunter (Charles
Causley)
I saw a jolly hunter
*Cau F 13; CCV 50; Fun 106; Once
138; PoWo I 42; P Sev 17; RMP 32;
Strict 141*

A Shot Magpie (Andrew Young)
Though on your long-tailed flight
CCC 92

SHRIMPS

I'm a Shrimp! I'm a Shrimp!
(Robert Brough)
I'm a shrimp! I'm a shrimp! Of
diminutive size
Pic 70

SINGING

Basso profundo (Sol Mandlsohn)
A singer, who sang
Til 18

Down in Yonder Meadow (anon.)
Down in yonder meadow where the
green grass grows
Pic 41

Euphonica Jarre (Jack Prelutsky)
Euphonica Jarre has a voice that's
bizarre
Pre 26

Everyone Sang (Siegfried
Sassoon)
Everyone suddenly burst out singing
PW 182

The Quartette (Walter de la Mare)
Tom sang for joy, and Ned sang for
joy
de la M P 44

The Serpent (Theodore Roethke)
There was a Serpent who had to sing
*AM 46; PG 62; Puf M 175; Walk 176;
Zoo 80*

The Solitary Reaper (William
Wordsworth)
Behold her single in the field
*Brave 18; Choice 21; Fab CV 119; Ox
PC 146; This W 145*

SISTERS

For Sale (Shel Silverstein)
One sister for sale
OTR 28

Listn Big Brodda Dread, Na!
(James Berry)
My sista is younga than me
Ber 24

My Sister is a Sissy (Jack
Prelutsky)
She's afraid of dogs and cats
Pre 138

My Sister Jane (Ted Hughes)
And I say nothing – no, not a word
*All 18; CCV 12; Fav 44; Floc 95; Hug
F 13; Once 77*

Poem for my Sister (Liz Lochhead)
My little sister likes to try my shoes
Scot 149

Sister (Judith Nicholls)
Tell me a story!
Nic F 12

Sisters (Wendy Cope)
My sister / was the bad one
Moon 96

SIZES

The Cricket (John Fuller)
The cricket like a knuckled rubber
band
Quin 90

Epistle to the Olympians (Ogden
Nash)
Dear Parents, I write you this letter
Nas C 58

Five-inch Tall (Norman
Nicholson)
I'm five-inch tall
Candy 40; WP 63

The Fly (Walter de la Mare)
How large unto the tiny fly
*Once 38; Ox T 105; Poem I 28; Pro II
77*

It Is Not Growing Like a Tree (Ben Jonson)
It is not growing like a tree
Puf V 239; Rat 216

Rain Sizes (John Ciardi)
Rain comes in various sizes
RT40

Small, Smaller (Russell Hoban)
I thought that I knew all there was to know
CCC 152; Gold 15; Poem I 28; Sort 57; Stoc 24

Ten Yards High (Norman Nicholson)
I'm ten yards high
Candy 38

SKATEBOARDS

Skateboard Flier (James Berry)
Please Mum please / not again back-to-school
Ber 80

SKATING

The Midnight Skaters (Edmund Blunden)
The hop-poles stand in cones
Cham 84; ND 238; O & A 66; Voi III 163

The Midnight Skaters (Roger McGough)
It is midnight in the ice-rink
McG PT 18; TG 27

Night-Skating (Vernon Scannell)
I skate on ice
Sca T 16

Our Village (John Yeoman and Quentin Blake)
Did you kow that the pond at the end of the lane
Vil 38-41

from *The Prelude* (William Wordsworth)
And in the frosty season, when the sun
Cham 86; Choice 23; Fab CV 57; GTP 281; KWP 217; Mot 22; ND 93; O & A 67; Stoc 50

Prizewinner (Caroline Ackroyd)
The ice skater
Mot 166

Skating (Herbert Asquith)
When I try to skate
Occ 92

Skating on Thin Lino or *Bedroom Skating* (Gareth Owen)
Because there is no Ice Rink
ATP 20; Bright 44

Watching You Skating (Adrian Mitchell)
I see two skates
Mit N 43

SKIES

The Unending Sky (John Masefield)
I could not sleep for thinking of the sky
Like 110; YD 137

SKIPPING

Skipping Rhymes *Sk 102-9*

Rope Rhyme (Eloise Greenfield)
Get set, ready now, jump right in
Blac 38

A Skip to Beat Bad Temper (Cynthia Mitchell)
An angry tiger in a cage
Tick 50

Skippers (Wes Magee)
Here comes Abigail
Mag W 10

Skipping Game (anon.)
Hello, hello, hello, sir
Mea 11

Skipping Rhyme (Alan Brownjohn)
Pain of the leaf one two
Six 83; Ten 182

Skipping Rope Song (Dionne Brand)
Salt, vinegar, mustard, pepper
Blac 39

Skipping Song (Gareth Owen)
Ann and Belinda
Bell 94; Owe C 79

Skipping Song (John Walsh)
When bread-and-cheese
RT 56

SKUNK

Skunk (Ted Hughes)
Skunk's footfall plods padded
Hug MW 40

SKYLARKS

The Skylark (Christina Rossetti)
The earth was green the sky was blue
NV 58

The Sky Lark (John Clare)
The rolls and harrows lies at rest
beside
Cla J 71

SKYSCRAPERS

Building a Skyscraper (James S. Tippett)
They're building a skyscraper
Once 16; P Sev 147

SLEEP

See also Dreams, Lullabies, Nightmares

Catching up on Sleep (Roger McGough)
I go to bed early
McG G 30; WS 76

Counting Sheep (Mark Burgess)
As I was going off to sleep
Bur 26

Counting Sheep (Wes Magee)
They said, 'If you can't get to sleep . . .'
All 123; AVF 41; Day 42; Shad 34

Half Asleep (Gareth Owen)
Half asleep / And half awake
Owe C 28

I'm Only Sleeping (John Lennon and Paul McCartney)
When I wake up early in the morning
KPC 117

Lights Out (Edward Thomas)
I have come to the borders of sleep
Floc 177; Mes 217; Wind 128

Saturday Night (Richard Edwards)
I've tried counting frogs
Edw W 24

Sweet Dreams (Ogden Nash)
I wonder as into bed I creep
Nas C 80; WP 93

SLEET

Sleet (Norman MacCaig)
The first snow was sleet. It swished heavily
Ox CP 12

SLIMMING

about auntie rose and her diet (Jenny Boult)
my auntie rose says
Aus R 62

Edible Anecdote No 24 (Julie O'Callaghan)
The first thing you say is
Moon 40

Give up Slimming, Mum (Kit Wright)
My Mum / is short / and plump
Gold 34; Pac 58; Wri R 20

SLOTHS

The Sloth (Theodore Roethke)
In moving slow he has no Peer
Walk 56; WS 77

SMELLS

See also Nif throughout

Smells (Christopher Morley)
Why is it that the poets tell
Nif 48; Open 59; Pic 58

from *Summoned by Bells* (John Betjeman)
Nose! Smell again the early morning smells
Nif 49

Wouldn't it be Funny if you Didn't Have a Nose? (Roger McGough)
You couldn't smell your dinner
McG PT 26

SMOKING

The Breath of Death (Lemn Sissay)
This cigarette of which I light
Life 11

SMUGGLERS

A Smuggler's Song (Rudyard Kipling)

157

If you wake at midnight and hear a horse's feet
Gold 96; KPC 111; NTP 174; Ox CV 322; Ox PC 52; Ten 75; YD 41

SNAILS

Considering the Snail (Thom Gunn)
The snail pushes through a green
Cam I 40; Floc 211; Foot 65

Living Tenderly (X. J. Kennedy)
My body a rounded stone
Ox A 271

The Odyssey of a Snail (Frederico Garcia Lorca)
Now over the path
Floc 211

The Snail (Charles Lamb)
The frugal snail, with forecast of repose
GTP 79

The Snail (James Reeves)
At sunset, when the night-dews fall
Ox PC 123; Puf Q 74; Ree C 3

Snail (John Drinkwater)
Snail upon the wall
CCC 35; Fab NV 74; Once 39; Pop 73; P Sev 135; Rog 11; Zoo 79

The Snail (William Cowper)
To grass, or leaf, or fruit, or wall
CCC 35; GTP 79

The Snail of the Moon (Ted Hughes)
Saddest of all things on the moon is the snail without a shell
Hug MW 45

Upon the Snail (John Bunyan)
She goes but softly, but she goeth sure
Gold 47; Like 23; ND 59; Ox CV 36

SNAKES

See also Adders, Rattlesnakes

A Narrow Fellow in the Grass (Emily Dickinson)
A narrow fellow in the grass

Floc 210; Foot 66; GTP 68; NTP 99; Ox A 109; Rat 307; WS 49

Sensemaya: A Chant for Killing a Snake (Nicolas Guillen)
Mayombe-bombe-mayombe!
Blac 60; HH 21; Stuf II 68

The Serpent (Theodore Roethke)
There was a Serpent who had to sing
AM 46; PG 62; Puf M 175; Walk 176; Zoo 80

Snake (Barbara Juster Esbensen)
The word begins to / hiss as soon as
Esb 17

Snake (D. H. Lawrence)
A snake came to my water-trough
Cam II 28; Earth 96; Fire 134; ND 62; NTP 100; Rat 395; Touch V 173

SNARES

See Traps

SNEEZING

Two of the Best (Richard Edwards)
Some people have lisps
Edw W 18

SNOOKER

The Hurricane [Alex Higgins] (John Jarvis)
The chattering dies as the players walk in
Cham 112; Mot 126

Pockets of Resistance (Peter Bond)
Life is a game of snooker
Mot 183

147 (Sheenagh Pugh)
It's the magic number: seven more
Ang II 15

SNORING

Louder than a Clap of Thunder (Jack Prelutsky)
Louder than an eagle screams
Pre 36

SNOW (L AND D)

Frying Pan's Theology (A. B. Paterson)
Scene: On Monaro
Iron 40

In Winter (Jean Kenward)
Where does it come from?
AFP 117

London Snow (Robert Bridges)
When men were all asleep the snow came flying
Fav 108; KWP 42

Outdoor Song (A. A. Milne)
The more it /SNOWS – tiddely-pom
Like 14; Pop 22; RMP 36

Snow (Walter de la Mare)
No breath of wind
de la M V 20; Once 58; WAS 150

Snow (Edward Thomas)
In the gloom of whiteness
NTP 134; Out 75; Voi III 157; WAS 151

Snow (Leonard Clark)
When winter winds blow
Nine 21

Snow and Ice Poems (Roger McGough)
Our street is dead lazy
Pro I 64

Snowfall (Eleanor Farjeon)
Oh, that first dazzled window-glance!
Far M 79

Snow in the Lamplight (Mark Burgess)
From my bedroom / In bare feet
Bur 20

Snow in the Suburbs (Thomas Hardy)
Every branch big with it
Out 80; Show III 5; This W 129; YD 114

Snow's Fall'n Deep (Walter de la Mare)
Now all the roads to London town
Star 12

Snowy Day in the Park (Sheila Simmons)
Across the park / the footprints go
AFP 119

When All the World is Full of Snow (N. M. Bodecker)
I never know / just where to go
Chris 38; Stoc 4; Walk 31

White Fields (James Stephens)
In the winter time we go
Ox T 147; RT 47; Stoc 8

Winter (Walter de la Mare)
Green Mistletoe!
Star 19

Winter Morning (Ogden Nash)
Winter is the king of showmen
Chris 37; King 181; Nas C 22; Out 76; Ox T 145

SNOW (N)

At Nine of the Night (Charles Causley)
At nine of the night I opened my door
Cau F 39; Chris 99; Quin 59; Sort 32; Stoc 70

Battle (Julie O'Callaghan)
We knew it would come all day –
Bright 28

Before a Fall (Alan Bold)
Once upon a sledge a boy called Bill
Bright 7

Explorer (Alan Brownjohn)
Two o'clock / Let out of the back door
ATP 44

The Kitten in the Falling Snow (James Kirkup)
The year-old kitten
Out 78

London Snow (Robert Bridges)
When men were all asleep the snow came flying
ND 12

The Mighty Slide (Allan Ahlberg)
The snow has fallen in the night
Ahl M 9

Only Snow (Allan Ahlberg)
Outside the sky was almost brown
Ahl P 66

Polar Bear Snow (Robert Heidbreder)
At Churchill, Manitoba
Hei 31

Snow (Robert Edwards)
I've just woken up and I'm lying in bed
ASP 15; Edw P 8

Stopping by Woods on a Snowy Evening (Robert Frost)
Whose woods these are I think I know
Cal 118; Choice 284; Fab CV 58; Fire 160; Floc 276; Foot 34; Gold 45; Iron 62; Like 67; NTP 136; Ox A 215; Pop 36; Pos 122; Rat 407; RMP 54; Shad 22; Show II 18; Sing 22; S Sun 35; Stoc 65; Talk 76; Ten 29; This W 156; Walk 31; WAS 154; YD 115

SNOWFLAKES

The Snowflake (Walter de la Mare)
Before I melt
Pos 125

Snowflakes (Clive Sansom)
And did you know
Ox CP 13

SNOWMEN

Boy at the Window (Richard Wilbur)
Seeing the snowman standing all alone
Mes 43

Death of a Snowman (Vernon Scannell)
I was awake all night
King 180; Pos 126; Sort 36; WS 103

The Snowman (anon.)
Once there was a snowman
Ox T 145

The Snowman (Roger McGough)
Mother while you were at the shops
Cal 116; King 182; McG P 34; Ox T 146; Stoc 48

Snowman (Shel Silverstein)
'Twas the first day of the springtime
Sil 65

SOLDIERS

Buckingham Palace (A. A. Milne)
They're changing guard at Buckingham Palace

*Fav 38; Fun 88; Mil VY 2; Nine 80; O\
CV 340*

The Duke of Plaza-Toro (Sir W. S. Gilbert)
In enterprise of martial kind
CBC 136

The Modern Major-General (W. S. Gilbert)
I am the very model of a modern Major-General
Show I 29

The Recruiting Sergeant (Philip Katz)
Come here to me, my merry, merry men
Howl 28

The Song of the Soldiers (Walter de la Mare)
As I sat musing by the frozen dyke
de la M P 112

Tommy (Rudyard Kipling)
I went into a public-'ouse to get a pint of beer
PW 72

SOLDIERS' SONGS

All the Hills and Vales Along (Charles Sorley)
All the hills and vales along
Fab CV 261; PW 42

Men who March Away (Thomas Hardy)
We be the King's men hale and hearty
Brave 95

Over the Heather the Wet Wind Blows (W. H. Auden)
Over the heather the wet wind blows
Choice 242; KPC 26; ND 144; NTP 171

from *Song for a Soldier* (A. A. Milne)
I march along and march along and ask myself each day
War 68

SORCERERS

from *The Sorcerer* (W. S. Gilbert)
Oh! My name is John Wellington Wells
CBC 124; Puf M 83

SOUTH AFRICA

Pockets of Resistance (Peter Bond)
'Life is a game of snooker'
Mot 183

Western Civilisation (Agostinho
Neto)
Sheets of tin nailed to posts
Afr I 61

SOWING

Sowing (Edward Thomas)
It was a perfect day
Cal 43; Choice 175

SPACE

See also 'Aliens' from space,
Astronauts, Earth destroyed,
Moon fantasy, Moon landing

Song in Space (Adrian Mitchell)
When man first flew beyond the sky
Five 49; Mit N 44; Spa 35

The Space Program (William
Eastlake)
People are so bored, bored
KCP 69

SPACE LAUNCHES

Interference (Edwin Morgan)
bringing you live
KCP 145

Man and Height (John Rice)
At times the success of a mission
Spa 34

Space Shot (Gareth Owen)
Out of the furnace
Spa 26

SPACE RACE

Space Race (Adrian Rumble)
. . . three . . . two . . . one . . . go
UD 39

The Space Race (Derek Stuart)
The space race! The space race!
Spa 33

SPACE TRAVEL

See also Foc 166-71

The Astronaut Talks to his Son
(Vernon Scannell)
Sometimes it seems like yesterday,
and yet
Sca T 60

In the Late Evening (Iain Crichton
Smith)
In the late evening
Spa 123

Limbo (D. M. Thomas)
The air-gauge clamped our heart-
beats. When we searched
Foc 167

The Space Explorer's Story (David
Harmer)
Having locked ourselves
Spa 95

Space Shanty (Adrian Rumble)
We are star-crazed
UD 42

SPACE TRAVEL:
IMAGINARY

The Ballad of Morgan the Moon
(Max Boyce)
Old Mog the mechanic, I remember
him well
Spa 38

Going Up (John Travers Moore)
Space-Suit Sammy / Head in glass
Walk 140

I Dreamed Earth was Dying
(Adrian Rumble)
I dreamed I was flying
UD 45

It's All Decided (Tony Bradman)
Right, it's all decided then
Bra A 48

Message from a Mouse (Patricia
Hubbell)
Attention, architect!
Walk 224

Mushrooms on the Moon (Ted
Hughes)
Mushrooms on the moon are
delicious
Hug MW 50

Nutty Nursery Rhymes (Max Fatchen)
'Jump over the moon?' the cow declared
Fat S 30; King 60; Spa 42

Off to Outer Space Tomorrow Morning (Norman Nicholson)
You can start the Count Down, you can take a last look
Candy 35; Spa 92; WP 102

The Owl and the Astronaut (Gareth Owen)
The owl and the astronaut
King 61; Owe C 9; Spa 44

Shed in Space (Gareth Owen)
My Grandad Lewis
King 62; Owe C 87; Spa 16

Space Shuttle (Judith Nicholls)
Monday / my Aunt Esmeralda
Nic F 32

Space Travellers (James Nimmo)
There was a witch, humpbacked and hooded
Open 110; Pos 9

Tea in a Space-ship (James Kirkup)
In this world a tablecloth need not be laid
Open 107

SPAGHETTI

Spaghetti (Frank Flynn)
A plate heaped high
Candy 23

Spaghetti (Shel Silverstein)
Spaghetti, spaghetti all over the place
Sil 100; SS 36

Spaghetti, Spaghetti (Jack Prelutsky)
Spaghetti! spaghetti!
Noisy 12; Pud 116

SPARROWS

The House Sparrow (John Heath-Stubbs)
Citizen Philip Sparrow, who likes
Sun 38

London Sparrow (Eleanor Farjeon)
Sparrow, you little brown gutter-mouse
Far M 18

Sparrow (Norman MacCaig)
He's no artist
CCC 100

SPEEDWAY RACING

Speedway Racing (Ana Balduque)
They line up together
Howl 34

SPELLING

Charlie Fook (Peter Mortimer)
Me name's Charlie Fook and me spelling's a laugh
Ang II 36

Gust Becos I Cud Not Spel (Brian Patten)
Gust becos I cud not spel
Pat 40

Spelling Rules, OK? (June Crebbin)
Each Monday we're given ten spellings
Cre 46

SPELL IT (Mike Rosen)
We didn't use to have POETRY
Ros F 28

SPIDERS

The Spider and the Fly (Mary Howitt)
'Will you walk into my parlour?' said the spider to the fly
Once 103; Ox CV 158

Who's There? (Judith Nicholls)
Knock, knock! / Who's there?
Nic F 6

SPIES

The Interrogation (Edwin Muir)
We could have crossed the road but hesitated
Show III 38; Wind 27

My Neighbour Mr Normanton
(Charles Causley)
My neighbour Mr Normanton
All 69; Cau F 74

Spy Story (Vernon Scannell)
He awoke in a strange bed
Strict 161

SPORTS

See also Boxing, Fishing,
Hunting, Mountaineering,
Shooting, Skating, Swimming

Judo Contest (J. Rathbone)
The novice grades had finished
Cham 50

SPOTS

Spell to Banish a Pimple (John
Agard)
Get back pimple
Life 6

Spots! (Shaun Traynor)
The spots say it all
Mea 16

SPRING

See also April

Alison (anon. *circa* 1300)
From middle March to April
Name 8

British Weather (Gavin Ewart)
It is the merry month of May
Touch IV 126

chanson innocente (e. e.
cummings)
in Just- / spring
*Fab NV 25; GTP 272; Pud 62; Rhy
145; RMP 30; Show I 12; This W 69;
Young 69*

The Corn Growing (Leonard
Clark)
Snow no longer snowing
Cla C 6

Cuckoo Song (Rudyard Kipling)
Tell it to the locked-up trees
Puf M 169

The Fight of the Year (Roger
McGough)
And there goes the bell for the third
month

*Cham 48; McRo 60; Out 16; Ox CP
154; Pro I 76*

from *The Georgics* (Virgil, trans.
from Latin C. Day Lewis)
Then are the trackless copses alive
with the trilling of birds
Floc 11

*Getting up Early on a Spring
Morning* (Po Chu-i China 9th
cent. trans. Arthur Waley)
The early light of the rising sun
shines on the beams
Floc 9

Good-by my Winter Suit (N. M.
Bodecker)
Good-by my winter suit
Occ 33

from *In Memoriam* (Alfred Lord
Tennyson)
Now fades the last long streak of
snow
Choice 97

Spring (Gerard Manley Hopkins)
Nothing is so beautiful as spring
*Choice 115; Earth 5; Out 30; Rat 405
(part) Touch IV 13*

Spring (Karla Kuskin)
I'm shouting / I'm singing
Walk 43

Spring (Song of Solomon)
For, lo, the winter is past
Like 61; PPP 17; Puf V 21

Spring (Thomas Nashe)
Spring, the sweet spring, is the year's
pleasant king
*Floc 6; Mes 95; Once 54; Ox PC 102;
Talk 15*

When Daisies Pied (William
Shakespeare)
When Daisies Pied and violets blue
This W 72

SQUIRRELS

Five Little Squirrels (anon.)
Five little squirrels
Fab NV 81; Pop 10

The Grey Squirrel (Humbert
Wolfe)
Like a small grey / coffee-pot
Show II 8; Touch IV 32; Young 21

Grey Squirrel (Wes Magee)
Noses against the classroom windows
ATP 70; Mag M 51

Squirrel (James Fenton)
Oh the elephant strolls, the turkey struts
Sort 52

Squirrel up a Pole (Gregory Harrison)
The engine roared in lower gear
CCC 117; Trio 29

Squirrels in my Notebook (Florence McNeil)
I went to Stanley Park
Til 48

To a Squirrel at Kyle-Na-No (W. B. Yeats)
Come play with me
Gold 81; Irish 173; KPC 215; O & A 63; Ox PC 131; Pop 72; PoWo I 40; P Sev 25; Rab 22; This W 45; Walk 55

Whisky Frisky (anon.)
Whisky Frisky
Ani 38; Fab NV 77; Read 58

STAGS

from *Peer Gynt* (Ibsen, trans. Peter Watts)
While I sheltered from the weather
KWP 100

from *A Runnable Stag* (John Davidson)
When the pods went pop on the broom, green broom
Ten 51

The Stag (Ted Hughes)
While the rain fell on the November woodland
Foc 61; KWP 96; Touch IV 198

STARLINGS

The Starling (John Heath-Stubbs)
The starling is my darling, although
Floc 91; Gold 22

The Starlings in George Square (Edwin Morgan)
Sundown on the high stonefields
Scot 85

STARS

Beware of the Stars (Ted Hughes)
That star / Will blow your hand off
Strict 37

Escape at Bedtime (Robert Louis Stevenson)
The lights from the parlour and kitchen shone out
All 115; KCP 193; Ox T 148; Shad 104; Ste 38; YD 129

I am . . . Star Counting (John Rice)
I am . . . lying here counting the stars
Spa 8

The Star (Jane Taylor)
Twinkle, twinkle, little star
NV 140; Ox CV 122; Ox Dic 397; Ox T 162; Puf V 217
(part) *Read 71; RMP 57*

The Starlight Night (Gerard Manley Hopkins)
Look at the stars! look, look up at the stars!
Choice 117; This W 105

Star-talk (Robert Graves)
Are you awake, Gemelli
Sort 101

When I Heard the Learn'd Astronomer (Walt Whitman)
When I heard the learn'd astronomer
Earth 28; KWP 213; PW 18

STEAM SHOVELS

Steam Shovel (Charles Malam)
The dinosaurs are not all dead
Poem I 36; P Sev 150; RMP 25; Walk 216

The Steam Shovel (Rowena Bennett)
The steam digger
Pop 80

STORM PETRELS

The Storm Petrel (John Heath-Stubbs)
Far out at sea, a little dark bird
Sun 37

STORMS

See also Thunder and Lightning

Hurricane (James Berry)
Under low black clouds
Ber 116

from *King Lear* (William Shakespeare)
Blow winds, and crack your cheeks!
rage! blow!
Floc 272

from *The Leech-Gatherer* (William Wordsworth)
There was a roaring in the wind all night
Floc 36; Iron 135; WAS 92

Lodged (Robert Frost)
The rain to the wind said
P Sev 124

Storm (Gillian Clarke)
The cat lies low, too scared
Five 75

Storm (Roger McGough)
They're at it again
ASP 36; Out 56; Ox T 142; P Sev 122; YD 111

Storm in the Black Forest (D. H. Lawrence)
Now it is almost night, from the bronzy soft sky
Cam I 64; Out 57

Storm on the Island (Seamus Heaney)
We are prepared; we build our houses squat
Touch IV 137

STORY-TELLING

Aunt Sue's Stories (Langston Hughes)
Aunt Sue has a head full of stories
World 16

STRAWBERRIES

For Strawberries (Eleanor Farjeon)
Ripe, ripe Strawberries
Pic 45

Strawberry Town (John Walsh)
Out there in the sunny fields they are gathering the strawberry crops
Pic 45

STREET CRIES

See Ox NR 72-3

SUGARCANE

Sugarcane (John Agard)
When I take
Aga 19; Pic 145; Stuf 53

SUMMER

A Hot Day (A. S. J. Tessimond)
Cottonwool clouds loiter
Out 41; Pro II 73

It's Hot! (Shel Silverstein)
It's hot!
DS 9

Knoxville, Tennessee (Nikki Giovanni)
I always like summer / best
Blac 15; Pic 92; Pop 91

Summer (Christina Rossetti)
Winter is cold-hearted
Ten 34

Summer Evening (Walter de la Mare)
The sandy cat by the Farmer's chair
Sing 10

Summer Farm (Norman MacCaig)
Straws like tame lightning lie about the grass
Out 34; Voi III 28

SUMMER-HOUSES

Gazebos (Roger McGough)
What I find wanting in gazebos
McG S 11

SUN

Joey (Shel Silverstein)
Joey Joey took a stone
Sil 26

Lucky Old Sun (U. S. A.)
Up in the morning
Afr I 45

Pods Pop and Grin (James Berry)
Strong strong sun, in that look
Ber 115; NTP 123

Poem about the Sun Slinking Off
(Roger McGough)
the sun
Out 37

Sun is Shining (Bob Marley)
Sun is shining, the weather is sweet
Life 86

Sunflakes (Frank Asch)
If sunlight fell like snowflakes
PG 27; Pop 26

The Sun's Travels (Robert Louis
Stevenson)
The sun is not a-bed when I
Ste 49

Sunstruck (Darien Smith)
There's a pencil of light
Aus R 5

There is Joy (anon., Arctic
Eskimo)
There is joy in
Earth 101

SUPERMARKETS

At the Super-market (Barbara
Ireson)
Take a trolley
RT 164

At the Supermarket (Hiawyn
Oram)
I wish they wouldn't do it
Ora 40

Cheeky Lee Babcott (Michael
McHugh)
Cheeky Lee Babcott
TG 18

*The Fate of the Supermarket
Manager* (Kit Wright)
There once was a supermarket
manager
Gang 109; Open 45; Pac 17; Wri R 70

Song of the Supermarket (Leslie
Norris)
COME IN ! COME IN! COME IN!
Pic 56

Supermarket (Felice Holman)
I'm / lost / among a / maze of cans
*KWP 88; Ox T 40; Pac 6; Pic 42; Sort
70*

Supermarket Thought (U. A.
Fanthorpe)
The kestrel's wide-fanned tail
Crys 33

SUPERNATURAL

See also Dwarves, Fairies, Ghosts,
Goblins, Gremlins, Ogres,
Poltergeists, Trolls, Vampires,
Werewolves, Witches

Anancy (Andrew Salkey, Jamaica)
Anancy is a spider
Blac 106; Stuf II 30

The House on the Hill (Wes
Magee)
It was built years ago
All 106; King 189

The Voice (Walter de la Mare)
As I sat in the gloaming
de la M V 11

Who's That? (James Kirkup)
Who's that / stopping at
King 198

SWALLOWS

Swallows Over the South Downs
(Mary Holden)
England, we're here again
WAS 40

The Swallow (Ogden Nash)
Swallow, swallow, swooping free
Read 23

SWANS

Roast Swan Song (Bavaria, 13th
cent., from latin trans. George F
Whicher)
Aforetime, by the waters wan
Floc 99

Short-cut for Swans (Gregory
Harrison)
Now why did they arrogant and
unafraid
Trio 26

The Silver Swan (Orlando
Gibbons)
The silver swan, who living had no
note
Fab CV 89; Rat 389; YD 66; Zoo 65

Swan (Leslie Norris)
Swan, unbelievable bird, a cloud
floating

CCC 106; Fab CV 96; Ox CV 314; Ox PC 30

The Wild Swans at Coole (W. B. Yeats)
The trees are in their autumn beauty
Fire 28; Floc 260; Ten 42; Touch V 170

SWIFTS

Swifts (Ted Hughes)
Fifteenth of May. Cherry blossom. The swifts
Show II 51

SWIMMING

See Cham 58-63

Advice to Swimmers (John Smith)
To clutch at straws is to drown surely
Mot 134

Come on in the Water's Lovely (Gareth Owen)
Come on in the water's lovely
Owe C 13

First Lesson (Philip Booth)
Lie back, daughter, let your head
Mot 135

Taking the Plunge (John Mole)
Flipping eck, cor blimey, strewth
Mol 11

Written after Swimming from Sestos to Abydos (Lord Byron)
If, in the month of dark December
Mot 47

SWINGING

A Swing Song (William Allingham)
Swing, swing, / Sing, sing
Tick 48

TABLE MANNERS

The Boy Serving at Table (John Lydgate, 1370?-1450)
My dear child, first thyself enable
Ox CV 4

Dave Dirt Came to Dinner (Kit Wright)
Dave Dirt came to dinner
Pac 55; Wri H 61

Hot Food (Michael Rosen)
We sit down to eat
Ros H 14

Little Bits of Soft-Boiled Egg (Fay Maschler)
Spread along the table leg
Pic 90; Walk 149

My Sister Sybil (Colin West)
Sipping soup, my sister Sybil
Corn 21

Standing on a Strawberry (John Cunliffe)
'You're standing on a strawberry'
Straw 6

Table Manners (Gelett Burgess)
The Goops they lick their fingers
BBGG 45; Mons 82; Ox A 209; Read 69; Sk 90; Walk 106

Table Rules for Little Folk (anon., c 1858)
In silence I must take my seat
Ox CV 226; Sk 89

The Visitor (Katherine Pyle)
John's manners at the table
BBGG 50; Once 74

With his Mouth Full of Food (Shel Silverstein)
Milford Dupree, though he knew it was rude
Pac 89

TADPOLES

Halfway (Judith Wright)
I saw a tadpole once in a sheet of ice
CCC 134; Sort 55

TALES, CAUTIONARY

Aunts and Nieces (A. E. Housman)
Some nieces won't, some nieces can't
Chat 336

The Chewing-gum Song (Roald Dahl)
Dear friends, we surely all agree
Gang 120

Goody Blake and Harry Gill (William Wordsworth)
Oh! what's the matter? what's the matter?
YD 37

I'm Much Better Than You (Colin
McNaughton)
My dad's bigger than your dad
McN 24

Kenneth (Wendy Cope)
The chief defect of Kenneth Plumb
King 66

Little Thomas (F. Gwynne Evans)
Thomas was a little glutton
BBGG 45

Meddlesome Matty (Ann Taylor)
One ugly trick has often spoiled
Ox CV 115

*Mrs Lorris, Who Died of Being
Clean* (Barbara Giles)
Mrs Lorris was a fusser
Trio 18

Purple William (A. E. Housman)
The hideous hue which William is
Chat 335

Roberta Hyde (Mark Burgess)
The trouble with Roberta Hyde
Bur F 36

Sarah Cynthia Sylvia Stout (Shelley
Silverstein)
Sarah Cynthia Sylvia Stout
BBGG 73; Ox A 280

TALES, CAUTIONARY:
BELLOC

Charles Augustus Fortescue
(Hilaire Belloc)
The nicest child I ever knew
Bel CV 48; Puf V 138

Franklin Hyde (Hilaire Belloc)
His Uncle came on Franklin Hyde
Fun 104

George (Hilaire Belloc)
When George's Grandmamma was
told
*Fab NV 159; Fun 122; GTP 216; Ten
148*

Henry King (Hilaire Belloc)
The Chief Defect of Henry King
*BBGG 48; Bel CV 22; FF 37; Fun 113;
Mea 36; Story 105; Ten 147*

Jack and his Pony, Tom (Hilaire
Belloc)
Jack had a little pony – Tom

*Bel CV 62; Fab NV 173; King 81; Ten
69*

Jim (Hilaire Belloc)
There was a Boy whose name was
Jim
*BBGG 70; Bel CV 15; Fab NV 161;
ND 109; Ox CV 312; Ox SP 25; P Sev
63; Young 62*

Matilda (Hilaire Belloc)
Matilda told such dreadful lies
*Bel CV 26; CBC 102; Fab CV 96; Fav
39; Ox CV 314; Ox PC 30; Puf V 152*

Rebecca (Hilaire Belloc)
A trick that everyone abhors
*Bel CV 42; Fab NV 156; Fun 116;
Name 70*

Tom and his Pony, Jack (Hilaire
Belloc)
Tom had a little pony, Jack
Bel CV 66; Ten 68

TALES, CAUTIONARY:
HOFFMAN

Caspar and the Soup (Heinrich
Hoffman)
Caspar was never sick at all
Fun 125

Flying Robert (Dr Heinrich
Hoffman)
When the rain comes tumbling down
Fab NV 158; Name 72

Harriet and the Matches (Dr
Heinrich Hoffman)
It's really almost past belief
Fab NV 157

Johnny Head-in-Air (Dr Heinrich
Hoffman)
As he trudged along to school
*All 62; BBGG 78; Fab NV 162; Ox C
206*

Little Suck-a-thumb (Dr Heinrich
Hoffman)
One day Mamma said 'Conrad dear
Fab NV 95; KCP 96

The Story of Augustus (Dr
Heinrich Hoffman)
Augustus was a chubby lad
*All 52; BBGG 48; Fab NV 101; Ox C
205; Pac 71; Walk 107; Young 57*

The Story of Fidgety Philip (Dr Heinrich Hoffman)
Let me see if Philip can
Ox CV 208
One evening Philip's father said
Fav 36; Fun 118; Name 67

TALES, TALL

See Ahl M throughout

Amazing Andy, Wonder Schoolboy (David Bateson)
Andy said he could tie himself
Aus B 56

Dahn the Plug'ole (anon.)
A muvver was barfin' 'er baby one night
Rat 120

desk (Dave Calder)
It was stuffy in the classroom
Rhy 139

The Green Eye of the Little Yellow God (J. Milton Hayes)
There's a one-eyed yellow idol to the north of Khatmandu
Show I 9

a heavy rap (Nikki Giovanni)
i can run faster than any gazelle
Blac 36

The Invisible Backwards-facing Grocer (Alasdair Clayre)
John Green the grocer lived a hesitant life
Gang 94

Lies (Kit Wright))
When we are bored
ATP 79

The Mad Professor's Daughter (Allan Ahlberg)
She came into the classroom
Ahl H 67

My Friend Edward Cole (Tony Bradman)
My friend Edward Cole says:
Bra A 38

Paul Bunyan (Arthur S. Bourinot)
He came / striding
Til 90

Paul Bunyan (Shel Silverstein)
He rode through the woods on a big blue ox
Sil 124

Tall Story for Fred Dibnah (Geoffrey Summerfield)
Jack Steeplejack / A joker
Ox T 80

Tall Timber (Len Fox)
Just south of the Murray where tall timbers grow
Aus R 90

Tom's Bomb (David Hornsby)
There was a boy whose name was Tom
Sort 88

Whoppers (Eric Finney)
I'm having a pony for Christmas
ATP 78

The Wonderful Derby Ram (anon.)
As I was going to Derby
Chat 362; Fab NV 70; Iron 2; Nine 102; NTP 216; Ox Dic 145; Ox NR 205; Pud 20

Yarns (Carl Sandburg)
They have yarns
GTP 196
(part) *WP 62*

TALKING

from *What Some People Do* (anon.)
Jibber, jabber, gabble, babble
DS 20; KCP 239

TATTOOS

'Blackie, The Electric Rembrandt' (Thom Gunn)
We watch through the shop-front while
Floc 130

TEA

On Making Tea (R. L. Wilson)
The water bubbles
Pic 96

A Nice Cup of Tea (A. P. Herbert)
I like a nice cup of tea in the morning
Pic 98

The Way of Tea (Chiao-Jen)
A friend from Yueh presented me
Pic 97

Stop Troubling that Phone (John Agard)
Telephone, telephone, you're so alone
Aga 11

Telephone (Mamman J. Vatsa)
I am a telephone
Blac 45

The Telephone (Robert Frost)
When I was just as far as I could walk
Fire 33

Telephone Conversation (Wole Soyinka)
The price seemed reasonable, location
Face 134; Fire 34; Floc 134; Touch V 116

Telephone Poles (John Updike)
They have been with us a long time
Earth 80; Floc 108

Telephones (Adrian Henri)
Grownups / Never stop complaining
Hen 22

True Love (Ian Serraillier)
My love was a thousand miles away
Occ 61

Waiting for the Call (Vernon Scannell)
Sitting in the curtained room
Sca L 49; Trio 45

TELEVISION

The Blind Eye of the Little Sony God (Mick Gowar)
There's a teak-topped, square-eyed idol standing silent in the room
Gow F 68

Jimmy Jet and his TV Set (Shel Silverstein)
I'll tell you the story of Jimmy Jet
Ox A 278; PoWo I 46; Sil 28; Story 38

Stephen (Wendy Cope)
Shed a tear for Stephen Kelly
DS 32

TeeVee (Eve Merriam)
In the house / of Mr and Mrs Spouse
KCP 137; King 73; Open 120

THE TEN COMMANDMENTS

The Ten Commandments (anon.)
I. Have thou no other gods but me
Ox CV 57; Ring 48; Sun 78

TERRORISM

Kill the Children (James Simmons)
On Hallowe'en in Ship Street
Strict 57

THAW

Last Snow (Andrew Young)
Although the snow still lingers
Out 15

Sudden Thaw (Andrew Young)
When day dawned with unusual light
NTP 137

Thaw (Edward Thomas)
Over the land freckled with snow half-thawed
Choice 171; Floc 10; Iron 39; NTP 136; Out 14; WS 116

The Thaw (Vernon Scannell)
The blue night was veiled with the slow
Trio 36

THEATRE

At the Theatre (A. P. Herbert)
Dear Madam, you have seen this play
Open 49

Chocolates (Guy Boas)
Here the seats are: George, old man
Open 50

THISTLES

Thistles (Ted Hughes)
Against the rubber tongues of cows and the hoeing hands of men
Fire 11; Pro III 43; Touch V 48; Voi III 171

THRUSHES

The Darkling Thrush (Thomas Hardy)
I leant upon a coppice gate
Cam II 130; Choice 134; Rat 120

Missel Thrush (Walter de la Mare)
When from the brittle ice the fields
Iron 143

A *Thrush in the Trenches*
(Humbert Wolfe)
Suddenly he sang across the
trenches
War 49

The Thrush's Nest (John Clare)
Within a thick and spreading
hawthorn bush
Ox PC 67

THUNDER AND LIGHTNING

Giant Thunder (James Reeves)
Giant Thunder, striding home
Mons 81; Ox T 143; Pac 105; Ree C 105

Rhyme (Elizabeth Coatsworth)
I like to see a thunder storm
Noisy 14

Song 21 (Australian Aborigine)
The tongue of the lightning flashes
along the top of the clouds
KWP 29

Thunder (Walter de la Mare)
Call the cows home!
Iron 6

Thunder and Lightning (James Kirkup)
Blood punches through every vein
Cal 110; Out 59; YD 111

Thunderstorm (Peter Skrzynecki)
Nearly every afternoon that summer
Aus R 102

TIDES

The Tide in the River (Eleanor Farjeon)
The tide in the river
Far M 21; NTP 236; Ox PC 136; Poem 1 40; P Sev 75; Puf Q 29

The Tide Rises, the Tide Falls (Henry W. Longfellow)
The tide rises, the tide falls
Gold 93; PG 43; Sea 54; Story 30

Tide Talk (Max Fatchen)
The tide and I had stopped to chat
Aus R 15

The Tides to Me (George Barker)
The tides to me, the tides to me
Sea 73

TIGERS

Auntie Agnes's Cat (Colin West)
My Auntie Agnes has a cat
West 43

India (W. J. Turner)
They hunt, the velvet tigers in the jungle
Jung 18; Ox PC 112

The Tiger (William Blake)
Tiger! Tiger ! burning bright
Choice 43; Fab CV 64; Fav 131; GTP 36; KCP 37; Mes 121; ND 80; NTP 105; Ox PC 111; Puf V 52; Rab 79; Rat 444; RMP 42; Talk 61; Ten 45

TIME

As I Walked Out One Evening (W. H. Auden)
As I walked out one evening
PW 197; Touch V 10

Blue Girls (John Crowe Ransom)
Twirling your blue skirts, travelling the sward
Foc 124; Rat 82

Cities and Thrones and Powers (Rudyard Kipling)
Cities and Thrones and Powers
NTP 147

Eating Habits (Vernon Scannell)
The whole world is a busy eating house
Sca 57

Lines on a Clock in Chester Cathedral (Henry Twells)
When as a child I laughed and wept
Puf V 214

Lines . . . Written on the Eve of his Execution (Sir Walter Ralegh)
Even such is Time, which takes in trust
ND 239

The Old Lord of Trecrogo (Charles Causley)
Long long ago-go
Cau J 40

Ramhead and Dodman (Charles Causley)
Said Ramhead to Dodman
Cau F 48

Sonnet LX (William Shakespeare)
Like as the waves make towards the
pebbled shore
ND 233

Then (Walter de la Mare)
Twenty, forty, sixty, eighty
de la M P 39

The Tree and the Pool (Brian
Patten)
'I don't want my leaves to drop,' said
the tree
AFP 123; Pat 125

Twenty-four Hours (Charles
Causley)
Twenty-four hours
Cau J 19

TOADS

A Friend in the Garden (Juliana
Horatia Ewing)
He is not John the gardener
CCC 137; Ox CV 256; Pets 50

Frog and Toad (Christina
Rossetti)
Hopping frog, hop here and be seen
CCC 137

Lullaby for a Baby Toad (Stella
Gibbons)
Sleep, my child / The dark dock leaf
CCC 221

Odd (Lillian Moore)
That's / odd
Ani 48

The Philosophic Taed (William
Soutar)
There was a taed wha thocht sae lang
Scot 20

Toad (Norman MacCaig)
Stop looking like a purse. How could
a purse
CCC 135; Scot 48

The Toads' Chorus (Rumer
Godden)
The Toads' choir will never tire
Zoo 48

TOOTHACHE

A Charm against the Toothache
(John Heath-Stubbs)
Venerable Mother Toothache
Poem I 58; Mea 41

TORTOISES

from *Baby Tortoise* (D. H.
Lawrence)
You know what it is to be born alone
*CCC 26; Choice 194; Pets 62; Touch IV
42*

My Tortoise (Stevie Smith)
I had a sweet tortoise called Pye
CCC 186

The Tortoise (Wes Magee)
Boxed for winter
Mag W 39; SS 18

TOWER BLOCKS

A Child of Our Time (Roger
Woddis)
I remember, I remember
Fav 24

Half Term (Mick Gowar)
Up and down / Up and down
Gow S 31

High Life (Julie O'Callaghan)
My home is on the eighty-ninth floor
Bright 25; O'Ca 20

The Jelly Piece Song (Adam
McNaughtan)
I'm a skyscraper wean, I live on the
nineteenth flair
NTP 155

Mary, Mary (Roald Dahl)
Mary, Mary, quite contrary
Dah S 55

My Animals (Elizabeth Jennings)
My animals are made of wool and
glass
Pets 79

Old Johnny Armstrong (Raymond
Wilson)
Old Johnny Armstrong's eighty or
more
Earth 25

I Robbed the Woods (Emily
Dickinson)
I robbed the Woods
Earth 18

Think of this Tower-block (Michael
Rosen)
Think of this tower-block
Ros W 67

The Last Steam Train to Margate
(John Hill)
Gosssh / I wisssh / I were a busss
World 12

Midnight on the Great Western
(Thomas Hardy)
In the third-class seat sat the
journeying boy
Face 74

The Night Mail (W. H. Auden)
This is the night mail crossing the
border
*Fav 94; KCP 23; Like 53; ND 17; Pro
I 65; Young 86*

On the Platform (Brian Lee)
The distance swims in the heat
where the rails reach far to the south
Six 224

*The Railway Historical Steam
Weekend* (Max Fatchen)
'Will you come,' says the letter, 'and
join our outing'
Fat W 15

Scene from a Slow Train (Martyn
Wiley)
'Man in Armchair'
Face 79

To a Fat Lady Seen from the Train
(Frances Cornford)
O why do you walk through the
fields in gloves
Face 78

The Train (Mary Coleridge)
A green eye – and a red – in the dark
Pos 25; PoWo II 22

The Train to Glasgow (Wilma
Horsbrugh)
Here is the train to Glasgow
*CBC 40; Fab NV 251; Nine 69; Once
11; Young 90*

TRAMPOLINES

The Trampoline (John Pudney)
You can weigh what you like for a
trampoline
Cham 107

TRAMPS

See also Hoboes, Swagmen

Minstrel (Michael Dransfield)
The road unravels as I go
Sort 24

Tramp (R. S. Thomas)
A knock at the door
Choice 301

The Vagabond (Robert Louis
Stevenson)
Give to me the life I love
ND 137; Puf V 175

TRAMS

Trams (Gregory Harrison)
Grandpa lived in that tall, lean
Trio 21

TRAPS

A Fellow Mortal (John Masefield)
I found a fox, caught by the leg
CCC 151

The Rabbit (W. H. Davies)
Not even when the early birds
CCC 216

The Snare (James Stephens)
I hear a sudden cry of pain
Irish 162; ND 84; Ox PC 130; WS 54

TRAVEL

See also Trains, Ulysses

from *Lines to Mr Hodgson* (Lord
Byron)
Huzza! Hodgson, we are going
Sea 114

TRAVEL, IMAGINARY

If Pigs Could Fly (James Reeves)
If pigs could fly, I'd fly a pig
*Nine 73; OSF 74; Ox T 53; Ree C 61;
World 31*

Kensey (Charles Causley)
Here's a card from Tangier, Kensey
Cau J 24

My Hat (Stevie Smith)
Mother said if I wore this hat
Gang 28

Rolling Down to Rio (Rudyard
Kipling)
I've never sailed the Amazon
Ten 172; World 20

Somewhere (Max Fatchen)
It's somewhere round the corner
Fat W 60

My new school calls it 'towning' or
else 'playing hookey'
Wad 10

Schule in June (Robert Bain)
There's no a clood in the sky
Kist 7

Truant (Phoebe Hesketh)
They call him dunce, and yet he can
discern
Six 141

The Truants (John Walsh)
So I cried 'We will!' and Roy echoed
'We will'
Quin 194

TRUMPETS

Trumpet Player (Langston
Hughes)
The Negro / With the trumpet at his
lips
Face 54

TULIPS

Moon-Tulips (Ted Hughes)
Tulips on the moon are a kind of
military band
Hug MW 35

TURKEYS

Three Turkeys (Marjory Fleming,
aged 7)
Three Turkeys fair their last have
breathed
Foot 42

Turkeys Observed (Seamus
Heaney)
One observes them, one expects
them
Floc 98; Pic 47

TURTLES

The Little Turtle (Vachell
Lindsay)
There was a little turtle
*Fab NV 85; KCP 118; Ox A 220; Ox
SP 123; Pop 74; Read 20; Tick 70;
Tim 5*

Tony the Turtle (E. V. Rieu)
Tony was a turtle
Fab NV 85

ULYSSES

Ulysses (Alfred Lord Tennyson)
It little profits that an idle king
Cam II 142; Choice 92; Fire 108

UNCLES

See also Aunts

Family Feeling (Charles Causley)
My Uncle Alfred had the terrible
temper
Cau V 59; Face 103

My Uncle Dan (Ted Hughes)
My Uncle Dan's an inventor, you
may think that's very fine
FF 16; Fun 51; Hug F 45

My Uncle Mick (Ted Hughes)
My Uncle Mick the portrait artist
painted Nature's creatures
Hug F 49

My Wicked Uncle (Derek Mahon)
His was the first corpse I had ever
seen
Wind 69

nobody loses all the time (e. e.
cummings)
i had an uncle named
Wind 68

The Spitfire on the Northern Line
(Brian Jones)
Harry was an uncle. I saw him twice
Poem I 87; Face 105

Uncle Albert (Vernon Scannell)
When I was almost eight years old
Fav 34

Uncle Alfred's Long Jump (Gareth
Owen)
When Mary Rand
Bright 40

Uncle Fred (Colin West)
My Uncle Fred / He went to bed
SS 5

Uncle Fred (Robert Fisher)
'There's no such things as ghosts'
ATP 51

UNEMPLOYMENT

Au Jardin des Plantes (John Wain)
The gorilla lay on his back
Cam II 109; Floc 220; Jung 56

I Don't Want your Millions, Mister
(anon.)
I don't want your diamond ring
KWP 20

UNICORNS

Ever See a Unicorn (Roger McGough)
Ever see / a unicorn
McG M 96

Fantasy in a Forest (Leah Bodine Drake)
Between two unknown trees I stood
O & A 140

The Strangers (Audrey Alexandra Brown)
Early this morning
Can 39

The Unicorn (E. V. Rieu)
The unicorn stood, like a king in a dream
AM 78; MT 73; Ox SP 126; Puf Q 138

The Unicorn (Shel Silverstein)
A long time ago when the earth was green
Sil 76

Unicorn (William Jay Smith)
The Unicorn with the long white horn
Walk 209

UNITED STATES OF AMERICA

See also USA

Stately Verse (anon.)
If Mary goes far out to sea
Fun 39; HH 78

UNKNOWN CITIZENS

The Man in the Bowler Hat (A. S. J. Tessimond)
I am the unnoticed, the unnoticeable man
Face 69

The Unknown Citizen (W. H. Auden)
He was found by the Bureau of Statistics to be
Cam II 107; Choice 244; Touch V 122

USA: PIONEERS AND THE WEST

The Last Song of Billy the Kid (anon.)
I'll tell you the story of Billy the Kid
Ten 110

USA: RAILROADS

Casey Jones (USA)
Come all you rounders I want you to hear
KWP 223

John Henry (USA)
Well, every Monday morning
Afr II 49
When John Henry was a little boy
Touch IV 109

USA: WAR BETWEEN THE STATES

Barbara Frietchie (John Greenleaf Whittier)
Up from the meadows rich with corn
GTP 190

Battle-Hymn of the Republic (Julia W. Howe)
Mine eyes have seen the glory of the coming of the Lord
GTP 311

USA: WAR OF INDEPENDENCE

Paul Revere's Ride (Henry Wadsworth Longfellow)
Listen, my children, and you shall hear
GTP 184; Nar 167; Ox A 45

The Dying British Sergeant (anon.)
Come all you good people where'er you be
Wheel 52

USELESSNESS

Useless (Paul Higgins)
You're as useless
Pro II 19

VAMPIRES

See also Mons 70-3

Ffangs the Vampire Bat (Ted Hughes)
Ffangs the vampire landed in London
Hug V 32

The Vampire (Jack Prelutsky)
The night is still and sombre
Mons 72; Shad 72
(part) *Nine 161*

The Vampire (Roger McGough)
Blood is an acquired taste
HH 97

VANDALISM

Chip the Glasses and Crack the Plates (J. R. R. Tolkien)
Chip the glasses and crack the plates!
Like 41; Poem I 42

On Monday Morning (Wes Magee)
There's been a break-in
Mag M 10

Outside (Anne Tibble)
The towered church squats
Foc 148

VAUGHAN

At the Grave of Henry Vaughan (Siegfried Sassoon)
Above the voiceful windings of a river
Sun 233

VEGETABLES

See also Asparagus, Bamboo shoots, Leeks, Mushrooms, Potatoes, Pumpkins, Rice, Salad

Gourds (Nicander, 2nd cent. BC)
First cut the gourds in slices and then run
Pic 66

I Hate Greens (David King)
I hate greens!
Pic 100

My Garden (Rodney Bennett)
I've a garden of my own
Pic 11

Turnip-Tops (Ann Taylor)
While yet the white frost sparkles over the ground
Pic 49

The Vegetable Garden and the Runaway Horse (Pam Ayres)
In everybody's garden now
Cal 62

VEGETARIANS

Eating Bamboo Shoots (trans. Arthur Waley)
My new Province is a land of bamboo-groves
Pic 107

I'm a Veggie (Judith Nicholls)
The day my Mum / went vegetarian
Nic F 17

Point of View (Shel Silverstein)
Thanksgiving Dinner's sad and thankless
Pic 105; Sil 98

Vegetarians (Roger McGough)
Vegetarians are cruel unthinking people
King 99

VIKINGS

Abbey Tomb (Patricia Beer)
I told them not to ring the bells
Wind 48

VIOLENCE

Beatings (Roger McGough)
My father beats me up
McG P 46

A Poem about Violence (Roger McGough)
If violence is what you want
McG P 45

VIOLINS

See also Fiddlers

At the Railway Station, Upway (Thomas Hardy)
There is not much that I can do
Open 59

THE VIRGIN MARY

As Mary was A-walking (Spanish, trans. E. C. Batho)
As Mary was a-walking
Story 12; Sun 118

I Sing of a Maiden (anon.)
I sing of a maiden
Fab CV 354; Floc 288; GTP 288; Puf V 256; This W 97

Mary's Song (Charles Causley)
Sleep, King Jesus
Ox CP 33

O, My Heart is Woe! (anon.)
'O my heart is woe!' Mary she said so
Sun 145

VISITORS

Domestic Asides (Thomas Hood)
I really take it very kind
Occ 87

A Good Hiding (Trevor Millum)
Why are we hiding in here, mother?
Boo 40

Silence (Marianne Moore)
My father used to say
Floc 62

VIXENS

See Foxes

VOICES

Their Voices (Adrian Mitchell)
One had a voice like an ancient wooden desk
Mit N 58

VOLCANOES

Mount Etna, a Volcano in Sicily (Virgil, trans. C. Day Lewis)
There lies a safe beach, sheltered from all four winds
KCP 202

THE VOWELS

AEIOU (Jonathan Swift)
We are very little creatures
Fun 67; Irish 163; Ox PC 21; Poem I 23; Stuf II 51

VULTURES

Vulture (Douglas Livingstone)
On ragged black sails
Touch V 172

The Vulture (Hilaire Belloc)
The vulture eats between his meals
Fab NV 77; Fun 21; Ox CV 312; Pac 95; P Sev 72; Walk 86; WS 78; Young 23

Vulture (X. J. Kennedy)
The vulture's very like a sack
Sort 43

WAGONDRIVERS

Song of the Wagondriver (B. S. Johnson)
My first love was the ten-ton truck
Ax 38; Cam I 21; Touch V 149

WAGTAILS

Little Trotty Wagtail (John Clare)
Little Trotty Wagtail, he went in the rain
CCC 101; Cla J 11; Fab NV 32; NTP 95; Once 43; Ox PC 65; Puf V 43; Rat 248; World 29

WAKING

Crack-a-Dawn (Brian Morse)
Good day and good morning
Mor 9

I Wake Up (Michael Rosen)
I wake up / I am not me
Life 6; Ros Q 13

Reveille (A. E. Housman)
Wake, the silver dusk returning
Show III 22

Waking (Lilian Moore)
My secret way of waking
Day 5; Walk 133

Waking-Up (Eleanor Farjeon)
Oh! I have just had such a lovely dream
Far R 11; Spi 8

WALES

A Welsh Testament (R. S. Thomas)
All right, I was Welsh. Does it matter?
Like 133

WALKING

Hiker's Haikus (Vernon Scannell)
This is the best way
Sca T 25

WAR

See also Battles, Chemical
warfare, Dirges and Laments,
Generals, Nuclear war,
Refugees, Sea battles, Soldiers,
Soldiers' songs, Spies

Beat! Beat! Drums (Walt
Whitman)
Beat! beat! drums! – blow! bugles!
blow!
PW 84

Buttons (Carl Sandburg)
I have been watching the war map
PW 67

Channel Firing (Thomas Hardy)
That night your great guns,
unawares
Rat 103

Christmas 1924 (Thomas Hardy)
'Peace upon earth!' was said. We sing
it
Ox CP 99

Embassy (W. H. Auden)
As evening fell the day's oppression
lifted
Foc 28

*History Teacher in the Warsaw
Ghetto Rising* (Evangeline
Paterson)
The schoolmaster once known as
PW 121

*In Time of 'The Breaking of
Nations'* (Thomas Hardy)
Only a man harrowing clods
PW 199; Rat 211

Masters of War (Bob Dylan)
Come you masters of war
Cam I 116

Proem (Richard Aldington)
Sixty years after the fall of Troy
FWW 62

A War Film (Teresa Hooley)
I saw / With a catch of the breath
War 35

The War Song of Dinas Vawr
(Thomas Love Peacock)
The mountain sheep are sweeter
KCP 154; NTP 170

Will It Be So Again? (C. Day
Lewis)
Will it be so again?
War 135

WAR: AFTERMATH

Aftermath (Siegfried Sassoon)
Have you forgotten yet?
FWW 76; War 62

Casualty (Miroslav Holub, trans.
E. Osers)
They bring us crushed fingers
Speak 109

Conquerors (Henry Treece)
By sundown we came to a hidden
village
Story 14

Does It Matter? (Siegfried
Sassoon)
Does it matter? – losing your legs?
PW 52; War 59

Fighting South of the Ramparts
(Chinese, trans. Arthur Waley)
They fought south of the ramparts
Floc 249; PW 64; Voi II 69

The Fly (Miroslav Holub, trans.
G. Theiner)
She sat on a willow trunk
Cam II 70; Rat 159

High Wood (Philip Johnstone)
Ladies and Gentlemen, this is High
Wood
FWW 91; PW 160

Home Thoughts from Abroad (John
Buchan)
After the war, says the papers, they'll
no be content at hame
Kist 71

The Horses (Edwin Muir)
Barely a twelvemonth after
*Cam II 83; Foc 172; PW 173; Rat 191;
Scot 3; Touch V 94*

How Sweet the Night (Rachael
Bates)
How sweet, how sweet will be the
night
PW 200

Johnny I Hardly Knew You (anon., Ireland)
With your guns and drums and drums and guns
World 53

The Lament of the Demobilized (Vera Brittain)
'Four years,' some say consolingly.
'Oh well . . .'
War 59

Lord Lovelace (Charles Causley)
Lord Lovelace rode home from the wars
Touch IV 45

A Protest in . . . AD 879 (Ts'Ao Sung, trans. Arthur Waley)
The hills and rivers of the lowland country
Touch V 132; Voi II 75

Reconciliation (Siegfried Sassoon)
When you are standing at your hero's grave
War 47

Remembrance Day (Judith Nicholls)
Poppies? Oh, miss
Cele 86

There Will Come Soft Rains (Sara Teasdale)
There will come soft rains
PW 201

There's a War On (Norman Nicholson)
Don't you know / there's a war on?
Ang I 99

Under the Hazy, Blossom-laden Sky (Okamoto Jun)
Under the hazy blossom-laden sky
Like 179

WARS: BOER

Boots (Rudyard Kipling)
We're foot – slog – slog – slog – sloggin' over Africa
Ten 138

Drummer Hodge (Thomas Hardy)
They throw in Drummer Hodge, to rest
PW 71

The Man He Killed (Thomas Hardy)
Had he and I but met
PW 117; Rat 267; Show III 47

WARS: CRIMEA

The Charge of the Light Brigade (Lord Tennyson)
Half a league, half a league
Brave 124; Like 43; ND 177; Story 40

WARS: SPANISH CIVIL

A Moment of War (Laurie Lee)
It is night like a red rag
PW 100

WARS: VIETNAM

Green Beret (Ho Thien)
He was twelve years old
Ax 78

Home-Coming (Bruce Dawe)
All day, day after day, they're bringing them home
Foc 39

What Were They Like? (Denise Levertov)
Did the people of Vietnam
Foc 40; PW 77; Voi III 108

WARS: 1914-18 (AIR)

Flying a Camel (Vernon Scannell)
'When I was young,' the old man said
Sca T 52

An Irish Airman Foresees his Death (W. B. Yeats)
I know that I shall meet my fate
Fab CV 270; Gold 20; Show III 24; War 17

WARS:1914-18 (THE DEAD)

Anthem for Doomed Youth (Wilfred Owen)
What passing-bells for these who die as cattle?

Choice 158; Fire 75; Floc 250; FWW 70; Like 169; ND 183; Voi III 125

The Death-Bed (Siegfried Sassoon)
He drowsed and was aware of silence heaped
FWW 48; War 52

Elegy in a Country Churchyard (G. K. Chesterton)
The men that worked for England
FWW 117

For the Fallen (Laurence Binyon)
With proud thanksgiving, a mother for her children
FWW 14
(part) They went with songs to the battle, they were young
War 58

Here Dead Lie We (A. E. Housman)
Here dead lie we because we did not choose
FWW 83; War 54

In Flanders Fields (John McCrae)
In Flanders fields the poppies blow
FWW 32; War 50

In Memoriam (Edward Thomas)
The flowers left thick at nightfall in the wood
Choice 172; War 55

Easter Monday: In Memoriam Edward Thomas (Eleanor Farjeon)
In the last letter that I had from France
PW 138; War 55

The Leveller (Robert Graves)
Near Martinpuich that night of Hell
War 23

Lost in France (Ernest Rhys)
He had the plowman's strength
Rhy 148

My Boy Jack (Rudyard Kipling)
Have you news of my boy Jack?
War 31

No One Cares Less Than I (Edward Thomas)
No one cares less than I
War 17

The Soldier (Rupert Brooke)
If I should die, think only this of me
Brave 123; Cam II 86; Fav 151; FWW 18; PW 39; Touch IV 177; War 16

The Volunteer (Herbert Asquith)
Here lies a clerk who half his life had spent
Foc 11; PW 113

The Ward at Night (anon.)
The rows of beds
War 52

WARS: 1914-18 (GAS)

Dulce et Decorum Est (Wilfred Owen)
Bent double, like old beggars under sacks
Cam II 74; Choice 156; Fire 110; FWW 74; ND 180; PW 55; Touch IV 175

WARS: 1914-18 (GENERAL)

See also Foc 10-25, FWW throughout, War 12-62

Base Details (Siegfried Sassoon)
If I were fierce, and bald, and short of breath
FWW 58; ND 173; Touch V 127

Dick Lander (Charles Causley)
When we were children at the National School
Cau V 5

Futility (Wilfred Owen)
Move him into the sun
Choice 161; Foc 21; PW 130; Rat 170; Show III 48; Touch V 76; Voi III 127; War 56

Gelibolu [Gallipoli] (Charles Causley)
The path, under a thin scribble of pine
Cau V 14

The General (Siegfried Sassoon)
'Good-morning, good-morning' the General said
FWW 61; ND 176; Touch V 81

from *Gold Braid* (A. A. Milne)
Same old trenches, same old view
FWW 90

Into Battle (Julian Grenfell)
The naked earth is warm with spring
FWW 23

The Last Laugh (Wilfred Owen)
'O Jesus Christ! I'm hit, ' he said; and died
War 43

next to of course god (e. e. cummings)
next to of course god america i
PW 40; Touch IV 163

Nineteen-Fifteen (John Drinkwater)
On a ploughland hill against the sky
War 20

The Parable of the Old Men and the Young (Wilfred Owen)
So Abram rose, and clave the wood and went
Cam I 119; Floc 250; FWW 101; Sun 212; Voi III 127

Recruited: Poplar (Margaret Postgate)
March 1917 They say – they say
Speak 106

The Send-Off (Wilfred Owen)
Down the close, darkening lanes they sang their way
Brave 35; Cam II 72; Choice 155; Foc 20; ND 160; PW 89; Rat 374

WARS: 1914-18 (TRENCHES)

Ballad of the Three Spectres (Ivor Gurney)
As I went up by Ovillers
FWW 55

Bombardment (Richard Aldington)
Four days the earth was rent and torn
Cam I 103

Break of Day in the Trenches (Isaac Rosenberg)
The darkness crumbles away
PW 102

Breakfast (Wilfrid Gibson)
We ate our breakfast lying on our backs
FWW 16, War 45

The Dead-Beat (Wilfred Owen)
He dropped, – more sullenly than wearily
Choice 157

The Dug-Out (Siegfried Sassoon)
Why do you lie with your legs ungainly huddled
Floc 252; FWW 100; War 24

Exposure (Wilfred Owen)
Our brains ache, in the merciless iced east winds
FWW 102; PW 103; Rat 145

I Tracked a Dead Man Down a Trench (W. S. Lyon)
I tracked a dead man down a trench
FWW 21

The Night Patrol (Arthur Graeme West)
Over the top! The wire's thin here, unbarbed
FWW 36

Strange Meeting (Wilfred Owen)
It seemed that out of battle I escaped
Choice 160; Face 93; FWW 94; Rat 407; Show III 40; Voi III 129

Suicide in the Trenches (Siegfried Sassoon)
I knew a simple soldier boy
Foc 15; PW 113; War 42

The Target (Ivor Gurney)
I shot him and it had to be
Foc 17; FWW 109

A Working Party (Siegfried Sassoon)
Three hours ago he blundered up the trench
FWW 38

Winter Warfare (Edgell Rickword)
Colonel Cold strode up the line
Show II 68

WARS: 1939-45 (AIR)

The Bull (Wilfrid Gibson)
Into the paddock from his parachute
War 86

The Death of the Ball Turret Gunner (Randall Jarrell)
From my mother's sleep I fell into the State
Rat 125

Fleet Fighter (Olivia Fitzroy)
'Good show!' he said, leaned his head back and laughed.
War 83

For Johnny (John Pudney)
Do not despair
War 88

184

Parachute Descent (David Bourne)
Snap back the canopy
War 72

Song of the Dying Gunner (Charles Causley)
Oh mother my mouth is full of stars
War 87

WARS: 1939-45 (AIR RAIDS)

The Black-Out (Mary Desiree Anderson)
I never feared the darkness as a child
PW 97

Black-Out (Valentine Ackland)
Night comes now
War 75

Bomb Incident (Barbara Catherine Edwards)
Stretcher to stretcher still they came
War 103

The Bombing of the Café de Paris, 1941 (Vernon Scannell)
Snakehips, the band leader, wore a gallant grin
Foc 29

Doodle Bug (Mike Rosen)
Sometime after / baked beans on toast
Ros F 50

Earlswood (Fleur Adcock)
Air raid shelters at school were damp tunnels
Touch V 85

I've Finished My Black-out (anon.)
I've finished my black-out
War 75

Ladybird, Ladybird (Ruth Tomalin)
Laybird, ladybird / fly away home
War 101

My Little Eye (Roger McGough)
The cord of my new dressing-gown
McG F 53

October 1940 (anon.)
When leaves like guineas start to fall
War 76

Picture from the Blitz (Lois Clark)
After all these years
PW 120; War 107

Song of the Bomber (Ethel Mannin)
I am purely evil
War 99

When Billy Brown Goes Out at Night (anon.)
When Billy Brown goes out at night
War 76

1940 (John Betjeman)
As I lay in the bath the air was filling with bells
PW 134

WARS: 1939-45 (CIVILIANS)

from *All-Clear* (John Latham)
Miss Ryder is showing us how to breathe
War 92

The Children's Party (Eiluned Lewis)
Quick as shuttles the children move
War 74

Drawing a Banana (Myra Schneider)
Forty of us looked longingly at the yellow finger
War 96

WARS: 1939-45 (THE DEAD)

Killed in Action (Juliette de Bairach-Levy)
His chair at the table, empty.
War 126

Lady in Black (Alun Lewis)
Lady in black / I knew your son
War 127

Lament (Frances Mayo)
We knelt on the rocks by the dark green pools
War 128

WARS: 1939-45 (EVACUEES)

Albert Evacuated (Stanley Holloway)

Have you heard how young Albert
Ramsbottom
War 78

Evacuee (Edith Pickthall)
The slum had been his home since
he was born
War 78

The Evacuee (R. S. Thomas)
She woke up under a loose quilt
Foc 31

WARS: 1939-45 (GENERAL)

See also Foc 26-36; War 64-135

from *Autobiography* (Adrian
Henri)
Carrying my gas-mask to school
every day
War 65

Bournemouuth, September 3, 1939
(Anthony Thwaite)
My summer ends, and term begins
next week
War 64

Cousin Sidney (Dannie Abse)
Dull as a bat said my mother
Face 102

Pebble (Michael Rosen)
I know a man who's got a pebble
Brave 76; Ros Q 102; War 131

The Question (Alexander McKee)
Perhaps I killed a man today
PW 68

The Second World War (Elizabeth
Jennings)
The voice said 'We are at War'
War 65

WARS: 1939-45 (HOLOCAUST)

Was Not There (Karen Gershon)
The morning they set out from
home
Foc 119

Massacre of the Boys (Tadeusz
Rozewicz, trans. Adam
Czerniawski)
The children cried 'Mummy! . . .'
War 91

More Light! More Light! (Anthony
Hecht)
Composed in the Tower before his
execution
Cam II 80

Pigtail (Tadeus Rozewicz, trans.
Adam Czerniawski)
When all the women in the transport
War 89

WARS: 1939-45 (HOME GUARD)

Watching Post (C. Day Lewis)
A hill flank overlooking the Axe
valley
PW 32

WARS: 1939-45 (SEA)

Night Patrol (Alan Ross)
We sail at dusk. The red moon
ND 161

WARS: 1939-45 (TRAINING)

All Day It Has Rained (Alun Lewis)
All day it has rained and we on the
edge of the moors
PW 30; Touch IV 176

*Lessons of the War I: Naming of
Parts* (Henry Reed)
Today we have naming of parts.
Yesterday
ND 159; PW 33; Touch V 83; War 70

*Lessons of the War II: Judging
Distances* (Henry Reed)
Not only how far away, but the way
that you say it
PW 82; Touch IV 179

Love Letters of the Dead (Douglas
Street)
Go through the pockets of the
enemy wounded
PW 76

WARTS

The Soul is the Breath in your Body
(Jeni Couzyn)
You can sell them for a penny
Puf M 26

WASHING

Bathroom Fiddler (Michael Rosen)
I'm the bathroom fiddler
Ros D 12

Washing (John Drinkwater)
What is all this washing about
Day 16

WASHING: CLOTHES

Bendix (John Updike)
This porthole overlooks a sea
Touch IV 139

Breakdown (Jean Kenward)
Rackerty clackerty
Pud 76; Tick 30

Clothes on the Washing Line (Frank Flynn)
On windy days
Candy 24; Ox T 141

Our Village (John Yeoman and Quentin Blake)
At the wash-house by the river
Vil 14

Stocking and Shirt (James Reeves)
Stocking and shirt
Once 62; Puf Q 78

They That Wash on Monday (anon.)
They that wash on Monday
Puf NR 90

Tumble Drying at the Laundrette (Grace Nichols)
Spin spin spin
Five 13

Washing Lines (Robert Sparrow)
Grandmother said
Nif 21

WASHING-UP

Sink Song (J. A. Lindon)
Scouring out the porridge pot
Corn 89; Pac 101; Poem I 42

Washing-Up (Michael Rosen)
On Sundays / my mum and dad said
Ros Q 7

Washing-up Song (J. R. R. Tolkien)
Chip the glasses and crack the plates!
Like 41; Poem I 42

WATCHMEN

Dan the Watchman (John D. Sheridan)
Dan the watchman / doesn't go to bed
Tick 161

WATER

Our Corrugated Iron Tank (James Hackston)
Our tank stood on a crazy stand
Aus B 102

Turn on the Tap (Norman Nicholson)
Turn on the tap!
Candy 43

Water (Philip Larkin)
If I were called to
Touch IV 122; Voi III 138

WATERFALLS

The Cataract of Lodore (Robert Southey)
How does the water
NTP 168; Ox CV 94

Waterfall (Seamus Heaney)
The burn drowns steadily in its own downpour
Touch IV 136

WATERLOO

The Eve of Waterloo (Lord Byron)
There was a sound of revelry by night
Fab CV 259; ND 157

The Field of Waterloo (Thomas Hardy)
Yes, the coneys are scared by the thud of hoofs
Fab CV 260

WAVES

There Are Big Waves (Eleanor Farjeon)
There are big waves and little waves
Once 61; Pos 95

WEASELS

The Weasel (Gregory Harrison)
It should have been a moment
CCC 122

WEATHER

See also Fab NV 230-1, Ox NR 117
See also Clouds, Frost and ice, Galoshes, Hurricanes, Moon, Puddles, Rain, Rainbows, Sleet, Snow, Spring, Thaw, Winds, Winter

December Leaves (Kaye Starbird)
The fallen leaves are cornflakes
S Sun 32

Glass Falling (Louis MacNeice)
The glass is going down. The sun
Fav 96; Irish 108; Out 49

It's Never Fair Weather (Ogden Nash)
I do not like the winter wind
Nas C 14; Out 12

So Long as There's Weather (Tamara Kitt)
Whether it's hot
Pop 14

Weather (Eve Merriam)
Dot a dot dot dot a dot dot
Like 29; Noisy 15; S Sun 27

The Weather (Gavin Ewart)
What's the weather on about?
Ox T 140; P Sev 129; Sort 31; YD 104

The Weather (anon.)
Whether the weather be fine
AVF 108; NV 18

The Weather Prophet (A. B. Paterson)
'Ow can it rain', the old man said, 'with things the way they are?'
Pat A 67

Weathers (Thomas Hardy)
This is the weather the cuckoo likes
Cal 53; Choice 133; Fab CV 59; NTP 124; NV 13; Out 8; Ox PC 96; Puf V 165; Rat 458; Sing 21; Ten 31; YD 105

Week of Winter Weather (Wes Magee)
On Monday icy rain poured down
Mag W 40; RT 43; WP 25

Willoughby (Charles Causley)
Willoughby Whitebody-Barrington-Trew
Cau J 80

WEATHER VANES

The Pedalling Man (Russell Hoban)
We put him on the roof and we painted him blue
Out 10; Six 163; YD 107

WEEKDAYS

See also Fab NV 228

Finger Nails (anon.)
Cut them on Monday, you cut them for health
Ox NR 16

Friday (Eric Finney)
Friday; the clock ticks on to four
Bell 127

Monday (Eric Finney)
Monday; not only that but it's pouring
SO 15

Monday's Child (anon.)
Monday's child is fair of face
Fab CV 93; Fab NV 226; Lob 134; NV 15; Ox Dic 309; P Sev 51; Voa 20; Young 44

Sneezing (anon.)
Sneeze on Monday, sneeze for danger
Mea 12; Tick 103; Young 45

Sunday (D. J. Enright)
My mother's strongest religious feeling
Sun 205

When to Cut your Fingernails (Roger McGough)
Cut them on Monday
McG PT 38

WENDIGOS

The Wendigo (Ogden Nash)
The Wendigo, / The Wendigo!

AM 29; Fab NV 80; MCF 3; Mons 35;
Nas C 36; Walk 207; WZ 88

The Wendigo (Ted Hughes)
The Wendigo's tread
Hug MW 33; Hug U 33

Windigo Spirit (Ken Stange)
The Windigo is a spirit of the North,
the Cree told us
Til 88

WEREWOLVES

The Farmer's Wife (Thomas
Blackburn)
Spring is the time for a wedding
Ax 13; Nar 42

The Griesly Wife (John Manifold)
Lie still, my newly-married wife
Story 134

The Werewolf (Jack Prelutsky)
The full moon glows, foreboding
Mons 76

WHALES

Killing a Whale (David Gill)
A whale is killed as follows
Ax 70

Leviathan (Pamela Gillilan)
You can't make whales
Earth 72

from *Paradise Lost* (John Milton)
. . . There leviathan / Hugest of
living creatures
AM 59

The Song of the Whale (Kit
Wright)
Heaving mountain in the sea
Jung 66; Pro II 55; Rab 85; Wri H 17

Whale (Alan Brownjohn)
I am a whale and
Six 53

Whale (Barbara Juster Esbensen)
An evenly balanced / word WHALE
Esb 7

The Whale (Middle English,
trans. Brian Stone)
The whale's a fish: of all that be
Sea 40

Whale (D. M. Thomas)
A whale lay cast up on the island's
shore
Gang 83

The Whale (Erasmus Darwin)
Warm and buoyant in his oily mail
GTP 69

Whale (Geoffrey Dearmer)
Wouldn't you like to be a whale
Fab NV 76; Young 12

Whale Poems (Roger McGough)
whales / are floating cathedrals
McG P 68; Rab 84

The Whale's Hymn (Brian Patten)
In an ocean before cold dawn broke
Pat 82

WHALING

The Whale (anon.)
O, 'twas in the year of ninety-four
Sea 223; Story 66

WILDERNESS

Inversnaid (Gerard Manley
Hopkins)
This darksome burn, horseback
brown
*Choice 113; Earth 39; Iron 139; ND
10; Rat 215*

Rannoch, by Glencoe (T. S. Eliot)
Here the crow starves, here the
patient stag
Choice 221

The Wilderness (John Cotton)
'This is the wilderness,' my uncle
said
Crys 17

WINDS (L and D)

*Address to a Child during a
Boisterous Winter Evening*
(Dorothy Wordsworth)
What way does the Wind come?
*NTP 130; Ox CV 128; Ox PC 100; Puf
V 226*

Child on Top of a Greenhouse
(Theodore Roethke)
The wind billowing out the seat of
my britches
Rhy 42

Moon-Wind (Ted Hughes)
There is no wind on the moon at all
Hug MW 34

The North Wind (anon.)
The north wind doth blow
Fab NV 29; Lob 110; Once 52; Ox Dic

426; Ox NR 50; Pop 28; Puf NR 178;
Puf V 28; Stoc 38

On Wenlock Edge (A. E. Housman)
On Wenlock Edge the wood's in trouble
Mes 216; ND 14; Rat 326

Snow-Bound (John Greenleaf Whittier)
Shut in from all the world about
Ox CP 14

A Song of Wind (Will Lawson)
Hark to the song of the scattering, scurrying wind
Pos 113

The Sound of the Wind (Christina Rossetti)
The wind has such a rainy sound
Howl 43; Once 65; Ox PC 58; S Sun 26

The Villain (W. H. Davies)
While joy gave clouds the light of stars
Rat 449

The Whirlwind is Wicked (J. M. Chamunorwa, trans. P. Berlyn)
It pulls the grass from the thatch
KWP 51

The Wind (James Reeves)
I can get through a doorway without any key
PG 30; Pos 113; Puf Q 91; Ree C 24; Walk 26; WAS 77

Wind (Ted Hughes)
This house has been far out at sea all night
Cam I 62; Floc 37; ND 13; Out 64

The Wind (Christina Rossetti)
Who has seen the wind?
Cal 95; Nine 20; NTP 127; NV 10; Ox CV 278; Ox PC 96; Pop 31; Walk 27

Wind (Dionne Brand)
I pulled a humming-bird out of the sky
Blac 13

The Wind (Richard Edwards)
The wind runs rivers through the grass
Edw P 42

The Wind was on the Withered Heath (J. R. R. Tolkien)
The wind was on the withered heath
Howl 44; MT 113

A Windy Day (Andrew Young)
This wind brings all dead things to life
GTP 259; Pos 110; This W 115

Windy Nights (Robert Louis Stevenson)
Whenever the moon amd stars are set
Bed 43; Fab NV 241; Fav 68; Gold 42; Howl 46; KCP 195; Like 13; NTP 127; NV 129; Ox CV 294; Ox T 140; Pop 34; P Sev 123; Puf M 185; Puf V 218; Shad 19; S Sun 25; Ste 24; Ting 6; Walk 27

Workings of the Wind (James Berry)
Wind doesn't always topple trees
Ang II 102; Ber 117; Stuf 86

WINDS (N)

Wedding-Wind (Philip Larkin)
The wind blew all my wedding-day
Foc 95

The Wind and the Moon (George Macdonald)
Said the Wind to the Moon, 'I will blow you out . . .'
Fab NV 127; GTP 258; King 185

The Wind in a Frolic (William Howitt)
The wind one morning sprang up from sleep
Ox CV 162; Tick 124

Winds Light to Disastrous (Spike Milligan)
As I sipped morning tea
King 173; Out 66

Wind-Wolves (William D. Sargent)
Do you hear the cry as the pack goes by
Walk 26

WINDIGO

See Wendigo

WINDMILLS

The Windmill (H. W. Longfellow)
Behold! a giant am I!
Pic 22

WINTER

Calling, calling (Wes Magee)
The sky is grey
DS 55

The Coming of the Cold (Theodore Roethke)
The ribs of leaves lie in the dust
Ox CP 10

December (R. Southey)
A wrinkled crabbed man they picture thee
Like 122

The Frozen Man (Kit Wright)
Out at the edge of town
ASP 16; Cal 16; Gold 14; Stoc 119; Wri R 74

Red Boots On (Kit Wright)
Way down Geneva
Occ 26; World 88

Some Winter Pieces (William H. Moore)
Tiny figures stand
Til 42

There Goes Winter (Matt Simpson)
Look at red-faced Winter
Occ 28

The Warm and the Cold (Ted Hughes)
Freezing dusk is closing
Pro III 76

When Icicles Hang by the Wall (William Shakespeare)
When icicles hang by the wall
Fab CV 56; Iron 57; ND 66; Ox PC 98; Puf V 128; This W 72; WAS 155; WS 111

Winter (John Clare)
Old January clad in crispy rime
Cla J 66

Winter Days (Gareth Owen)
Biting air
Out 77; Ox CP 11; Stoc 62; Tick 123

Winter Time (Robert Louis Stevenson)
Late lies the wintry sun a-bed
Ox CV 298

Working in Winter (John Mole)
Silently the snow settles on the scaffolding
Rhy 29

WITCHES (L AND D)

See also Puf M 71-85, Wit throughout
See also Charms and spells, Hallowe'en, Sorcerers, Wizards

The Garden's Full of Witches (Colin McNaughton)
Mum! The garden's full of witches!
McN 62

The Hag (Robert Herrick)
The hag is astride
Fab CV 221; GTP 107; MT 135; Ox PC 85; Poem I 57; Pos 7; WS 95

The Hour When the Witches Fly (John Foster)
When the night is as cold as stone
AFP 53

from *Macbeth* (William Shakespeare)
Double, double, toil and trouble
Like 9; Walk 202; Wit 12
Thrice the brindled cat hath mew'd
ND 193; Puf M 79; Show II 45

from *The Masque of Queens* (Ben Jonson)
I have been all day looking after
Puf M 80

Mrs Gulliver (Leonard Clark)
As she slinks by
Cla C 26

The Ride-by-Nights (Walter de la Mare)
Up on their brooms the witches stream
de la M P 92; Pos 8; PoWo I 102; P Sev 95

The Spell of a Witch (Gillian Parker, aged 9)
I am making a magic spell
Nif 57

Wild Witches' Ball (Jack Prelutsky)
late last night at wild witchhall
Boo 78; HH 62; Wit 17

Witches' Charms (Ben Jonson)
Dame, dame! the watch is set
MT 136; Ting 23

The Witches Ride (Karla Kuskin)
Over the hills
P Sev 91; Pud 40; Wit 9

The Witches' Wood (Mary Coleridge)
There was a wood, a witches' wood
PoWo II 17

The Witch's Brew (Wes Magee)
Into my pot there now must go
AVF 98

The Witch's Cat (Ian Serraillier)
'My magic is dead,' said the witch
MT 138; PG 68

WITCHES (N)

Alison Gross (anon.)
O Alison Gross, that lives in yon tow'r
Fab CV 222; MT 30; Nar 12

The Allansford Pursuit (Robert Graves)
Cunning and art he did not lack
Rat 26

Annabel and the Witches (Mick Gowar)
Once upon a time there was a girl called Annabel
Gow T 20

As Lucy Went A-walking (Walter de la Mare)
As Lucy went a-walking one morning cold and fine
Ox SP 18

A Moon-Witch (Ted Hughes)
A moon-witch is no joke
Hug MW 74

Moon-Witches (Ted Hughes)
The moon is a dusty place
Hug MW 47

Space Travellers (James Nimmo)
There was a witch, hump-backed and hooded
Open 110; Pos 9

The Two Witches (Robert Graves)
O sixteen hundred and ninety-one
MT 29; PoWo II 16

Wanted – a Witch's Cat (Shelagh McGee)
Must have vigor and spite
Gold 39; Walk 202

The Witch (Mary Coleridge)
I have walked a great while over the snow
Shad 61; PoWo II 38

Witch Goes Shopping (Lilian Moore)
Witch rides off / Upon her broom
Open 108; Shad 83; Wit 21

Witch Spawn (Beth Cross)
It's true I knew her Mother burned
Strict 55

WIZARDS

The Wizard (Jack Prelutsky)
The wizard, watchful, waits alone
MT 28

WOLVERINES

The Wolverine (Ted Hughes)
The gleeful evil Wolverine
Hug MW 14

WOLVES

A Night with a Wolf (Bayard Taylor)
High up on the lonely mountains
Foot 32; GTP 33, Jung 80; O & A 14

WOMBATS

The Diggers (A. B. Paterson)
Bristling Billy the porcupine
Pat A 20

Weary Will (A. B. Paterson)
The strongest creature for his size
Pat A 19

WOODMEN

Throwing a Tree (Thomas Hardy)
The two executioners stalk along over the knolls
KCP 87

WOODPECKERS

Green Woodpecker (Reginald Arkell)
When I were a-coming
WAS 84

A Legend of the Northland (Phoebe Cary)
Away, away in the Northland
Ox SP 147

The Woodpecker (Elizabeth Madox Roberts)
The woodpecker pecked out a little round hole
Ox A 224

Woodpecker (John Agard)
Carving
Ani 30

Woodpecker (Ted Hughes)
Woodpecker is rubber-necked
Hug MW 26

WOODS

The Way Through the Woods (Rudyard Kipling)
They shut the road through the woods
Fab CV 377; Gold 62; Like 96; MT 110; ND 18; NTP 183; Ox CV 323; Shad 82; Show I 5; Ten 37; This W 163; Ting 8

WORDS

Feelings about Words (Mary O'Neill)
Some words clink / As ice in drink
Walk 197

Full House (Moira Andrew)
Words inhabit my head
Pro III 79

Nice Work (Judith Nicholls)
Never use the word NICE
Nic F 20

Sam Groom (Charles Causley)
What are you writing down there, Sam Groom
TG 42

The Word Party (Richard Edwards)
Loving words clutch crimson roses
Edw P 13

Words (Brian Lee)
Sticks and stones
Sort 72

Words (Edward Thomas)
Out of us all
Iron 104

WORK

Toads (Philip Larkin)
Why should I let the toad work
Fire 186; Touch V 150

Toads Revisited (Philip Larkin)
Walking around in the park
Fire 188; Touch V 166

Woman Work (Maya Angelou)
I've got the children to tend
Touch V 158

Work (D. H. Lawrence)
There is no point in work
Touch V 151

WORMS

See Earthworms

YAKS

The Mad Yak (Gregory Corso)
I am watching them churn the last milk
Ark 85; WZ 118; Zoo 51

The Yak (Hilaire Belloc)
As a friend to the children commend me the yak
Fab NV 166; Ox CV 310; Ox PC 117; Pets 26; Zoo 50

The Yak (Jack Prelutsky)
Yikity-yackity, yickity-yak
Noisy 22; Walk 197

The Yak (Virna Sheard)
For hours the princess would not play or sleep
Can 24

Yak (William Jay Smith)
The long-haired Yak has long black hair
Fun 32; GTP 55; OTR 32

194

Books to Which Reference is Made

Explanations of the symbols used for books

The abbreviation used for a book of poems by a single author begins with the first three letters of the poet's name: e.g. *Aga L*, John Agard's *Laughter is an Egg*; *Hug M W*, Ted Hughes's *Moon-Whales*.

Anthologies are coded by title, e.g. *Floc*, A Flock of Words; *Chris*, Poems for Christmas; *Day*, All in a Day. When a series of volumes is graded for classroom use, the volumes are indicated by Roman figures, the pages by Arabic numbers: e.g. *Pro II 24* is *The Poetry Processor* volume II page 24.

The abbreviations used for publishers, such as *Fab*, Faber; *Ox*, Oxford, are easily recognisable.

A very brief comment on each book will, I hope, give some indication of its type, and of the age range for which it is designed, though most anthologies contain some poems which can be enjoyed by all ages.

Abi

In Abigail's Garden (comp. and ill. Helen Williams)
Methuen 1986; 24pp
Twelve passages of poetry concerned with gardens, matched with exquisitely detailed pictures in various styles. Unique.

AFP, ASP, ATP

A First (Second) (Third) Poetry Book (comp. John Foster, ill. various)
OUP 1987 (1988) (1988); 128pp
Following the editor's earlier successful series, this has the same reliable virtues Many new poems, all expertly graded, popular with the suggested age ranges.

Afr I, Afr II

African Poetry for Schools I, II (ed. Noel Machin)
Longman Group 1978, 6th imp. 1982, (1978, 3rd imp. 1981); 87pp (101pp)
'African' includes Caribbean and USA. Perhaps too much elucidating and too many comprehension questions in notes, but the poems themselves are unhackneyed and the photographs striking.

Aga

I Din Do Nuttin (John Agard, ill. Susanna Gretz)
Bodley Head 1983; 40 unnumbered pp
The Guyanese poet re-creates for young children their experiences – buying new shoes, having a birthday – with sympathy and gaiety.

Aga L

Laughter is an Egg (John Agard, ill. Alan Rowe)
Viking 1990; 72pp
Agard writes, in this celebration of laughter, of 'a small joke . . . dying to share itself', and shares with the reader moods of pure fun.

Ahl H

Heard It in the Playground (Allan Ahlberg, ill. Fritz Wegner)
Viking Kestrel 1989; 110pp
Splendid mixture of 'short ones', 'songs' (to popular tunes) and 'long ones' (narratives). Widely varying and precisely right whether celebrating simply kicking a ball, or covering every detail of the primary school day.

Ahl M

The Mighty Slide (Allan Ahlberg, ill. Charlotte Voake)
Viking Kestrel 1988; 96pp
Tales in flowing verse admirable for reading aloud. Fantastic events on solid familiar backgrounds.

Ahl P

Please Mrs Butler (Allan Ahlberg, ill. Fritz Wegner)
Kestrel 1983, Puffin 1984; 94pp
Children and teachers, their triumphs and disasters, are sketched and summed up with point and wit. Immensely popular with all ages, particularly 8-11s.

All

All the Day Through (coll. Wes Magee, ill. David Sim)
Evans Bros 1982; 128pp
Through the day in home and school from waking till bedtime. Some pleasantly
unfamiliar verses, often very short. For 8–12s.

AM

Amazing Monsters (ed. Robert Fisher, ill. Rowena Allen)
Faber 1982; 96pp
Monsters, both traditional and newly-invented; poets from Tennyson and Lear
to Ogden Nash and Michael Rosen.

Ang I, Ang II

New Angles I, II (comp. John Foster, ill. various)
OUP 1987 (1987); 120pp (128pp)
Contemporary poets white and black write on adult subjects for 13-16s. Many
poems previously unpublished.

Ani

Animals Like Us (chosen Tony Bradman, ill. Madeleine Baker)
Blackie 1987; 64pp
Pleasant mixture of contemporary and traditional verses about many different
creatures, for younger juniors.

Ark

Noah's Ark (Michael Harrison and Christopher Stuart-Clark, ill. various)
OUP 1983; 144pp
The story of the Flood from many cultures, followed by an alphabet of animal
poems, many of them (like the illustrations) striking and unusual.

ASP, ATP

See AFP

Aus B

Someone is Flying Balloons (sel. Jill Heylen and Celia Jellett, ill. Kerry Argent)
Omnibus Books (Adelaide) 1983, 1884, 1986, CUP 1985; 136pp

Aus R

Rattling in the Wind (sel. Jill Heylen and Celia Jellett, ill. Maire Smith)
Omnibus Books (Adelaide) 1987, CUP 1987; 142pp
Fresh voices from Australia fill these companion anthologies for 8-12s.
Outstanding illustrations. Great variety of styles and themes including some
aboriginal material.

AVF

A Very First Poetry Book (comp. John Foster, ill. Jan Lewis, Inga Moore and Joe
Wright)
OUP 1984; 128pp
Teachers will value this book for its wealth of hitherto unpublished poems, many
very short.

Ax

Axed Between the Ears (ed. David Kitchen)
Heinemann 1987; 102pp
This teaching anthology contains many unhackneyed poems chosen and enjoyed

(says the compiler) by upper secondary pupils. Splendid. But the poems are almost swamped by comment and 'comprehension work'.

Bab

News for Babylon (ed. James Berry)
Chatto and Windus 1984; 212pp
This volume of West Indian British poetry allows older pupils to sample 154 poems by 40 black poets, in languages from standard English to Creole. Sad in that the frequent underlying feelings of pain and anger seem justifiable.

BBGG

Beastly Boys and Ghastly Girls (ed. William Cole, ill. Tomi Ungerer)
Methuen 1970, continually reprinted; 125pp
Self-explanatory title. Spidery drawings enhance the crazy humour, often American, which delights primary classes.

Bed

When the Dark Comes Dancing (ed. Nancy Larrick, ill. John Wallner)
Heinemann 1983; 79pp
Beautifully produced American picture book for bedtime reading.Unfamiliar verses and lullabies from Eastern Europe, Africa, Canada, etc.

Bel CV

Selected Cautionary Verses (Hilaire Belloc, ill. B.T.B. and Nicolas Bentley)
Puffin 1940, continually reprinted, 1987; 185pp
Belloc's immortal Jim, Matilda, Henry King and other children, beasts and peers. Enjoyable, easily memorised light verse for juniors.

Bell

Nine O'Clock Bell (ed. Raymond Wilson, ill. Jon Riley)
Viking Kestrel 1985; 174pp
Poems which mirror every aspect of school life today, with glimpses too of education in China, Norway, Russia and Germany.

Ber

When I Dance (James Berry)
Hamish Hamilton 1988; 120pp
A mixture of two cultures, British and Caribbean. The poems may supply the real need for children black and white to share each others' experiences and to hear each others' voices. Much for reading and chanting aloud.

Blac

Black Poetry (comp. Grace Nichols, ill. Michael Lewis)
Blackie 1988; 143pp
Something new to many teachers (see also *Stuf* and *Stuf II*). A poet's selection of 'voices from the Caribbean, Afro-America, Asia, Africa and Britain'.Fresh point and captivating rhythms. Brilliant black and white illustrations. Also available a *Poetry Jump-Up*, Puffin 1990.

Boo

Never Say Boo to a Ghost (chosen John Foster, ill. Korky Paul)
OUP 1990; 96pp
One of the popular 'horror' anthologies, full of vampires, werewolves, etc. A few blood-curdling pieces, a few comic.

ll Together Now! (Tony Bradman, ill. Julie Park)
'iking Kestrel 1989; 128pp
imple verses about their experiences for the youngest children.

rave

'one but the Brave (comp. Jennifer and Graeme Curry, ill. David Arthur)
\rrow Books 1986; 156pp
oems old and new celebrating many and various forms of courage.

right

right Lights Blaze Out (Alan Bold, Gareth Owen, Julie O'Callaghan)
)xford 1986; 48pp
ee *Trio*. Others in the series: *Candy, Crys, UD*.

ur

an't Get to Sleep (written and ill. Mark Burgess)
1ethuen 1990; 64pp
ubtitled 'Poems to read at bedtime', these are mainly short tinkling verses
1itable for the youngest at other times also. See *Ora, Raw, Sam*

ur F

eeling Beastly (written and ill. Mark Burgess)
1ethuen 1989; 64pp
imple verses for the youngest, with drawings which exactly fit the words.

al A

alendar of Poems (coll. Wes Magee, ill. Gary Wing)
ell and Hyman 1986; 128pp
or each month there is a group of poems (usually 20th-century) capturing
3propriate sights, sounds, activities and weather.

am I, Cam II

Cambridge Poetry Workshop 14+ (Lynn and Jeffrey Wood)
UP 1990; 140pp
: *Cambridge Poetry Workshop GCSE* (Jeffrey and Lynn Wood)
UP 1988; 167pp
eaching anthologies using well-known poets from Shakespeare onwards, half
` them from this century. Each poem or pair of poems is very thoroughly
troduced, explained, discussed and followed by a choice of assignments.

an

1e New Wind Has Wings (comp. Mary Alice Downie and Barbara Robertson, ill.
izabeth Cleaver)
UP 1984; 112pp
supplemented edition of a book which has been a tried favourite in Canada
1ce 1968. A delightful collection, for juniors, of poems little known in England.
istinguished illustrations alternating collage and lino-cuts.

andy

1e Candy-Floss Tree (Gerda Mayer, Frank Flynn and Norman Nicholson)
xford 1984; 48pp
e *Trio*. Others in series: *Bright, Crys, UD*.

Cau E

Early in the Morning (Charles Causley, ill. Michael Foreman, music Anthon Castro)
Viking Kestrel 1986; 64pp
New poems for the youngest, half of them set to music, with the flavour genuine nursery rhymes.Full of Causley's inimitable invention. A beautiful boo

Cau F

Figgie Hobbin (Charles Causley, ill. Jill Bennett)
Macmillan 1970, Puffin 1979, rep. 1983; 96pp

Cau J

Jack the Treacle-Eater (Charles Causley, ill. Charles Keeping)
Macmillan 1987; 96pp
Two collections of his own poems by this favourite anthologist. Ostensibly f juniors and accessible to them, but readers of all ages will appreciate the w wisdom and imagination that abound in these books.

Cau V

A Field of Vision (Charles Causley)
Macmillan 1988; 68pp
Nearly 40 poems (for adults, but accessible to older pupils) reflecting Causle travels and his return to his home county, Cornwall.

CBC

The Children's Book of Comic Verse (chosen Christopher Logue, ill. Bill Tidy)
Batsford 1979, rep. 1980; 162pp
This includes some little-known verses, and a long bibliography of anthologie But what seems comic to one class may not raise a smile in another.

CCC

Of Caterpillars, Cats and Cattle (chosen Anne Harvey, ill. William Geldert)
Viking Kestrel 1987; 233pp
Over 200 poems about creatures of all kinds. Teachers will find old favourites well as many new verses. Fascinating juxtapositions. Outstanding illustrations.

CCV

Comic and Curious Verse (chosen Zenka and Ian Woodward, ill. Pat Oakley)
Ladybird 1983; 52pp
A tiny brightly-coloured beginner's book with comic-strip style illustration Favourite ridiculous verses.

Cele

Let's Celebrate (comp. John Foster, ill. various)
Oxford 1989; 112pp
Worldwide festivals – with explanatory notes – are described in verse, most of not published before.

Cham

We are the Champions (comp. Caroline Sheldon and Richard Heller, ill. Virgin Salter)
Hutchinson 1986; 124pp

Unusual 'Collection of sporting verse' celebrating myriad forms of physical skills, including golf, skating, snooker, trampolining and many more. See also *Mot*.

Chat

The Chatto Book of Nonsense Poetry (ed. Hugh Haughton)
Chatto and Windus 1988; 530pp
An encyclopaedic review of nonsense poems from the 11th century to the present day. Many from Eastern Europe as well as from America, France and Germany, and much of Carroll and Lear. A learned introduction for the interested teacher. An adult reference book.

Choice

Choice of Poets (comp. R. P. Hewett)
Harrap 1968, rep. 9 times by 1975; 318pp
Fourteen acknowledged poets from Wordsworth to R. S. Thomas, for readers of 14+. Too many notes, perhaps, but the reader is invited to use only what is actually needed for full appreciation.

Chris

Poems for Christmas (Zenka and Ian Woodward, ill. Liz Graham-Yooll)
Hutchinson 1984, Beaver 1985; 144pp
Pleasant collection of favourite carols and less well-known poems for the Christmas season.

Cla C

The Corn Growing (Leonard Clark, ill. Lise Kopper)
Hodder and Stoughton 1982; 56pp
Delicate pencil drawings closely fit quiet poems, most of them set in a slightly romanticised countryside. For young children.

Cla J

Clare's Countryside (John Clare; sel. Brian Patten, ill. Ann Arnold)
Heinemann 1981; 78pp
A beautifully illustrated selection of Clare's poetry, evoking vividly sights, sounds, smells and animals of the English countryside.

Corn

Cohen's Cornucopia (coll. Mark Cohen, ill. Colin West)
Patrick Hardy Books 1983; 112pp
Scraps of verse and prose 'to twist the tongue and jerk the jaw' – and to delight lovers of zany nonsense. Illustrations in exactly the same spirit.

Cow

I Never Saw a Purple Cow (chosen and ill. Emma Chichester Clark)
Walker Books 1990
Over 100 nonsense verses, mostly very short, very attractively illustrated and produced. For 5-7s.

Cre

The Jungle Sale (June Crebbin, ill. Thelma Lambert)
Viking Kestrel 1988: 80pp
Delightful book for 6-9s, with great variety of verses on home and school, for singing and reciting. Riddles, concrete poems. All attractively presented.

Crys

The Crystal Zoo (U. A. Fanthorpe, John Cotton, L. J. Anderson)
Oxford 1985; 48pp
See *Trio*. Others in series: *Bright, Candy, UD*.

Dah R

Revolting Rhymes (Roald Dahl, ill. Quentin Blake)
Jonathan Cape 1982, rep. six times; 32 unnumbered pp
Perversions of 6 standard nursery tales, told in slangy quick-moving verse, the burlesques of nursery classics are immensely popular.

Dah S

Rhyme Stew (Roald Dahl, ill. Quentin Blake)
Cape 1989; 80pp
Again the perfectly paired Dahl and Blake present popular perverted versio of favourite nursery tales and rhymes. This book is rather more sophisticat and 'rude' than *Dah R*, and is popular with slightly older children.

Day

All in a Day (sel. Kaye Webb, ill. Kathie Layfield)
Ladybird 1985; 43pp
Kaye Webb, skilled anthologist, has chosen poems written from a 'child's e view'. She takes the reader from waking to bedtime, accompanied by attracti pencil sketches on coloured paper.

de la M P

Peacock Pie (Walter de la Mare, ill. Edward Ardizzone)
Faber Fanfares 1958, continually reprinted; 121pp
For 50 years regarded as the outstanding poet for children, even now much de la Mare's poetry still appeals, especially to the imaginative. This is a well-tri selection with excellent pictures.

de la Mare V

The Voice (Walter de la Mare, chosen and ill. Catherine Brighton)
Faber 1986; 26 unnumbered pp
Thirteen poems by de la Mare take the reader from dawn to dusk, following t children and animals who live in the castle and gardens depicted in such lovi detail. A fascinating creation.

Down

Down Our Street (Jennifer and Graeme Curry, ill. Scoular Anderson)
Methuen 1988, Magnet 1989; 96pp
'A collection of streetwise poems' introduces the lower juniors to t heterogeneous inhabitants of 'Our Street'.

DS

Poetry One: Dragon's Smoke (coll. Wes Magee, ill. Catherine Brighton)
Basil Blackwell 1985; 64 pp
A popular poet's choice of popular verses (many very brief)
for the youngest listeners. Immense variety of matter, manner and writers.

Earth

What on Earth . . .? (ed. Judith Nicholls, ill. Alan Baker)
Faber 1989; 118pp
An alarming indictment showing poets' reactions to the shameful pollution of
our country and planet.

Edw M

A Mouse in my Roof (Richard Edwards, ill. Venice)
Orchard Books 1988, Puffin 1890; 76pp
Edward's third collection of well-crafted verses, beautifully illustrated and
presented. He has an engaging habit of giving the reader a witty surprise in the
last line.

Edw P

The Word Party (Richard Edwards, ill. John Lawrence)
Lutterworth Press 1986, Puffin 1987; 64pp

Edw W

Whispers from a Wardrobe (Richard Edwards, ill. John Lawrence)
Lutterworth Press 1987; 64pp
Light-hearted rhymes for the youngest; everyday events touched by fantasy and
nonsense.He revels in words, and in delightful lists. More conventional in style
than is usual today.

Edw Ph

Phoots! (Richard Edwards, ill. Stephen Lambert)
Orchard Books 1989; 68pp
A book describing these mysterious creatures (kin to the Jumblies?)
in quick-moving verse. Ingenious lists of Phoots' language, superstitions, etc. For
7+.

Eli

Old Possum's Book of Practical Cats (T. S. Eliot)
Faber 1939, continually reprinted; 64pp
Both illustrators (Edward Gorey 1939 and 1982, Nicholas Bentley 1974 and
1985) are admirable. These poems, written by the distinguished poet for his
friends' children, and later inspiration for the musical *Cats*, are classics which are
much enjoyed.

Esb

Words with Wrinkled Knees (Barbara Juster Esbensen, ill. John Stadler)
OUP 1990; unnumbered pp
Animals seen as words – 'an evenly balanced word WHALE', 'a short word
covered with fur BAT', 'a moonstruck word OWL' – and 18 more. Splendidly
appropriate black and white illustrations.

Ewar

Caterpillar Stew (Gavin Ewart, ill. Ronald Ferns)
Hutchinson 1990; 79pp
Short witty poems and notes about animals (particularly Australian)
with suitably witty illustrations. Fact and fancy mingle, the aim being to teach
about conservation while entertaining.

Fab CV

The Faber Book of Children's Verse (comp. Janet Adam Smith)
1953, continually reprinted; 384pp
Admirable selection for children already interested in poetry. Thoughtf[
grouping by themes: Marvels and Riddles; The Sea; Kings Queens and Heroe
Top juniors to adults.

Fab NV

The Faber Book of Nursery Verse (ed. Barbara Ireson, ill. George Adamson)
Faber 1958, rep. 1975, 1983; 286pp
Splendid perennial collection for younger children, going well beyond th
nursery. Emphasis on rhythmic verse easy to speak aloud and remember.

Face

Faces in a Crowd (ed. Anne Harvey)
Viking 1990; 167pp
'Poems about people' in immense variety. Poets of both sexes and of mar
periods and cultures, poems in many styles and moods not usually met i
anthologies.

Fan

Selected Poems (U. A. Fanthorpe)
King Penguin 1986; 124pp
Adult subjects explored in the author's distinctive voice, with wit and dee
feeling, for students attracted by the flavour of her poems in anthologies.

Far M

Invitation to a Mouse (Eleanor Farjeon, chosen Annabel Farjeon, ill. Anto[
Maitland)
Pelham Books 1981, Knight Books 1983, 1986; 96pp

Far R

Something I Remember (Eleanor Farjeon, ed. Anne Harvey, ill. Alan Marks)
Blackie and Son 1987, Puffin 1989; 160pp

Two selections from Eleanor Farjeon's vast output of chiming verses. Still mu[
that is relevant to modern children, as well as glimpses of the far-off wor
between the wars.

Fat S

Songs for my Dog and Other People (Max Fatchen, ill. Michael Atchison)
Kestrel 1980; 64pp

Fat W

Wry Rhymes for Troublesome Times (Max Fatchen, ill. Michael Atchison)
Kestrel 1983; 79pp
Fresh humour (sometimes black) from Australia. Juniors enjoy these ingenious
rhymed verses picturing a surprising mixture of everyday events and fantas[
situations, plus limericks and sheer nonsense.

Fav

One Hundred Favourite Poems (chosen Zenka and Ian Woodward, ill. Doug[
Hall)
Hutchinson 1985; 160 pp

These indefatigable anthologists the Woodwards determined 'to provide in a single volume the very best in children's poetry'. Inevitably some choices will seem remarkable.

F

Funny Folk (ed. Robert Fisher, ill. Penny Dann)
Faber 1986; 80pp
It is difficult to sustain uninterruptedly an atmosphere of 'funniness'.The really 'funny' verses are the well known. Useful to have at hand, with few discoveries.

Fifth

Fifth Poetry Book (comp. John Foster, ill. various)
OUP 1985; 128pp
As usual John Foster has mixed many previously unpublished poems with some well-tried ones, and made an anthology suitable for the suggested age range.

Fire

Touched with Fire (comp. Jack Hydes)
CUP 1985, 4th imp. 1988; 208 pp
Poems of the last 400 years. A rich and interesting selection for top forms, interspersed with advice on tackling poetry in examinations.

Five

There's a Poet Behind You (ed. Morag Styles and Helen Cook, ill. Caroline Holden)
A & C Black 1988; 128pp
Five poets write about their approaches to poetry, illustrated by their own and children's verses. Grace Nichols, Adrian Mitchell, Gillian Clarke, Michael Rosen, John Agard.

Floc

A Flock of Words (coll. David Mackay, ill. Margery Gill)
The Bodley Head 1969, rep. 1973, 1979; 323pp
Distinguished timeless collection 'for children and others', well tested in the classroom. Poems from many centuries and countries, arranged with great skill and sensitivity to benefit by juxtaposition.

Foc

Poems in Focus (ed. Christopher Martin, ill. various)
Oxford 1985; 192pp
Adult poems on adult subjects for top forms, thematically arranged. Notes and teaching suggestions are discreetly grouped separately.

Foot

A Footprint on the Air (ed. Naomi Lewis, ill. Liz Graham Yooll)
Hutchinson 1983; 72pp
'Nature Verse' chosen by the compiler of *Mes*, with the same insistence on quality and choice of unhackneyed poems. Top juniors upwards.

S

Facing the Sea (comp. Anne Walmsley and Nick Caister, ill. Errol Lloyd)
Heinemann 1986; 151pp
The poems in this mixed anthology are a good introduction to the Caribbean for teenagers. The convenional examination 'exercises' can be ignored. The explanatory notes are helpful to British readers.

Fun

The Children's Book of Funny Verse (comp. Julia Watson, ill. various)
Faber 1979, rep. Puffin 1980; 128pp
Many snatches of verse, tongue twisters, riddles, and some longer story poem
cautionary tales, ruthless rhymes.

FWW

Poetry of the First World War (sel. Edward Hudson, ill. photographs)
Wayland (Publishers) Ltd 1988; 128pp
Arranged in chronological order and accompanied by contemporary pho
tographs, this collection has great immediacy and illustrates clearly and moving
the shifts in feelings and beliefs from 1914 to 1919.

Gang

Gangsters, Ghosts and Dragonflies (chosen Brian Patten, ill. Terry Oakes)
Allen and Unwin 1981; 160pp
Unconventional poems, almost all by living poets, that tell or imply a story. Live
with much fantasy in varied modes and moods, for top juniors upwards.

Gho

Ghosts Galore (ed. Robert Fisher, ill. Rowena Allen)
Faber 1983, pback 1986; 91pp
Some poems justify the subtitle 'Haunting verses'. Many aspects of and attitudes
the supernatural, from Ann Boleyn walking the Tower to Thomas Hardy's 'T
Glimpse'.

Gh P

Ghost Poems (ed. Daisy Wallace, ill. Tomie de Paola)
Pepper Press 1981, Unwin Hyman 1985; 32pp
A slim picture book for juniors, with not-too-frightening verses on t
supernatural.

Gold

Golden Apples (ed. Fiona Waters, ill. Alan Marks)
Heinemann 1985; 118pp
Poems of tried attraction, and great variation of style and substance, primarily f
children of 9-12, but for all ages an excellent introduction to 20th-century poetr

Gow F

So Far so Good (Mick Gowar, ill. Barry Thorpe)
Collins 1986; 80pp
Mick Gowar goes deeply into the trials and worries of teenagers faced with n
feelings and relationships, treating them sympathetically and frankly and qu
unsentimentally.

Gow S

Swings and Roundabouts (Mick Gowar, ill. Alan Curless)
Collins 1981, Lions 1987; 77pp

Gow T

Third Time Lucky (Mick Gowar, ill. Caroline Crossland)
Viking Kestrel 1988; 78pp

Child's-eye view of life in the family and at school in the city.Comic moments
well as serious insights. For upper juniors and above.

206

ran

ay it Again, Grannie! (John Agard, ill. Susanna Gretz)
odley Head 1985; unnumbered pp
Vit and wisdom and fun for 5-9s; poems elaborating 20 Caribbean proverbs.
ympathetic illustrations.

ro

lanifold Manor (Philip Gross, ill. Chris Riddell)
aber 1989; 68pp
 sequence of intriguing poems centred on a deserted manor house: ghosts,
phabets, riddles, an impudent jackdaw, puns, jostle each other. Of particular
terest to top forms interested in writing poetry are the poet's short notes.

TP

he Golden Treasury of Poetry (sel. Louis Untermeyer, ill. Joan Walsh Anglund)
olden Press NY 1959, Collins 1961 etc., 1982; 324pp
he commentary, though sensitive and helpful, is naturally dated in tone. But
is remains an admirable selection for juniors, with standard English poets,
nusual American poets, and anonymous jingles, all well represented.

ei

on't Eat Spiders (Robert Heidbreder, ill. Karen Parker)
UP (Toronto) 1985; 48pp
ustrations alternately in black and white and in brilliant colour enhance a
elightful set of short poems for 6-9s, from Canada. Lots of simple jokes.

en

he Phantom Lollipop Lady (Adrian Henri, ill. Tony Ross)
ethuen 1986; 96pp
he Mersey sound' for top juniors upwards; enticing quick-moving verses,
nny, eerie, nonsensical, serious, shrewd.

H

etry through Humour and Horror (Chris Webster, ill. various)
ssell Educational 1987; 122pp
 teaching anthology which is full of ideas for presenting the humorous and
rrifying poems used as examples, and for encouraging children to write their
n poems. The publishers will supply free an accompanying teacher's book.

wl

e Howling Pandemonium (comp. Zenka and Ian Woodward, ill. Julie Park)
ackie 1990; 64pp
ese experienced anthologists have collected verses on sounds, from the whizz
a humming-bird's wings to speedway racing. For 7-10s.

g F

et My Folks (Ted Hughes, ill. George Adamson)
ber 1961, with additions 1971 and 1977, rep. 1987, 1988; 61pp
ourites for 30 years, Ted Hughes's extraordinary family still delight.

Hug MT

Moortown Diary (Ted Hughes)
Faber 1979, rep. with notes 1989; xii + 68pp
Ted Hughes as farmer: a diary strongly re-creating earth, weather and animal
birth and death. Adult poems.

Hug MW

Moon-Whales (Ted Hughes, ill. Chris Riddell)
Faber 1963, 1976, rev. 1988; 96pp
This is basically a reprint of 'The Earth-Owl and Other Moon-People', with extr
poems adding detail to the poet's fantastic and sinister moon world.

Hug U

Under the North Star (Ted Hughes, ill. Leonard Baskin)
Faber 1981; 47pp
Impressive partnership with Baskin in a very large beautifully produced pictu
book. Poems and pictures combine powerfully to evoke the bleak Arctic Circ
and the harsh life of the animals that inhabit it.

Hug V

Ffangs the Vampire Bat (Ted Hughes, ill. Chris Riddell)
Faber 1986; 96pp
The first adventures are in verse, the cock Attila suffering many tri
(wonderfully well illustrated) till rescued by Ffangs, whose unfinished sto
continues in verse and prose. Immensely popular.

IC

Island of the Children (comp. Angela Huth, decorated Jane Ray)
Orchard Books 1987; 128pp
Previously unpublished poems by living writers, invited to contribute to a
anthology for children. Extremely handsomely presented.

Irish

The Wolfhound Book of Irish Poems (ed. Bridie Quin and Seamus Cashman,
drawings T. O'Connell, photographs D. Larkin, M. Cashman)
Wolfhound 1975, new ed. 1987, rep. 1992
Timely reminder of how much 'English' poetry was written by Irishmen, a
how much appealing and too-little-known poetry other Irish poets ha
achieved. A very interesting read.

Iron

Iron Honey Gold (comp. David Holbrook)
CUP 1961, 1965, 1988; 156pp
Scraps of anonymous children's game rhymes and folksongs rub shoulders wi
the work of some of the greatest English poets, in no discernable arrang
ment. Exhibits the astounding variety of writing called 'poetry'. A period pie
poems that were current in the 1960s.

Jon

The Curse of the Vampire's Socks (Terry Jones, ill. Michael Foreman)
Pavilion Books 1988; 128pp
Self-described as 'doggerel', nonsense stories with a mixture of smelly soc

ewer rats, a vampire, a sewer kangaroo who bobs up in the loo, and similar 'ude' people and happenings.

ung

Headlines from the Jungle (ed. Anne Harvey and Virginia McKenna, ill. Tessa .ovatt-Smith)
'iking 1990; 112pp
oems, many little-known, about wild creatures and man's dealings with the nimal kingdom. A fresh collection, beautifully illustrated, on a favourite subject.

CP

he Kingfisher Book of Children's Poetry (sel. Michael Rosen, ill. various)
ingfisher 1985, 7th rep. 1990, pback 1991; 255pp

WP

World of Poetry (sel. Michael Rosen, ill. Larry Wilkes and others)
ingfisher 1991; 256pp
wo very handsome and enjoyable books. 'Hundreds of thoughts, dreams and eas trapped in words', old and new, make up these deservedly popular •llections.Infinite variety: poems grave and gay, long and short; poets famous nd unknown, from many lands. Useful indexes of poets, titles, first lines and •bjects.

ing

he Kingfisher Book of Comic Verse (sel. Roger McGough, ill. Caroline Holden)
ingfisher Books 1986, 6th rep. 1990; 256pp
ver 200 items, showing how variously comic poetry can be. Much recent riting. A feast of sense and nonsense, poking fun at many sacred cows.

ist

Scots Kist (intro. D. Gifford)
liver and Boyd 1979; 154pp
new enlarged edition of *The New Scots Reader* giving Sassenachs a taste of the :hness, robustness and humour of Scottish poetry.

a B

Book of Bosh (Edward Lear, chosen Brian Alderson, ill. Lear)
iffin 1975, rep. 1982, 1986, 1988; 216pp
'rics and prose, a generous supply of the limericks and songs of this master of •nsense, with lots of his own drawings.

a C

e Complete Nonsense of Edward Lear (ed. Holbrook Jackson, ill. Edward Lear)
ber 1947, 17th imp. 1987; 288pp
1 essential book for juniors and their teachers, in print for over 40 years. Lear's n inimitable drawings.

fe

e Doesn't Frighten Me At All (comp. John Agard ill. various)
:inemann 1989; 96pp
ie British Guyanese poet has compiled an anthology for teenagers, reminding :m that 'poets come from all sorts of cultures' and can be inspired by 'a tiny nple' as well as by 'the big wide questions about life and death'. Eye-opening 'iety of poems, poets and presentation.

Like

I Like This Poem (ed. Kaye Webb, ill. Antony Maitland)
Puffin 1979, rep. 18 times; 192pp
Unique: the only anthology chosen by children voting (with reasons)
for their own favourites. Arranged by ages; good reading for everyone.

Lob

Arnold Lobel's Book of Mother Goose (chosen and ill. Arnold Lobel)
Walker Books 1987; 176pp
306 favourite rhymes with fresh, robust, inventive illustrations by a muc
honoured illustrator. See also *Walk*.

Love

The Language of Love (comp. Anne Harvey)
Blackie 1989; 176pp
Love poetry from snatches of song to complete formal poems, from music hall
Shakespeare, John Donne to Dorothy Parker, the 5th to the 20th century; fro
Russia, Korea, Sweden, America; about first love and last love, being in love at
out of love. A comprehensive treatment of the theme.

Mad

The Mad Family (chosen Tony Bradman, ill. Madeleine Baker)
Blackie 1987; 64pp
Simple episodes from family life, mostly pictured in a humorous light,
contemporary rhymers.

Mag M

Morning Break (Wes Magee; ill. Valeria Petrone)
CUP 1989; 62pp

Mag W

The Witch's Brew (Wes Magee; ill. Marc Vyvyan-Jones)
CUP 1989; 46pp

Bright attractive covers open on bright fresh verses (*Mag W* for young
children, *Mag M* for 8-10s). Magee shows life at home and in school from
child's standpoint, with both humour and sympathy, mixing the prosaic with t
fantastic.

McG F

Melting into the Foreground (Roger McGough)
Viking 1986, Penguin 1987; 77pp
Teenagers who, as juniors, enjoyed McGough's work, will like to tackle the
adult poems. A slightly acid flavour, but humour still persists.

McG G

In the Glassroom (Roger McGough)
Cape 1976, 4th rep. 1985; 60pp
An early collection of McGough's verses for adolescents, many of which ha
become widely popular.

McG M

An Imaginary Menagerie (Roger McGough, ill. Tony Blundell)
Kestrel 1988, Puffin 1990; 108pp
From Aardvark and Allivator to Yak and Zouk, tiny sparkling nonsense verses and absurd comical drawings amuse and delight with every variety of word-play.

McG P

Sky in the Pie (Roger McGough, ill. Satoshi Kitamura)
Kestrel 1983, rep. 1984; 88pp
A surprise on every page, beginning with the man who found it so delicious to have sky in his pie that he demanded the moon.

McG PT

Pillow Talk (Roger McGough, ill. Steven Guarnaccia)
VUP 1990; 80pp
Brief verses for the youngest, crafted with McGough's unfailing skill.

McG S

Nailing the Shadow (Roger McGough, ill. Marketa Prachaticka)
Viking Kestrel 1987; 96pp
A much more sombre tone than is usual in McGough's work, though his mastery of words is always a delight to the reader.

McN

There's an Awful Lot of Weirdos in our Neighbourhood (Colin McNaughton, ill. author)
Walker Books 1987, new edn 1990; 126pp
The well-known illustrator's first book of verses, quite zany, ingenious nonsense, for 6-9s.

McG Ro

You Tell Me (Roger McGough and Michael Rosen, ill. Sara Midda)
Kestrel 1979; 72pp
Boy's-eye views of home and school, the daily triumphs and disasters treated with empathy and humour. As ever both poets explore all possible meanings of each word. Enjoyed by 10-13s.

MF

Monstrosities (ed. and ill. Charles Fuge)
Hutchinson 1989; 72pp
The illustrations are even more monstrous than the poems, which include verses by Causley, Graves, Hughes, Magee, McGough and many more.

Ma

Measles and Sneezles (comp. Jennifer Curry, ill. Susie Jenkin-Pearce)
Hutchinson 1989, rep. 1991; 96pp
Glimpses, mainly light-hearted, of children's attitudes to illness, doctors and hospitals.

Mes

Messages (ed. Naomi Lewis, ill. Brian Grimwood)
Faber 1985; 255pp
An unusual, valuable anthology. New poems, little-known poems by famou
authors, well-known poems that will bear re-reading. Free verse and sonnet
Poets writing from the 14th to the 20th century. A permanent standby fo
readers of 11 upwards.

Mill

Warning: Too Much Schooling can Damage your Health (Trevor Millum, ill.
Wright)
E. J. Arnold and Son 1988; 144pp
Poems written over many years of schoolmastering, penetrating and pointed ar
often very funny. For top juniors upwards. There are also some helpful ide
about writing poetry.

Mil VY
Mil NS

When We Were Very Young
Now We Are Six (A. A. Milne, ill. Ernest Shepard)
Methuen 1924 and 1927, continually reprinted; 100 and 103pp
Many of the poems – bar the over-sentimental – still give much pleasure
children under 7. Milne is a brilliant craftsman, and his best verses a
effortlessly memorised. Some, e.g. 'The Old Sailor', *Mil NS 36*, delight all ages.

Mit N

Nothingmas Day (Adrian Mitchell, ill. John Lawrence)
Alison and Busby 1984; 80pp
The first collection of Adrian Mitchell's very individual poems made especia
for children, accompanied by John Lawrence's distinguished woodcuts. There
something for all ages.

Mol

Boo to a Goose (John Mole, ill. Mary Norman)
Peterloo Poets, Cornwall 1987; 68pp
Something for every junior, jokes, snatches of verse and riddles alternate wi
thought-stirring poems, finally a sequence on the circus. Added pleasure fro
John Mole's extensive vocabulary and craftsmanship.

Mons

There are Monsters About (Zenka and Ian Woodward, ill. Virginia Salter)
Blackie 1987; 92pp
This 'fiendish poetry anthology' is a blood-curdling collection of monstro
creatures: one-off Kraken, Jabberwocky and Marrog, and more plentiful giar
vampires and werewolves. Authors from Edmund Spenser to Jack Preluts
Suitably scarey illustrations.

Moon

Is That the New Moon? (ed. Wendy Cope, ill. Christine Roche)
Lions Teen-Tracks 1989; 128pp
Poems by women (some from overseas) chosen by a woman poet for girls
13-16. Adult but accessible.

[or

[P]icnic on the Moon (Brian Morse, ill. Joep Bertrams)
[T]urton and Chambers 1990; 112pp
  [A] varied collection of original poems for 9-12s, appropriately illustrated. They
[r]ange from fact to fantasy, from a latch-key kid to space travel and magic.

[o]t

[T]he Poetry of Motion (ed. Alan Bold)
[M]ainstream Publishing no date; 200pp
  [Fr]om 18th-century archers, boxers and cricketers to the football, snooker and
[da]rts players of today, these verses celebrate physical activity, both the sports
[th]emselves and individual practitioners. See also *Cham.*

T

[Th]e Magic Tree (chosen David Woolgar, ill. various)
[O]UP 1981, rep. 1985; 160pp
  [T]he subtitle 'poems of fantasy and mystery' is abundantly justified, and there are
[so]me fine poems rarely anthologised, in a handsome volume.

[N]ame

[M]y Name, My Poem (comp. Jennifer and Graeme Curry, ill. John Richardson)
[H]utchinson 1986; 96pp
  [Cl]ever collection of poems containing names from Alexandra to Zoe.

[a]r

[Na]rrative Poems (ed. Michael Harrison and Christopher Stuart-Clark, ill. various)
[Ox]ford 1981; 188pp
  [Gr]eat variety: over 50 stories in verse, from ancient ballads to Auden, Kipling
[an]d Causley.

[a]s C

[Cu]stard and Company (Ogden Nash, ill. Quentin Blake)
[Ke]strel 1979, rep. 1980, 1982; 128pp
  [Li]ght verse in Nash's inimitable style, with perfectly fitting illustrations. Children
[esp]ecially enjoy his animals.

[D]

[Th]e New Dragon Book of Verse (ed. Michael Harrison and Christopher
[St]uart-Clark, ill. various)
[O]UP 1977, rep. 1978; 267pp
  [A] rich if conventional collection of mainly adult poems from many centuries,
[arr]anged by theme. Chosen for ages 9-15, suitable for the more academic classes.
[Co]mpanion volume to *YD*.

[C]

[Co]me On Into My Tropical Garden (Grace Nichols, ill. Caroline Binch)
[A] & C. Black 1988; 41pp
  [Lu]cky children accepting the title's invitation will share episodes in a Caribbean
[chi]ldhood with the Guyanese British poet. Most attractive verses and
[illu]strations: a happy book.

213

Nic M

Magic Mirror (Judith Nicholls)
Faber 1985; 48pp

Nic F

Midnight Forest (Judith Nicholls)
Faber 1987; 53pp

Great variety: re-creation of Biblical characters, poems of school and of space travel, of family meals and of the tragic despoiling of the rain forest. For 10-14s.

Nif

Niffs and Whiffs (comp. Jennifer Curry, ill. Susie Jenkin-Pearce)
The Bodley Head 1991; 92pp
Indefatigable anthologist, Mrs Curry, has compiled an anthology of smell (mostly unpleasant) in unfamiliar poems, many written for this book.

Nine

Poems for 9-Year-Olds and Under (ed. Kit Wright, ill. Michael Foreman)
Kestrel 1984, Puffin 1985; 192pp
Superb collection of poems, mainly contemporary, in every mood, chosen by one of the most popular children's poets to amuse, astonish, provoke and enlighten. See also *Ten*.

Noisy

Noisy Poems (coll. Jill Bennett, ill. Nick Sharratt)
OUP 1987; 24pp
Bright endpapers are covered with every imaginable 'noisy' word, and there are 12 attractively decorated onomatopaeic poems to be spoken, chanted and shouted. Ages 5-8.

NTP

A New Treasury of Poetry (sel. Neil Philip, ill. John Lawrence)
Blackie 1990; 256pp
John Lawrence's superb woodcuts decorate almost every page of this handsome volume, which is a library in itself. Neil Philip deliberately tried to choose 'poems which last', accessible to children but not necessarily written for them. Poems are arranged in sections, by theme, and range widely in mood, style, period and country of origin.

NV

A Golden Treasury of Nursery Verse (ed. Mark Daniel, ill. Victorian painters)
Pavilion Books 1986; 153pp
A sumptuously re-created book for Victorian children. Short traditional verse along with poems from Wordsworth to Chesterton. Full-colour reproductions of Victorian paintings abound. A really splendid period piece.

O & A

Out and About (chosen Raymond Wilson, ill. Mike Daley)
Viking Kestrel 1987; 191pp
Poems of the open air (less about what is happening to our environment than say, *Rab*). For age 11 upwards.

214

'Ca

...king my Pen for a Walk (Julie O'Callaghan)
...rchard Books 1988; 76pp
...his slim volume presents an attractive new voice, of great immediacy. Girl
...enagers in particular will find their dilemmas sympathetically revealed.

cc

...casions (sel. Anne Harvey, ill. Angela McAllister)
...ackie 1990; 160pp
...he all-embracing title allows the excellent anthologist, Anne Harvey, to offer a
...ry wide selection of verses long and short, familiar and strange, celebrating
...ery imaginable 'occasion'.

nce

...ce Upon a Rhyme (ed. Sara and Stephen Corrin, ill. Jill Bennett)
...ber 1982, Puffin; 157pp
...1 favourite poems for juniors, mainly light-hearted. Attractively printed and
...ustrated.

pen

...en the Door (comp. A. Greenwell and M. Peek, ill. various)
...hn Murray 1984; 132pp
...useful anthology of rather conventional poems, grouped according to theme:
...eather, Old Age, People, etc. The questions and exercises suggested are
...osaic and often impractical.

ra

...eaking for Ourselves (Hiawyn Oram, ill. Satoshi Kitamura)
...ethuen 1990; 64pp
...ead aloud poetry' in voices aged 6, 4 and 1. Good for the youngest. See also
...r, Raw, Sam.

SF

...t Such Foolishness (ed. William Cole, ill. Tomie de Paola)
...ethuen 1980; Magnet 96pp

TR

..., That's Ridiculous ((ed. William Cole, ill. Tomi Ungerer)
...agnet 1972, often reprinted; 96pp

at

...t of the Blue (chosen Fiona Waters, ill. Veroni Barge)
...ntana Lions 1982; 96pp
...very useful and attractive collection of poems, many little-known, about every
...rt of weather. Children can hunt for verses to match each day's climate.

WN

..., What Nonsense (ed. William Cole, ill. Tomi Ungerer)
...ethuen 1968, rev. 1972, rep. 1978
...onsense rhymes, many very short, mainly by contemporary versifiers. Exactly
...titles. Immensely popular in primary schools. See also *BBGG*.

Owe C

Song of the City (Gareth Owen, ill. Jonathan Hills)
Fontana Young Lions 1985; 94pp

Owe K

Salford Road (Gareth Owen, ill. John Warwicker)
Kestrel 1979; 79pp

Owe Y

Salford Road (Gareth Owen, ill. Alan Marks)
Fontana Young Lions; 1988

The poet of the urban child. Boy's-eye views of home, family, school, stre
cricket, vividly recalled with telling detail.

Ox A

The Oxford Book of Children's Verse in America (ed. Donald Hall)
Oxford 1985; 320pp
A book for the teacher who is looking for enjoyable little-known poems. Fro
the 17th century to the 20th, a historic survey with much that will give pleasur
and many surprises.

Ox CP

The Oxford Book of Christmas Poems (ed. Michael Harrison and Christoph
Stuart-Clark, ill. various)
OUP 1983, rep. 1984, 1985, pback 1988; 160pp
A lavishly produced volume, invaluable in December, with such abundance a
variety of Christmas poems that every teacher will find some appropria
material.

Ox CV

The Oxford Book of Children's Verse (chosen Iona and Peter Opie)
OUP 1980; 407pp
'The classics of children's poetry'. 332 poems specifically written for childre
from Chaucer (1343-1400) to Ogden Nash (1902-71). Notes on authors a
sources. Perhaps surprisingly, many early poems still appeal.

Ox Dic

The Oxford Dictionary of Nursery Rhymes (ed. Iona and Peter Opie, ill. from earli
books for children)
OUP 1951, rev. 1966; 467pp
The authoritative volume on the origins and history of the best 500 songs a
rhymes for the youngest children. A source book for the teacher: childr
reading for themselves can have *Fab NR*, *Lob*, *Puf NR*, *Voa*.

Ox NR

The Oxford Nursery Rhyme Book (assembled by Iona and Peter Opie, ill. fro
earlier children's books)
OUP 1955, often reprinted; 224pp
The most complete collection: 800 rhymes and songs, most of them very brief.
most valuable book for teachers of the youngest children.

216

The Oxford Book of Poetry for Children (comp. E. Blishen, ill. Brian Wildsmith)
OUP 1963, rep. 1980, 1982, 1984, 1985; 168pp
Shows how accessible and enjoyable 'real' poetry can be. Meant for younger children but much is appropriate for all juniors. Delightful illustrations in lavish colour. Should be in every class library.

The Oxford Book of Story Poems (ed. Michael Harrison and Christopher Stuart-Clark, ill. various)
OUP 1990; 176pp
Useful collection for reading aloud: old favourites mixed with new narrative poems.

The Oxford Treasury of Children's Poems (Michael Harrison and Christopher Stuart-Clark, ill. various)
OUP 1988, rep. 1989; 174pp
Brilliant colours invite children to look for treasure within this book, to be rewarded by abundant examples of favourite poems, starting with those for the very young, and gradually growing in complexity.

A Packet of Poems (picked by Jill Bennett, ill. Paddy Mounter)
OUP 1982; 112pp
Very light verses, many limericks, brightly illustrated, and all concerned with food. For 5-8s.

Gargling with Jelly (Brian Patten, ill. David Mostyn)
Viking Kestrel 1985; 128pp
Jokes jostle serious musings, riddles and epigrams neighbour narratives, making fine mixed reading. The drawings catch the mood of overflowing energy.

The Animals Noah Forgot (A. B. Paterson, ill. Norman Lindsay)
Arlington Books 1982; 71pp
'Banjo' Paterson (1864-1941) singer of the people, scenery and animals of Australia, provides a refreshingly different world, full of wombats, dingos and other unusual animals. Perfectly appropriate illustrations.

Thawing Frozen Frogs (Brian Patten, ill. David Mostyn)
Viking 1990; 127pp
Apparently nonsense verses which turn out to have more than 'a grain or two of truth among the chaff', expressed with Brian Patten's typical deftness and energy.

Pet Poems (ed. Robert Fisher, ill. Sally Kindberg)
Faber 1989; 86pp
Over 60 varied poems, many unhackneyed, on pets, including several by children. Warmly recommended.

PG

A Pot of Gold (ed. Jill Bennett, ill. Paddy Mounter)
Doubleday 1989; 112pp
As ever with Jill Bennett the poems are just right for juniors, tried and tested in the classroom. The illustrations will entice any reluctant reader.

Pic

A Picnic of Poetry (sel. Anne Harvey, ill. Helen Read)
Blackie 1988; 160pp
'Food, food, glorious food' from many countries and centuries, celebrated in many aspects, growing it, cooking it, and eating it with varied table manners. A real feast of unusual verses.

Poem I

Poems I (Michael Harrison and Christopher Stuart-Clark, ill. photographs)
OUP 1979, rep. twice 1981
Wonderfully diverse collection, grave and gay, short and long, concrete and abstract. Something for everyone from elephant jokes to R. S. Thomas. For 9-13s.

Pop

Sing a Song of Popcorn (sel. B. S. de Regniers *et al.*, ill. Marcia Brown *et al.*)
Hodder and Stoughton NY 1988, UK 1989; 142pp
Beautiful picture book, illustrated by nine Caldecott Medal artists, of poems 'children will sit still for'. A revised version of an American book which sold over a quarter of a million copies in the last 20 years.

Pos

The Possum Tree (sel. Lesley Pyott, ill. Andrew and Julian Wong)
A. & C. Black 1985; 160pp
First published in Australia as 'The best primary poetry anthology', it certainly has a rich variety. New Australian voices mix with a careful selection of children's favourite poetry, thematically arranged. Unique in being illustrated by child artists.

PoWo I, II

Poetry World I, II (coll. Geoffrey Summerfield)
Bell and Hyman: I: ill. Per Dahlberg, 1985; 122pp
                II: ill. Peter Lomax. 1985; 96pp
Anthologies for 10-13s, despite the title mainly English poets.

Ppp

Here a Little Child I Stand (ed. Cynthia Mitchell, ill. Satomi Ichikawa)
Heinemann 1985; unnumbered pp
'Poems of prayer and praise' from all over the world. An outstanding picture book for 6-9s, truly ecumenical.

Pre

The New Kid on the Block (Jack Prelutsky, ill. James Stevenson)
Heinemann 1986; 159pp
Light nonsense verse of a high quality, lots of word-play, many good jokes and surprises. Much enjoyed by under 9s.

218

o I, II, III

he Poetry Processor I, II, III (Paul Higgins, ill. Tim Archbold)
lackwell 1989, (1990) (1991); 80, (80) (96)pp
eaching anthologies with a remarkable variety of illustrative poetry, ranging
om concrete poetry, riddles and word-play to sonnets and villanelles. The
uality of some of the poems by children who were being taught testifies to the
ccess of the methods suggested.

Sev

oems for 7-Year-Olds and Under (chosen Helen Nicoll, ill. Michael Foreman)
estrel Books 1983; 160pp
nglish poetry for the youngest, from Shakespeare to Gavin Ewart. Good big
int and apt illustrations to encourage young readers.

ad

admuddle Jump In (sel. Beverley Mathias and Jill Bennett, ill. David McKee)
ethuen 1987, Magnet; 128pp
jolly collection, with many unusual poems and entertaining illustrations,
osen to give pleasure to the younger juniors.

of M

he Puffin Book of Magic Verse (chosen Charles Causley, ill. Barbara Swiderska)
uffin 1974, reissued 1988
narms and spells and supernatural tales, ranging over 900 years and including
lish, Red Indian and Anglo-Saxon verses. A really magical collection for 8s
wards.

of NR

he Puffin Book of Nursery Rhymes (gathered by Iona and Peter Opie, ill. Pauline
ynes)
63, in print 1990; 220pp
ntaining 150 rhymes from *Ox NR*, and 200 less well-known, and illustrated by
uline Baynes' delicate drawings. An ideal introduction for the youngest
aders. Notes and index of subjects help the teacher.

of Q

Puffin Quartet of Poets (chosen Eleanor Graham, ill. Diana Blomfield)
nguin 1958, still in print; 190pp
eanor Farjeon's gentle humour, James Reeves' delightful animals, E. V. Rieu's
arper, often fantastical verses, Ian Serraillier's stories, all now have classic
tus and still attract many children from 8 to 14. See also *Quin* and *Six*.

of V

he Puffin Book of Verse (ed. Eleanor Graham)
53, rep. 16 times; 286pp
old-style anthology of poems by recognised poets 1600-1950. Still a very
und introduction to the main body of English poetry. 9 years upwards.

V

ace and War (chosen Michael Harrison and Christopher Stuart-Clark, ill. Alan
rks)
JP 1989; 208pp
early 200 poems, covering 2500 years and countries all over the world. A

valuable, unhackneyed selection, with juxtapositions arranged to provok
thought. Brilliant cycle of illustrations.

Quin

Poets in Hand : A Puffin Quintet (chosen Anne Harvey)
Puffin 1985; 241pp
Five contemporary poets with individual voices. Charles Causley needs n
introduction, and John Fuller, Elizabeth Jennings, Vernon Scannell and the la
John Walsh also have much for top juniors upwards. A boxer-poet surpris
many. A good introduction to adult poetry. See also *Six*.

Rab

The Last Rabbit (sel. Jennifer Curry)
Methuen 1990; 112pp
'Green' poems (by children as well as adults) rejoicing in the remaining natur
pleasures of our planet and dreading its degradation.

Rat

The Rattle Bag (sel. Seamus Heaney and Ted Hughes)
Faber 1982; 498pp
Some 500 poems, mainly 20th-century, in alphabetical order, chosen by tw
distinguished poets. Invaluable to the teacher of older pupils. Every pup
ideally, should have a copy.

Raw

Dog's Dinner (Irene Rawnsley, ill. Simone Abel)
Methuen 1990; 44pp
'Read aloud poetry' for the youngest. See also *Bur, Ora, Sam*.

Read

The Walker Book of Read-Aloud Rhymes for the Very Young (sel. Jack Prelutsky, i
Marc Brown)
Walker 1987; 98pp
Such an attractive book that children will be enticed to read for themselves
well as asking to be read to. Over 200 poems, many by American wome
unfamiliar in England.

Ree

Ragged Robin (James Reeves, ill. Emma Chichester Clark)
Walker Books 1990; 80pp
A distinguished picture book using 26 poems by James Reeves (1961)
alphabetical order. The varying moods of the poems are reflected in the rainbo
colours of the delightful illustrations.

Ree C

Complete Poems for Chilldren (James Reeves, ill. Edward Ardizzone)
Heinemann 1973, pback 1987; 195pp
Reprinted as *The Wandering Moon*. Very varied moods in rhymed verses from t
nonsensical 'Prefabulous Animiles' to sensitive evocations of nature. Ve
consistent quality. A classic poet for juniors.

Rhy

This poem doesn't rhyme (ed. Gerard Benson, ill. Sarah-Jane Stewart)
Viking 1990; 160pp
All the possible ways of writing poems which don't rhyme are paraded with expertise and some humour.

Ring

Ring Out Wild Bells (chosen Zenka and Ian Woodward, ill. Virginia Salter)
Hutchinson 1987; 128pp
The compilers describe this as a 'celebration of Christian verse', and have chosen hymns, carols, prayers and narrative poems. Useful for assembly.

RMP

Read Me a Poem (chosen Caroline Royds, ill. Inga Moore)
Kingfisher Books 1986, rep. 1987; 64pp
A large, beautifully laid-out book for 5-7s, with exceptional illustrations. Poems, mostly rightly familiar, range from serious to comic, and from nursery rhymes to Blake and to Michael Rosen.

Rog

Roger Was a Razor Fish (comp. Jill Bennett, ill. Maureen Roffey)
Bodley Head 1980, 1983; 48pp
Bright attractive pictures and a brilliant choice of jingly verses for the very youngest readers, with a few cleverly chosen 'real' poems slipped in.

Ros D

Don't Put Mustard in the Custard (Michael Rosen, ill. Quentin Blake)
Deutsch 1985; 30 unnumbered pages
For the youngest, but the sheer zaniness is enjoyable at any age.

Ros F

When Did You Last Wash Your Feet? (Mike Rosen, ill. Tony Pinchuck)
Deutsch 1986; 92 unnumbered pp
Disguised as a peculiarly loud 'comic', with Tony Pinchuck's graffiti and seemingly crude pictures as an integral part of stories and poems, this book is unique. Teenagers' troubles – acne ('Spots / I gottem'), relationships with parents and teachers, bad teaching, anti-Semitism, a dying mother – vividly, sometimes bitterly, felt and presented.

Ros H

The Hypnotiser (Michael Rosen, ill. Andrew Tiffen)
Deutsch 1988; 128pp
This and *Ros F* may be Rosen's most controversial books. 'Can this be poetry?' ask some adults. Children find many facets of their personal relationships truly re-created and presented as dramatic monologues or playlets. Lots of fun, some very serious ideas.

Ros M

Mind Your Own Business (Michael Rosen, ill. Quentin Blake)
Deutsch 1974, Young Lions; 96pp

Ros W

Wouldn't You Like to Know? (Michael Rosen, ill. Quentin Blake)
Deutsch 1977, Puffin; 96pp

Ros Q

Quick, Let's Get Out of Here (Michael Rosen, ill. Quentin Blake)
Deutsch 1983, Macmillan 1988; 128pp

A most successful partnership. Blake and Rosen, each so individual, combine
perfectly to picture in dialogue and drawings many aspects of a child's life – no
subjects barred.

Ros Y

You Can't Catch Me (Michael Rosen, ill. Quentin Blake)
Deutsch 1981, Puffin 1982; 30pp
Some favourites from *Ros M* and *Ros W*, with some new verses, made into a
lavishly coloured picture book popular with younger children.

RT

Rhyme Time (coll. Barbara Ireson, ill. Lesley Smith)
Arrow Books 1977, latest reissue 1989; 188pp
200 poems to delight young children and encourage them to sing and to count
and to read verse for themselves.

Sam

Beams (Vyanne Samuels, ill. Paul Dowling)
Methuen 1990; 55pp
'Read aloud poetry' for the younger children, evoking the Caribbean. See also
Bur, Ora, Raw.

Sca

The Clever Potato (Vernon Scannell, ill. Tony Ross)
Hutchinson 1988; 64pp
Thirty-six poems about food, all but three written for this book and so quite new.
An adult's poet writing for 9-13s with wit, humour and great ingenuity.
Reminiscences, jokes, fantasy and finally reminders of the shocking contrast
between our banquets and Third World starvation.

Sca L

Love Shouts and Whispers (Vernon Scannell, ill. Tony Ross)
Hutchinson 1990; 79pp
Over 40 poems, all but four published for the first time, exploring the meaning
of 'love' to children and adults, headmaster, policeman, pop star, school girl and
boy. Extra interest for some readers in the formal shaping of several poems.

Sca T

Travelling Light (Vernon Scannell, ill. Tony Ross)
The Bodley Head 1991; 64pp
Another Scannell/Ross collaboration, for 8s upwards. Every form of transport
and travel, described in varied, accomplished verse suitably illustrated.

Scot

Voices of Our Kind (ed. Alexander Scott)
Chambers 1971, rev. 1975 and 1987; 154pp
Modern Scottish poetry from 1920. Sturdy poems in three languages, English, Scots and Gaelic (with glossaries and translations). Delightfully different from the usual anthologies.

Sea

The Puffin Book of Salt Sea Verse (comp. Charles Causley, ill. Antony Maitland)
Kestrel 1978, pback 1978, in print 1990; 272pp
A varied and comprehensive collection by a sometime seaman. From Homer to Seamus Heaney, tragedy to music-hall choruses.

Shad

Shadow Dance (coll. Adrian Rumble, ill. Rowena Allen)
Cassell 1987; 112pp
Celebrating night and darkness, often in their sinister and supernatural aspects.

Show I, II, III

The Poetry Show I, II, III (David Orme and James Sale, ill. David Eyre)
Macmillan 1987 (1987) (1988); 84, (92) (104)pp
Carefully planned from middle school to GCSE, these teaching anthologies are divided into sections (Form, Sound, Imagery, etc.), each with a relevant mini-anthology, containing many unusual choices. At the end of each volume two poets describe the creation of a poem.

Side

Our Side of the Playground (comp. Tony Bradman, ill. Kim Palmer)
The Bodley Head 1991; 96pp
Ingeniously presented, to be read from opposite ends, this book purports to give the boys' view of girls (B), the girls' view of boys (G).

Sil

Where the Sidewalk Ends (written and ill. Shel Silverstein)
Jonathan Cape 1984, rep. 1987, 1990; 174pp
Poems and drawings combine to create a fantastic world, where 'ANYTHING can be'. We are bidden to 'Come in!'. Immensely popular.

Sing

Sing a Song of Seasons (comp. Linda M Jennings, ill. Sally Gregory)
Hodder & Stoughton 1985; 12pp
Essentially a picture book illustrating favourite seasonal poems.

Six

Six of the Best: A Puffin Sextet of Poets (chosen Anne Harvey)
Puffin 1989; 238pp
cf Q and *Quin* are followed by Anne Harvey's choice of six poets: George Barker, Alan Brownjohn, Leonard Clark, Phoebe Hesketh, Russell Hoban and Brian Lee. Each has a distinctive voice, and all are distinguished by their success in writing for both children and adults.

Sk

Beaver Book of Skool Verse (Jennifer Curry, ill. Graham Thompson)
Hamlyn 1981; 159pp
Poems on every school situation; less subversive than Ahlberg and Rosen nevertheless frank.

SO

School's Out (comp. John Foster, ill. Alastair Graham)
Oxford 1988, rep. 1988, 1989, 1990; 128pp
Mainly light-hearted glimpses of many aspects of school, by poets black and white. Another successful anthology by John Foster.

Sort

All Sorts of Poems (ed. Ann Thwaite, ill. Patricia Mullins)
Angus and Robertson 1978, Magnet 1980; 128pp
Many fresh poems specially written for Ann Thwaite's annual 'Allsort' (1968-76), plus others written since. Much that younger childdren can enjoy with their elders. Many good verses too short to list.

Spa

Spaceways (coll. John Foster, ill. various)
OUP 1986; 128pp
Verses related to every aspect of 'Space', many in print for the first time, and assembled by a very experienced anthologist.

Speak

Speaking to You (sel. M. Rosen and D. Jackson, photographs S. and R. Greenhill)
Macmillan 1984; 128pp
Pieces specifically to be spoken aloud, often in dialect. Much Jamaican English The voice of the underdog is heard and relationships are explored.

Spi

A Spider Bought a Bicycle and Other Poems (sel. Michael Rosen, ill. Inga Moore)
Kingfisher Books 1987; 115pp
Amazing mixture of verses, to give pleasure to 5-10s. Often very short, taken from oral as well as written sources, they come from Siberia and the Caribbean from the USA and Greenland, from Shakespeare and Dr Seuss. Engaging illustrations for each poem.

SS

Poetry Two: A Shooting Star (coll. Wes Magee, ill. Lorraine White)
Basil Blackwell 1985; 63pp
Attractive successor to *DS*, for slightly older children, addressed to children concerns at school and home, their friends and relations.

S

Sun Singing in the Sun (chosen Jill Bennett, ill. Vanessa Julian-Ottie)
Viking Kestrel 1988; 96pp
The slightly twee cover belies the contents – a collection of sturdy verses, old and new, many American, for the youngest children.

224

Single Star (comp. David Davies, ill. Margery Gill)
he Bodley Head 1973, Puffin 1976, 1978, 1982, 1988; 96pp
his 'Anthology of Christmas poetry'contains poems old and new, highly valued
y teachers looking for something unhackneyed.

Child's Garden of Verses (Robert Louis Stevenson, ill. Michael Foreman)
ollancz 1985; 124pp
he first book of poems written from a child's viewpoint, 100 years old and still
uch loved. An essential book for the youngest. Many editions available, e.g.
rian Wildsmith's blaze of colour (OUP 1966 rep. 5 times); Annie Owen's
entenary edition (Arum Press 1985); paperback with Eve Garnett's drawings
uffin Classic).

Christmas Stocking (comp. Wes Magee, ill. Jill Bennett)
assell 1988, 1989, Puffin 1990; 140pp
n appropriate title for a book crammed with Christmas goodies, some
aditional favourites and some new surprises, chosen with discrimination by
es Magee, poet and teacher.

very Poem Tells a Story (chosen Raymond Wilson, ill. Alison Darke)
iking Kestrel 1988; 166pp
early 100 stories in verse, in variety of lengths, styles, dates and subjects. Good
r reading aloud and inspiring drama at secondary level.

anding on a Strawberry (John Cunliffe, ill. David Parkins)
ndre Deutsch 1987; 64pp
hildren disliking school (and family, except 'Gran') are frequently the subject
these verses. Was the poet very bored at school?

rictly Private (chosen Roger McGough, ill. Graham Dean)
estrel 1981, Puffin; 185pp
xcellent bold anthology for teenagers, chosen by a very popular poet 'for the
% of kids who do not come top in English'.The poets are 'for the most part
ve and British'. Something for every mood, nothing feeble.

ike that Stuff (sel. Morag Styles, ill. Joanne Smith and Bernard Georges)
JP 1984, 5th imp. 1989; 96pp

u'll Love this Stuff (sel. Morag Styles, ill. Bernard Georges)
JP 1986, 3rd imp. 1989; 112 pp
nique collections of poems very rarely otherwise anthologised, written by
ildren as well as adults and coming from a great many cultures. Chosen and
ranged by an expert and inspiring teacher for children of 8-13, but much for
ler pupils too.

225

Sun

The Sun Dancing (comp. Charles Causley, ill. Charles Keeping)
Kestrel 1982, Puffin 1984; 284pp
Invaluable collection of unusual poems on religious themes for 10-14s, but as usual with Charles Causley's books, there is much for everyone.

Talk

Talking to the Sun (sel. Kenneth Koch and Kate Farrell, ill. see below)
Holt Rinehard NY 1985, Viking Kestrel 1986; 112pp
A unique book showing 'how great and how likeable poetry is', also how vario in form, coming from how many countries and cultures, from how ma centuries. Illustrations of treasures from the great Metropolitan Museum in Ne York. Perfect for browsing.

Ten

Poems for Over 10-year-olds (chosen Kit Wright, ill. Michael Foreman)
Viking Kestrel 1984; 192pp
Many favourite poems for people up to and beyond school leaving age, group skilfully by theme, with wide variation of mood in each section. See also *Nine*.

TG

Ten Golden Years (ed. Sally Grindley and Chris Powling, ill. various)
Walker Books 1989; 45pp
Well-known poets have contributed new verses, and ten artists (all winners of t Mother Goose Award) have illustrated them. A distinguished book. Royalties to the Great Ormond Street Hospital for Sick Children.

This W

This Way Delight (sel. Herbert Read)
Faber 1957, rep. 1958, 1960, 1965, 1970; 192pp
Poems mainly lyrical and fantastical. 17th-century English and 20th-centu American poets mingle happily. A truly delightful timeless collection f over-10s to adults, well worth reviving.

Tick

Is a Caterpillar Ticklish? (coll. Adrian Rumble, ill. Mary Budd)
Robert Royce Ltd 1986; 192pp
Poems, many brief, grouped ingeniously by theme, to enhance each other and make a substantial book, handsomely printed, for 7s upward.

Til

'Til All the Stars have Fallen (sel. David Booth, ill. Kady MacDonald Denton)
Viking 1990; 93pp
A very widely-ranging miscellany of unfamiliar poems, chosen by a Canadi Professor of Children's Literature.

Tim

Tiny Tim (chosen Jill Bennett, ill. Helen Oxenbury)
Heinemann 1981; unnumbered pp
Two experts produce a perfect blend of old and new verse, exactly a brilliantly illustrated, for the youngest children.

226

Ting

Spine Tinglers (ed. Zenka and Ian Woodward, ill. Chris Russell)
Ladybird 1983; 51pp
A tiny brightly coloured book, crammed with ghosts, witches, corpses and bats.

Touch IV, V

Touchstones IV, V (ed. Michael and Peter Benton, ill. various)
Hodder and Stoughton 1968, 1970, 1988 (1968, 1988); 208pp (208pp)
Excellent teaching anthologies now revised and extended. Groups of well-chosen and ingeniously arranged poems from many parts of the world. Book V contains many poems too complex to classify simply, some on painful subjects, and interesting pairs for comparison in sixth forms.

TPS

Dancing Teepees (sel. Virginia Driving Hawk Sneve, ill. Stephen Gammell)
OUP 1989; 32pp
An out-of-the-way picture book of very short poems of American Indian youth, translated from oral cultures of various tribes. Beautifully and appropriately illustrated.

Trio

Catch the Light (Vernon Scannell, Gregory Harrison, Laurence Smith)
Oxford 1982; 48pp
The 'Three Poets' series was launched to give teenagers larger samples of contemporary poets than the odd poem in an anthology. Two well-known poets are teamed with one less familiar. See also *Bright, Candy, Crys, UD*.

UD

Upright Downfall (Roy Fuller, Barbara Giles, Adrian Rumble)
OUP 1983; 48pp
See *Trio*, and also *Bright, Candy, Crys*.

Vil

Our Village (John Yeoman, ill. Quentin Blake)
Walker 1988; 40pp unnumbered
A delightful and distinguished book by two masters of their crafts. A picture map of the village shows where eveyone lives. We meet Mr Crumb the baker at daybreak and end with general skating by lantern light. Ages 6 to 10.

Voa

Over the Moon: a Book of Nursery Rhymes (chosen Selina Hastings, ill. Charlotte Voake)
Walker Books 1985, rep. 1988; 128pp
A lovely book for the unfortunates who have not been given nursery rhymes at home. Full-colour spreads alternate with delicate black and white sketches.

Voi II, III

Voices II, III (ed. Geoffrey Summerfield, ill. various)
Penguin 1968, still in print; 192pp, (190pp)
Geoffrey Summerfield chose little known poems from all over the world and combined them with surprising illustrations, so well assembled that *Voices* affected all later anthologists. Still well worth using from age 11 upward.

Wad

Barley Barley (Barrie Wade, ill. Irene Wise)
OUP 1991; 64pp
Shrewd and sensitive re-creation of lives of children and adults at school and home, by a teacher of both children and students.

Walk

The Walker Book of Poetry for Children (sel. and intro. Jack Prelutsky, ill. Arnold Lobel)
Walker Books 1983; 248pp
The subtitle 'A Treasury of 572 poems' is indeed justified. Lavishly produced and decorated by this leading illustrator, well mixed, with many favourite poems as well as verses (often American) which are unfamiliar. Something for everyone in the primary school. Useful indexes of authors, titles, first lines and subjects. See also *Lob.*

War

In Time of War (sel. Anne Harvey, ill. from Imperial War Museum)
Blackie 1987; 160pp
A remarkably varied and poignant collection from the two World Wars recreating the home front as well as active service. Contemporary posters, cartoons and popular songs add immediacy. Invaluable for pupils studying these periods.

WAS

Words for All Seasons (chosen Malcolm Saville, ill. E. and P. Wrigley)
Lutterworth Press 1979; 192pp
A popular author's personal choices, often short extracts, relating the Christian year to the natural year. A cheerful wholesome book, with several unanthologised poems.

West

The Best of West (written and ill. Colin West)
Hutchinson 1990; 192pp
Selected by the writer from six earlier books, here is a batch of brief ingenious nonsense verses, clerihews, ruthless rhymes, tongue twisters, 'stories in stanzas' sheer absurdities, all with matching illustrations.

Wheel

Wheel Around the World (comp. Chris Searle, ill. Katinka Kew)
Macdonald 1983; 62pp
An index lists the many countries from which these poems come. Equal variety of poets young and old, unknown and famous. Admirable collection for 10 upward.

Wind

The Windmill Book of Poeetry (ed. David Orme, ill. Peter Melnyczuk)
Heinemann 1987; 128pp
A teaching anthology of poems, often unfamiliar, cleverly arranged in twos and threes for comparison. Worth having for the new voices. Aimed at GCSE.

Wit

Witch Poems (ed. Daisy Wallace, ill. Trina Schart Hyman)
Bell and Hyman 1980; 32pp
Eighteen verses on witches, suitably eerily illustrated, in a well-produced slender book.

World

Around the World in Eighty Poems (comp. Jennifer and Graeme Curry, ill. Mark Southgate)
Hutchinson 1988; 96pp
A mixed bag from home and abroad.

WP

Writing Poems (ed. M. Harrison and C. Stuart Clark, ill. various)
Oxford 1985; 136pp
To be used with *Poem I* or on its own. A splendidly varied anthology with helpful ideas for encouraging the writing of poetry by 10-13s.

Wri C

Cat among the Pigeons (Kit Wright, ill. Posy Simmonds)
Viking Kestrel 1987; 80pp

Wri H

Hot Dog and other Poems (Kit Wright, ill. Posy Simmonds)
Kestrel Books 1981, Puffin 1982; 72pp

Wri R

Rabbiting On (Kit Wright, ill. Posy Simmonds)
Fontana Lions 1978; 95pp

Irreverent witty verses, with irresistible rhythms, some very short, some narratives, about family life. Often very funny but sometimes serious. Juniors recognise themselves. Posy Simmonds' illustrations match perfectly.

WS

Word-Spells (chosen Judith Nicholls, ill. Alan Baker)
Faber 1988; 131pp
A rich collection of high quality with poems which readers of different ages can enjoy. Mainly contemporary writers of accessible verse.

WZ

The Way to the Zoo (chosen David Jackson)
OUP 1983; 128pp
Unusual poems about animals, from many cultures, arranged in well-contrived sections from 'Birth' to 'Death' and 'Extinction'. Thought-provoking juxtapositions. Brilliant black and white illustrations, unattributed.

YD

The Young Dragon Book of Verse (Michael Harrison and Christopher Stuart Clark)
Oxford 1989; 168pp
Companion volume to *ND*, for younger age-groups. Mainly contemporary with a few earlier poets, Crabbe, Wordsworth, Kingsley, Yeats.

Young

Fontana Lions Book of Young Verse (chosen Julia Watson, ill. Quentin Blake)
Collins 1973, 10th imp. 1983; 96pp
Julia Watson's practised hand has arranged a delightful collection for the 5-8s
and Quentin Blake's drawings add to the gaiety.

Zoo

A Children's Zoo (ed. Julia Watson, ill. Karen Strachey)
Collins Fontana Lions 1978, 2nd imp. 1982; 96pp
Julia Watson has actually found some unfamiliar poems, many American, on this
most popular subject. She groups the animals by the number of their feet from
'six' to 'none'. Appeals to all juniors.

89, 91, 94, 95, 96, 115, 129, 137, 147, 156, 157, 161, 162, 167, 177, 191

Owen, Wilfred 1, 182, 183, 184

Pacheco, J.E. 113
Packenham-Walsh, Rev. William 154
Palmer, Herbert 76
Palmer, Samuel 58
Park, Frances 98
Parker, Edgar 67, 122
Parker, Gillian 191
Parker, James 121
Parker, Martin 27
Parry, Edward Abbot 12
Parvin, Betty 72
Pasternak, Boris 115, 118, 194
Pasternak, Lydia (trans.) 194
Paterson, A.B. 9, 11, 16, 42, 71, 127, 132, 153, 159, 188, 192
Paterson, Evangeline 181
Patrickson, Kit 65
Patten, Brian 1, 4, 6, 10, 16, 21, 29, 30, 31, 36, 49, 51, 54, 62, 63, 70, 78, 87, 89, 99, 101, 103, 113, 115, 116, 117, 124, 130, 133, 142, 147, 162, 170, 173, 189
Payne, Basil 46
p'Bitek, Okot 68, 75
Peacock, Thomas Love 181
Peake, Mervyn 9, 25, 101
Peele, George 28
Pender, Lydia 106, 144, 151
Peter 132
Pettit, Millicent L. 133
Petty, Noel 30
Phillips, Gordon 78
Phillips, Redmond 88
Philpotts, Eden 6, 11
Pickthall, Edith 186
Pierpont, James 16
Pilling, Christopher 57
Plath, Sylvia 10, 11, 13, 71, 98, 115, 130
Plomer, William 115, 126
Po Chu-i 37, 95, 133, 163, 176
Poe, Edgar Allan 16, 55, 93, 140
Pollock, Danny 45, 72
Pope, Alexander 74, 130
Porter, Cole 102
Porter, Margaret 132
Porter, Peter 124, 141
Postgate, Margaret 184
Poulson, Joan 120

Pound, Ezra 98
Pratt, E.J. 150, 152
Prelutsky, Jack 2, 25, 35, 36, 38, 5 68, 77, 83, 84, 86, 105, 110, 13 155, 158, 162, 179, 189, 191, 19 193, 194
Prevert, Jacques 17, 53, 107
Pudney, John 175, 184
Pugh, Sheenagh 54, 158
Purdy, Alfred 140
Pyle, Katherine 167

Raine, Kathleen 98
Rajendra, Cecil 10
Ralegh, Sir Walter 98, 102, 112, 1: 172
Randall, Dudley 40
Rands, W.B. 52, 62, 129
Ransom, John Crowe 46, 172
Rasmussen, Knud (trans.) 57
Rathbone, J. 163
Rawling, Tom 66, 152
Rawnsley, Irene 17, 31, 41, 52, 73, 120
Reaney, James 94
Redmond, Seamus 45
Reed, Henry 186
Rees, James 4
Reeves, James 5, 6, 7, 11, 18, 27, 31, 37, 49, 56, 65, 73, 74, 75, 108, 109, 110, 111, 121, 122, 1 135, 139, 144, 149, 158, 172, 1 187, 190
Reid, A. (trans.) 113
Rhys, Ernest 48, 183
Rice, John 39, 151, 161, 164
Richards, Laura E. 31, 108, 122
Richards, Michael 4, 117
Riche, Clive 68
Rickword, Edgell 184
Riddell, Elizabeth 101, 174
Ridley, George 101
Rieu, E.V. 1, 15, 26, 37, 46, 67, 103, 127, 129, 137, 138, 152, 1 178
Riley, James Whitcombe 10, 75, 11
Rilke, R.M. 128
Roberts, Elizabeth Madox 193
Roberts, T.G. 132
Robeson, Paul 129
Robinson, Edwin Arlington 134
Robinson, Ted 8
Rodgers, W.R. 57
Roethke, Theodore 13, 57, 63,

240